THE PITTSBURGH THEOLOGICAL MONOGRAPH SERIES

General Editor

Dikran Y. Hadidian

25

The Semiotics of the Passion Narrative

THE SEMIOTICS OF THE PASSION NARRATIVE
TOPICS AND FIGURES

by

LOUIS MARIN

●

translated

by

Alfred M. Johnson, Jr.

THE PICKWICK PRESS

Pittsburgh, Pennsylvania

1980

Originally published as *Sémiotique de la Passion. Topiques et figures.* Copyright 1971. Paris: Aubier, Cerf, Delachaux & Niestlé, and Desclée de Brouwer.

Library of Congress Cataloging in Publication Data

Marin, Louis, 1931-
    The semiotics of the Passion narrative.

    (Pittsburgh theological monograph series ; 25)
    Translation of Sémiotique de la Passion.
    Bibliography: p.
    Includes indexes.
    1. Jesus Christ--Biography--Passion Week.
2. Typology (Theology) I. Title. II. Series.
BT414.M3513   232.9'6   80-18199
ISBN 0-915138-23-9

BT
414
.M3513

Copyright© 1980 by
THE PICKWICK PRESS
5001 Baum Boulevard
Pittsburgh, PA 15213

To my father

CONTENTS

Second Part

THE SEMIOTICS OF THE TRAITOR

APPENDICES

INTRODUCTION

> *"What makes the nobility of a legend, as of a* Langue, *is in condemning both to make use of only the elements brought before them and in whatever meaning, they reunite them and take from them continually a new meaning."*
> —Ferdinand de Saussure

A single problem connects the two essays which we are going to read, but at some different levels and at some different points of the text: that of the place, the function, and the nature of mediation in the narrative logic. If an ordinary narrative—being worth the trouble of being said—presents itself, in one way or another, as the resolution—in a text—of an opposition or an antinomy which is at the same time its outer limit and its origin; if an ordinary narrative, in order to be produced, finds its necessity in the form of a text—in the development of this opposition and thereby, in the search of an intelligibility, whatever may be the plan where that is established; if an ordinary narrative, in order to anchor its "story elements" [*"racontants"*], in a point of origin and connect them by a discursive sequence, refers to the textual establishment of a meaning in an insignificant, and for that very reason, a threatening place; then an ordinary narrative is, in one segment determined by its succession, the use of a mediatory operation which tends to bring together [p. 10] the sides of the opposition to stick together again the elements disjoined by the antinomy, and to reduce the scandalous fracture of the nonsense.

We are given a specific narrative, which has received the archaic name of the Passion of Jesus Christ, and we are examining the opposition which the narrative finds necessary to be told and the mediation by which it overcomes that opposition. In other words, we have considered the narrative as the narrative figure of a dialectic of origin and change. It is a figure which it is a matter of transforming into its "property" in order to find its primary elements and their relationships, and in order to find the successive, necessarily connected operations, and in order to construct a model from it and thereby to progressively encircle the structure. A structure of a

1

2

figure which reveals a dialectic, i.e. the beginning of a
change, the promise of a transformation, the drawing of an
intelligibility to come, in a primary ensemble of stable and
articulated relationships, or in a homeostasis[1] without either
imbalance or disorder. This was indeed the other* of the narrative opposition on the epistemological plane. Can a structure of change be spoken of? Thus the narrative which, in its
immanence, aimed at the dialectic solution of its original opposition, presented itself as its original opposition in the
analytical--interpretive--discourse that we hear made about it.
The metadiscourse reflected or represented in its epistemological relation of antinomy where the latter found its negative
raison d'être, its point of departure proportionally more necessary that it must be transformed and reduced, under the penalty of succumbing to the threat of nonsense.

Thus the notion of mediation in the narrative logic referred to that antinomic origin of the narrative which is indeed "the other of the text"* by which this logic is developed: or again its referent. Again it is necessary from the
beginning, to determine the position of this referent of the
text. There is great danger here of falling into the traps of
exteriority, as if the referent of the text referred, at first
and essentially in their independence and their transcendence,
to a bit of the world, to a moment of history, to a piece
[*lieu*] of space, and to a subject who is somewhere else and
from another time. The referent is indeed what the text
speaks about, but it is this to the same extent to which it
is spoken by the text. It is not from transcendent existence
that the text (re)produces on the mode of the discourse. It
is the movement of transcendence of the discourse, that [p.
11] which the discourse brings back when it is produced. It
is what the discourse produces when it speaks and communicates.
This is indeed the other of the text, the opposite side by
which the text is produced, and which it produces for that
very reason: indissociable from the *parole* by which it is
brought into use--that is to say precisely by which it is
shaped or produced--but without which the *parole* would not be
uttered. This is a necessary condition for the transitivity
of the *parole*, and every communicativity. Let us recall here
the definition of "reference" given by E. Benveniste, whose
remarkable tautology expresses the indissociability of the
referent and discourse: "The sentence is a unit(y)* of which
it is a segment of discourse....But it is a complete unit(y)*

---

*"other" in the sense of alterity or the "alter ego" in psy-
  chological terms.
unité may mean either a unit or a unity.

which carries meaning and reference at the same time: meaning
because it is information about signification and reference because it *refers* to a given situation. Those who communicate
have precisely this in common, a certain reference of situation without which communication as such does not take
place[2]...."

That being said, its otherness is clearly indicated at no
better point of the discourse than its "origin" because it is
at this "utopian moment" that this twofaced existence is established, at once, of which all reality is only a reciprocal
reflection. But this is not a specular and fruitless point,
since this reality is the movement and the power of production
which is named "discourse". Must not "the original impulse
which has compelled men to 'exchange' *paroles* be sought in a
representation which is doubled back on itself, resulting from
the symbolic function making its first appearance? As soon as
an acoustic object is apprehended as offering an immediate
value, at the same time for the one who speaks and the one who
hears, *it acquires a contradictory nature whose neutralization
is only possible by this exchange of complementary values* to
which all social life is reduced."[3] Let us not hesitate to
project this powerful hypothesis of Lévi-Strauss on the narrative as an instance of discursive communication in order to
construct this "second generation semiology", which Benveniste
evoked, formed by "the translinguistic analysis of texts...by
the elaboration of a meta-semantics constructed on a semantics
of enunciation".[4] *The narrative* will then be in its specific
*logic the neutralizer exchange by the mediatory operation of
the original elements of its antinomy.*

For that very reason, we understand two elements of the
notion of [p. 12] mediation. It is an exchange of signifier
elements of the opposition, that is to say, some elements connected by a reciprocal disjunction. But this exchange is not
a pure and simple exchange. It isolates the empty space, where
the conjunction of contraries will be able to be produced, but
at another level, i.e. in another sense. It is the condition
of possibility of the dialectic change, the empty introduction
as the sheer "zero" of the opposition, an addition in the face
of the "complementary values" of the elements of the opposition. It is perhaps by distinguishing the neutral term as a
moment of the neutralization of opposites, and the synthetic
term as a moment of their conjunction, that we can determine
with greater accuracy the meaning of the dialectic mediation
and see how the exchange of complementaries is productive of
an additional element which replaces them: in short, how it
can have excess and synthesis in it; *"coincidentia oppositor-
um"*, and have in this coincidence, something more and else
than the opposites. Henceforth the addition far from being

4

only the necessary condition of the relationship of complemen-
tarity which is constitutive of the symbolic mind in action,
as it is for Lévi-Strauss,[5] is also, and no less necessarily,
the product of the exchange of disjoined complementaries,
characteristic of this symbolic act.

Perhaps it will be said that this production is illusory
and that the remainder is found in the "exit" of the exchange
process is nothing else than the same thing which has permitted it to begin. Every narrative would then be the interplay
of this illusion. The opposition which provokes it, far from
dissipating it, would only be repeated interminably all along
its incidents and episodes. And the "solution" which these
caused at the end of the tests, the exiles, and the meetings,
by which the signifiers are exchanged in the internal communication of the discourse, would be only the representation of
the initial opposition, in a bifurcation which would have the
only innovation of the decoy. It is possible; but it is also
possible that the neutralizing function of the exchange may be
forgotten, in this hypothesis--that it may be inside the discourse or outside between speakers--which annuls the opposites
in an instant in the intersection of a gift and a counter-gift
but which instead of making them return to the primary unity
and the primary indistinctness--those where nothing is done
and nothing is said: the obscurity of the thing [p. 13] it-
self--maintains them in their pure difference and entertains
them as different at the end of the process. This operation
is not a mystery, nor a magical trick. It only makes apparent
the intimate connection* of "saying" and "doing" in the discourse of the narrative.

If the narrative speaks about something that is the antimony of its origin, and if the initial opposition speaks it by
causing it, that means that in the process of exchange and communication which constitutes the narrative in all its dimensions of its transmission and reception, and of its coding and
expression, a transformation begins and a "travail" of contraries develops. A fixed production of meaning, and an "act
of meaning" in and by a "speaking",[6] are disconnected by the
surprising threat which constitutes this symbolic thing, which
is at the same time full and double, in itself and different
than itself, coexisting in itself at a distance from itself, in
order to repeat the remark by Lévi-Strauss: vacillation from
the thing of the being, violence of a fracture in the thing and
in the being which are precisely "the other of the discourse"
that they cause and which unceasingly annuls them and reinvests

---

articulation may mean either "connection" or "articulation".

them in the empty space of their difference. Such is the function of the reference in the discourse of the narrative. It is at the same time its condition of existence and the material which ceaselessly transforms it into a product; which unceasingly shapes it because this material is not a thing, but a gap in the things. It is not a being, but a difference in the being, a productive disjunction. It is the travail of the discourse of the narrative on this difference that we have tried in turn to recover in a metadiscourse of the Passion narrative; a representation divided in two and in an exchange process, no longer narrative, but meta-narrative, of the narrative of an exchange and a communication.

The problems of mediation and reference are thus fundamentally connected to the narrative logic. Again it was necessary to determine precisely the strategic plan of the analysis and the point on which in fact the weight bears. This point and this plan appeared to us to be the proper name. Why? Because the proper name has the characteristic of being an element of the textual surface, of a "manifestation" which is endowed with very remarkable properties for our purposes. It refers "by definition" to a referent and is depleted in this aim. But for that very reason it indicates a singularity, and it only has a linguistic existence in this [p. 14] indication. In other words, and to repeat Benveniste's terms from the text which we cited above, the proper name would be that sign of language which, in the closed world of signs, would function as a "sentence", by only having access to the meaning by its reference, less in a given situation, than in a singular *existant* which it would cause to occur in the "parole", entirely by referring it to this *other* of the language which cannot be spoken, but only indicated by a kind of verbal gesture. Thus the proper name has in language a single strength and a no less remarkable weakness. If it is at the border of the *parole* and silence, marking the inferior zone of language, it is also the transgression of this border, not at this level, but between *langue* and *parole*, and in the caesura of the symbolic bifurcation since in some way it is the presence in the language of the being itself as such, in its attributed transcendence.

Our first approach has taken aim at the proper place names or the toponyms of the Passion narrative. Their organization inside of the narrative, the relationships which they were able to maintain, in their recurrences or their absences, in their arrangement along the narrative line, permit us then to construct what we have called the productive scene of the narrative, as a network of named textual places. This scene was productive, in so far as the network of places which marks it out and articulates it is a double process of transformation: in the system of the text defined here by four variants in a position of reciprocal representation (the four canonical gospels) and in the large syntagmatic of the narrative articulated in ensembles, which are at the same time in a hierarchical system and ordinate of segments, sequences, functions, and qualifications. The scene of the narrative, as a network of places in the names which specify them, is thus simultaneously the product of the narrative and the ensemble of textual marks of its production: the traces of the work on this other of the text [autre-du-texte] (or its referent) of which the narrative is composed. Or to take an example and set it forth schematically. "Bethany" is the toponymic name of two sequences of relations and correlations, the name of a textual place where a meaning is produced. It is a toponym of the resurrection of Lazarus and the performative mortuary anointing of Jesus. But it is also a toponym of his "messianic" entrance into Jerusalem and his ascension. "Bethany" is the figure of the articulation of his Life and Death and of the [p. 15] contradictory messianic Kingship. This name is the textual mark of the *effectuation* (or of the mediation) of this double opposition seized then as the other of the text [autre-du-texte].

Therefore the proper (place) noun has this ambiguous value, or this transgressive power of indicating the back side of the text as transcendence, but considered as a textual element and as such, capable of entering into a signifier network, that of the places where the meaning is produced. It is this borderline function which Lévi-Strauss has well placed in a prominent position in a series of texts from *The Savage Mind* and of which our own reflections constitute at the same time an extension and an application. Setting aside the logical-philosophical hypothesis of the insignificance of proper names, Lévi-Strauss considers them in the edifice of a specific language, as the edge of the cut [coupure] which separates the language of the world from things. More precisely, the proper names would constitute the boundary of a classificatory work in the heart of a specific cultural system, while remaining "always in the direction of the classification". And the author continues: "Consequently in each system the proper names represent some *quanta of signification* underneath which one does nothing more than show." Certainly, the proper name is not reducible to a pure index, nor to a simple demonstrative pronoun as Peirce or Russel were able to conceive of it; for the simple reason that they are names and therefore belong to the language. To be sure, it will never be possible to pass by imperceptible degrees from "showing" to "speaking". And one can say with Lévi-Strauss that "the more or less 'proper' character of names is not determinable in an intrinsic way, nor by their comparison with the other words of language", but that "it depends on the moment at which each society declares its work of classification finished".[7]

But it does not follow at all that the proper name is a boundary of the operative power of a signifier system in a culture, and that some phenomena of interferences and turbulences are always produced on the boundaries which reveal the contact between the system and what could be metaphorically called its environment. In other words, a boundary is not an inert cutting [*coupure*]: there is a frame of the boundary, a place of confrontation of opposing forces, a place where the other of the system [*l'autre-du-systeme*] points. It is this place that marks the proper name. "It is always in the direction of the classification"; but it is also the end of the [p. 16] classification in a specific culture, the point beyond which one does nothing more than exist in immediate contact with the same thing, even if this contact and this immediacy are pure utopia. Because it would be necessary to ask if "showing" is not already signifying the thing as an object to be studied in common. Therefore already it is not a communication between indicators producing meaning, and hence the transmission of a useful sign, of an information intended to control and orient a force for a task to be accomplished.[8] But that is not the point. Because the proper name is at the boundary of the system, and it sets forth the frontier, it constitutes the place of exchange of the system, the zone where it strives to integrate elements which are "external" to it, and to inflect the forces which threaten its integrity, but also where the first fractures are produced, the first "changes" which will lead to a general transformation of the system, and to its re-structuration: threatened with nonsense and struggle and triumph of sense. To ask what these forces are, and what these "external" elements are is not a relevant question. To accept it would be to lapse into the illusion of exteriority which is attached almost inexorably to every reflection about the referent, to every thought about the boundary. These forces and elements are only interesting to us to the extent to which they appear in their relation to the system as its otherness which produces the boundary in it and which the boundary shapes [*travaille*].

But it is precisely in this epistemological area that we set forth our hypothesis concerning the toponyms in the Passion narrative. If in order to mark it out, it is true that the place name indicates a geographic space, but also simultaneously articulates it in a topic discourse which arises itself from a specific cultural system in the story and in the tradition, that is to say in the last resort, in an ensemble of texts, the following is the problem: What changes the topics, what changes the system--or what remains the same--what restructures it on another level, without changing space and without creating a new world, "a new earth from a new heaven"? Even better, what preserves certain names, and makes them become "different" without however ceasing to indicate a specific space? In other words, what will mark the *passage*, the transformation of a "cultural" system into another system which is at the same time in continuity with the first and in a state of rupture? How can a topography be preserved, [p. 17] at a time when the topic which is necessarily connected to it must change? Such is the *"Aufhebung"* of this dialectic that our hypothesis inspired us to describe, which referred us to the analysis of the mediatory operation which the Passion narrative also displays on this plane. Moreover is not its "hero" the Mediator par excellence? Therefore what comes to be revealed in the textual structure--understood as a productive space, by its names--the change of system, in the ambiguous sense of this term, preservation and inversion?

It will be seen how the narrative will attempt the *neutralization* of the names in their propriety in order to make them become *different* by their passage to the "common": a diversified *neutralization* since it will take the form of an etymological interpretation or that of a radically new occurrence, or else that of a pure and simple obliteration, into a common noun whose substitution is accomplished, either in a narrative metonymy or in a discursive metaphor. On the other hand, and at the same time, the neutralizer processes will expand through the system of the text, defined by its four variants, and on the different isotopies where the narrative is articulated (narrative, narrative discourse, discourse), and thanks to their remarkable interferences. Then and only then the proper names can make a return to the narrative. It is because the exchange of the proper name has been accomplished as an indicative designation and as a signifier structured in a specific system (contrary to the common noun, which in any case belongs to the deepest zones of the system, and not to that of its boundary) that the change can then occur. At first the change lies in this neutralizing exchange of the nominal signifiers. Not between them, as will be the case in the semiotics of the traitor, but between two lexical zones of different levels: neutralizing exchange, but by this neutralization, an exchange productive of the change restructuring the system on another plane. By it the opposition is annuled in the same interplay of its difference. The same thing is conjoined to another thing because it has been made different by the interference of the other-of-the-system [*autre-du-système*] at its boundary.

In other words, the ancient toponyms can then be born again, but articulated through the narrative in a new topic. These are the same, but they become different because they function in the same topographic indication as a boundary of a new system. If, as R. Jakobson points out, the significa-

tion [p. 18] of a proper name is defined by its return to the
code,[9] we are dealing in the specie with a change of code.
While saying "Jerusalem" or "Temple" or "Mount of Olives" the
new community (new within the old) no longer considers "Jerusalem" or "Temple" as ancient. The Temple or Jerusalem have become different by themselves. Therefore all our analysis is
based on the hypothesis of a neutralizing mediation which is
the "moment" of the change of code. At that moment the Temple
is no longer the Jewish Temple. But it is not only the Temple
(of the Christian community). It is the common place which the
hero *leaves*, which is then established as a Temple by his discourse. "He spoke of the Temple of his body" (Jn. 2:21). Thus
at the "center" of the Passion narrative, there is the interplay of obvious toponyms, in the unit(y) of the same place, a
transference of synchronic-diachronic sense, a metaphor. Or
to be more precise, since the proper name belongs to the superficial leximatic ensemble of the text, the dialectic of toponyms, between "proper" and "common", with the double moment of
the neutral and the mediation, is established as the productive
scene of a *metaphoric event* in the system of the text.

We conclude then by referring to the event itself of which
the toponymic dialectic was only the representation (*Vorstel-
lung*): metaphoric event or arrival of the mediation itself in
the neutralization of the hero by the traitor. It is not a
question here of repeating the analyses which will be read in
the second part of the work, but only of emphasizing the double
appurtenance of the personage and his name on the one hand, and
of the name and the narrative event on the other. In general
at first the personage is a proper name which appears as an
event of reading; but which, at the same time, functions along
the narrative line as the figure of an exchange of functions
and qualifications, of "logical" classes where they are grouped
at narrative places where they articulate the story. Thus what
Paul Ricoeur writes of the word in general can be applied more
particularly to the proper name of the personage in the narrative enchainment of a text. It is the exchanger between the
system and the act, the structure and the event. "On the one
hand," Paul Ricoeur continues, "it belongs to the structure as
a differential value, but then it is only a semantic virtuali-
ty, on the other, it belongs to the act and the event, in so
far as its [p. 19] semantic actuality is contemporary with the
fading actuality of the [narrative] statement". It is what we
call an event of reading in the system of the text. But, he
adds, "the word outlives the sentence...at the transitory instant of the discourse....Thus loaded with a new value of
use...it returns to the system and by returning to the system, it gives it a history".[10]

One will see in our analyses how we are at the same time close to and far from this remark: close by the epistemological demand which we reveal in the most rigorous structural analysis which has been made of the narrative, by reverting to the level of the narrative itself, in the pure succession of its events. Certainly returning to the story, but in so far as it is a narrated-recited [racontée-récitée] story in the system of the text, but it is at no point a return by some illusion of referential exteriority, to a historical transcendent of which the narrative would be the simple duplication. This is why the event of which we are speaking is a reading event, that which appears in the complex relationship of evocation of the meaning between reading and read, that is to say in the relationship of the text. But the distance and the difference that we observe in the presence of the instructions of P. Ricoeur are no doubt due to the dimension of the textual ensembles which we are dealing with, myth, narrative, and discourse, and not only, at a higher level of abstraction, the word, the sentence--because the word is for us the proper name, only vocable, which is able to play at the boundary of the structure and the event because it is only of the boundaries of the whole structure by having the value of an existential index (without being an index properly speaking). We have shown, on the way, the operations of a neutralizer exchange which punctuate the transformation of the system, i.e. its restructuration at another level. Simon becomes Peter because he is a (foundation) stone, Jesus becomes Christ because he is Christ--the anointed one....

But even more precisely, it is, in this narrative, a name in which the neutralizing function of the mediation is catalyzed bit by bit through some duplications and recurrences, some iterations and displacements, in the form of a character who--in the same narrative--will carry out the synchronic-diachronic transference of the meaning. It is he who, in the text itself, "will act out" the metaphor of breaking open the system, thanks to which the narrative is structured, and by being structured triumphs over its originating opposition, over the other [p. 20] where it has found its anchorage and its starting point. One will see that it is the traitor who is the other of the hero--the one by whom the hero can accomplish his mission, which is first to establish a recitable narrative, i.e. to *be* established in narratable *parole* by the community which, in a characteristic movement of retroaction, will only be such by this *parole* in action: a discourse--narrative "act"--spoken and consumed--by the community which it produces and which produces it from an exchange of this *parole*. Such is the referential event that the proper name of the traitor specifies and metaphorizes inside of the system, in order to break it open, so that it will reproduce.

Two reading notes in order to end:

1. We have moved the relevant notes to the end of the work. They constitute a critical re-reading of the text by the one who has written it, in fact by those who have been in communication with him before publication. Also they can for the most part be read between them as a second text having its relative autonomy in relation to the first which however has produced it. Therefore here is repeated in a commentary what laborously we have tried to explain from the text criticized: that it is a producer of meaning, a meaning which is collected in the second commentary which doubles it, but which by criticizing it, elucidates it, and produces it in its turn. It is in this way that the text engenders in some way the metatext which in turn produces it with its rules and its productive laws.

2. Some appendices will be found at the end of the book dealing with some other more general texts or belonging to another theoretical domain. They were needed not to close the volume, but to open it to an intertextuality, in order to show the infinite task of interpretation in action and to a certain extent to break the circle by which it produces the text which engenders it, by indicating the new plane where it is reconstituted. Moreover, the collective set of works in *Le Récit évangélique* which follows our study, in the perspective of the collection, are equally one of the privileged places of the critical overture which we have, even here, only begun.

First Part

THE PLACES OF THE NARRATIVE

Chapter One

PROBLEMATIC AND WORKING HYPOTHESES

While dealing with the analytical description of the toponymy of the Passion narratives, this study pursues a double objective: first, to investigate with this particular case the general problem of proper names which is known to present a very complex problem for semiotic structural theory; and to accede then in this way to one of the possible organizations of the meaning in the Passion narratives. From one objective to another, however, the status of this work changes its nature, since according to the first perspective, it is only one example of one general semiotic problem among other studies of the same kind centered on the same problem,[1] whereas in the second perspective it is a preparatory, and no doubt fundamental, moment of a structural analysis of the Passion narrative, and as such one piece of a structural exegesis of the Gospel. These indications are not superfluous because they can contribute to posing the problem of the relationships between a theory, its fields of application or its validity and the extension and the level of the problems which it is capable of integrating.

TEXTS AND CORPUS

At the center of the complex interplay of relations which generally defines textual semiology, the question appears of the relation of one text in its individuality and the corpus in which the text is included, and of which it is an element. Depending upon whether the problem presented will be that of the proper name, as a specific problem of textual semiology, then the gospel texts [p. 24] will come into comparison with those of [Sir Thomas] More or Pascal[2] or still others, and the question will then be to make clearer the reasons, other than subjective ones, why these different texts have been chosen as constituting the primary elements of the corpus on which the problem of the proper name will be based. According to the other research intention, the problem of grappling with the toponymy of the Passion narratives in the Gospels will relate to a specific level of structuration of the meaning; in other words, one code of deciphering the texts among other codes. And the ulterior demand of semiological research will be to articulate this code with other codes that the total analysis of the text will have to reveal and of which semiological research also takes account. It would then be necessary to ask how these codes, of which the texts considered constitute some kinds of citations,[3] enter into coherence and according to what rules and laws they form a system. These two points of view are not independent; but they no longer constitute two different versions of a single theoretical text. Without giving for the moment a rigorous definition of the concept of a level,[4] let us say that these two points of view are connected, despite their heterogeneity of levels, and that one of the theoretical efforts to be promoted will be to show how some levels of the problematic are connected* [lit. articulated] to one another. We have formulated some propositions for a model of textual analysis on this point in another study: which we should be permitted to refer to.[5]

However, our work will intentionally place the two perspectives in a hierarchy by subordinating the first to the second. This is another way of admitting that the problem of the proper name cannot receive its general solution again and in particular in the framework of this study. However, in order to be able to execute correctly the constituent movement of the problematic of our work,[6] it is appropriate again to set forth very quickly the essential questions which we will pose concerning these texts.

THE PROPER NAME INDEX

The first statement of the definition suggested for the proper name in general is, if not an index,[7] at least an intermediary between language and gesture, between "meaning" it and "showing" it. According to [p. 25] this orientation, the proper name would designate an individual and would be at the same time not only devoid of every classificatory value in its usage, but equally of every signification by itself;[8] since entirely by belonging to the language (the articulated phonematic ensemble) it would only be defined by a single extra-linguistic relationship: the one by which it designates that object in the world, and not by the system of relationships that it should maintain with other names. In other words, it is possible to mark a series: "Dupont, Durand, Dunand, Duchamp, etc."; but at first sight, the differences between these vocable names (of saints), to the extent to which they are proper, are not relevant. They are insignificant. And it can be thought that the singularity of this relationship of naming

---

*See n. bottom p. 4.

[*nomination*] and the extra-linguistic position of one of its poles offers a privileged means of access to the problem of the referent in the constitution of the semiotic model of the sign: What would be the position, in the system of the *langue*, of an element whose every signification would be uniquely referential? Thus this element which would be designated in some way closer to the gesture than to the name is a name which indicates the exterior of language. And at first this would be by some names of this kind as the discourse makes use of them. The text in which they are written down would be concentrated on the external, not linguistic, "reality".

But in another sense, the proper name flows again from the material exteriority to which it seems to be linked, in order to be enclosed in the code of the *langue* where it is used, and it never leaves it. Consequently, the proper name, unlike the demonstrative noun, does not designate. It does not specify, properly speaking, this individual here. It does not point at all, but only designates in so far as it carries the proper name. It rises on the surface of the being in order to withdraw at the very moment when it rises. It says nothing about being; it is used of being.[9] It is an interaction of the language which R. Jakobson characterized by speaking of the circularity of the code.[10] "Socrates" is the name of a person named "Socrates". The departure of the name "Socrates" out of the code into the message is a false departure, because "Socrates" has no "meaning" in the message, except by reference to the element of the code "Socrates". The interplay of the proper name plays a game in this way superficially with the individual being who determines at one moment this linguistic element at the mercy of meaning. Also the proper name which says nothing about being, says everything about being immediately [p. 26] and at once. If I say "Dupont", I am saying *nothing* about Dupont in one sense, because the name "Dupont" cannot be the starting point of a movement of knowledge. But in another sense, I am saying *everything about Dupont*, but it is empty; it is taken in its totality, but derived from its name.[11]

THE PROPER NAME IN THE SYSTEM

If on the other hand, textual analysis shows that the proper name belongs to a signifier system, and if it is possible for us to describe this system in its pertinent oppositions in the very interior of the texts studies, then one step will be made in the establishment of a theory of the proper name, integrated in the general theory of the language. On the critical plane, one will then have shown that the problem of the referent in the establishment of the theory of the sign is a non-pertinent problem and must not be taken into consideration. But it could also be true that this demonstration itself may not be relevant to a general theory of the proper name. The latter would indeed remain what we have said: at the same time unimportant and aiming to empty an existential totality, considered as a proper name attached as such to its definition. But when it is used in a discourse,[12] when it appears in this ensemble of structurally connected sentences which we call a "narrative", then it acquires meaning from this appurtenance. Far from making us accede to a theory of the proper name, the proper name would give us one of the key-(stones) of a theory of the narrative, in that it would permit us to construct it on its specific level. Since the proper names are articulated in their signifier relationships inside of a narrative, they would never risk the introduction of some other significances [sic], from which they are themselves, by themselves, deprived, nor of causing other levels of analysis to interfere in the specific plan of the narrative syntax, since they would be shown to be inoperative in the search for meaning.

TOPICS

A second set of preliminary remarks is also necessary. It is also necessary for us in effect to justify the reason why we have chosen to study the proper *place* name in the [p. 27] Passion narratives. What is the reason for this limitation of the field of study? It is caused by the interference of a second problematic which concerns the fundamental relationship of space and meaning in the narrative.[13] Taken seriously, this relationship would permit us to come to a kind of minimal definition of the narrative in its most obvious manifestation. It would be the account in language of the *journeys* of human individuals[14] in space, and of their *positions* in some places of this space, without it being immediately useful for the moment to ask if these are the human individuals who, by their positions, constitute some places in this space,[15] or if these places "preexist" as some points of privileged articulations which give to the (individual) elements what goes through them or what establishes their qualifications and their functions.[16]

The Productive Scene

Nevertheless, such a definition has the double disadvantage of being too general and too superficial: too general, because it would be necessary to specify with more clarity and precision some rules, resolutions, and laws allowing us to understand the orientation and direction of these journeys

and the modalities of these positions;[17] too superficial, because it is not certain that a complete and systematic analysis of the texts, in which such accounts are given, does not
compel us to abandon the concept of man in order to keep only
those of functions and qualifications grouped in some ensembles
of which the analysis would have to describe the laws of interference, integration, or transformation. If it were possible
to arrive at such laws, the meaning of a narrative would then
be established by the specific way in which the space of the
narrative would be organized in the text which presents it in
the reading: space then would not simply refer to the different settings in which some "actions" of "personages" would be
developed. It would not only be a setting, but "a scene which
produces", on which some complex interactions of relationships,
groups, and knots of relationships are displayed--a scene
which, at the same time, discloses and envelops by giving a
combinatory to be read, not only whose internal and external
differences it would be appropriate to describe assiduously,
but also its constitutive rules.[18]   [p. 28]

The problem which would then be posed to a narrative
semiotics would be to define the way in which the space is
established on stage in and by a narrative which leads the
establishment of the meaning to be seen, that is to say to be
read,[19]--because there is a scene which is the text--but which
also conceals it in this same establishment, since the meaning
is established at all other levels and on all the other planes
where they are given to be read. The text-scene as a product
would receive in this way its "other", which is the very production of the text-scene. All the ambiguity of the narrative
would consist in passing itself off as a mirror product of the
"reality" when it is the production of the meaning in the space
of the text. If it is kept, at least in an operative and hypothetical title, the starting point of the analysis will then
have to be this textual constitution of the space by the journeys and the positions which articulate it.

The Topographic Code

Now it appears from the most superficial reading of the
gospel texts that this articulation is already made before
every journey, every position, of the "hero", his companions,
and his adversaries in the "heroic achievement" with which we
began the analysis. The space is marked by the proper place
names which--like every other proper name--point to the insignificance of the places of the world which they show, like
some sign posts at the border of a path which is already
traced out.[20] But perhaps that may be too much to say in
speaking of an articulation already made: it would imply

prior to the narrative that what concerns us is a more primitive narrative which is already written and where the scene of the text would already be drawn up. We do not set aside this direction of analysis which, by degrees, would return us to the open totality of the biblical texts, the New and Old Testaments.[21] But since, by a methodological decision,[22] our object is constituted by the Passion Narratives, and for some reasons of heuristic efficacy its progressive extension to all the biblical text would prohibit its examination practically from the start, it is possible to find a starting point which, while giving the presuppositions of the analysis, the foundation on the very inside of its textual object: the place name then appears in a contingent punctuality (by assumption), without any other relationship connecting them than the journey [p. 29] of Jesus, his "anabasis" to Jerusalem and to the Temple which will reverse[23] the movement of leaving to the Place of Skull and the nearby sepulchre.

Therefore it is at the level of the narrative that the toponyms have some chance of entering into a signifier system. But henceforward they will have to comply with the requirements of the laws of the narrative, while giving to it its drama, while establishing it in a space which is clearly stated from then on. In this way the place names come to appear simultaneously as one of the codes of the narrative, a code articulated in an open way[24] by the journeys and the positions that the narrative reveals superficially, but also as designating its referential in the geographic or historical "reality". The insignificance of the toponyms,[25] their radical contengency with respect to the actions and thoughts of personages, the empty aim that their indicial character implies, this collection of remarkable traits that the toponyms carry in themselves because they are proper names, will undergo an essential transformation, while becoming the ensemble of the points and places of spatial articulation of the narrative. It will accede to the narrative significance; but it will keep from its first definition the superficial appearance of contingency intended to anchor the narrative in "reality", offering to the narration of the being without the form of the reality of its scene.

THE DOUBLE INTERPLAY OF THE PLACE NAME

This will be therefore—at least hypothetically—the double interplay of the toponyms whose primary referential insignificance is—as in the Hegelian dialectic—at the same time preserved and transcended; transcended by their integration in the narrative in which they become the signifier articulations, (but then they cease to refer to some sites and places of the world); preserved because the proper names appear on the reading surface and will always appear as the duplication, in language, of the purely personal, of what is "here and now" unique in its facticity and its transcendence, in short as the upheaval in the text of the absolute referential, of that by which it cannot have of reducing knowledge. Thanks to this appearance which in the text, where they acquire their significance, preserves their original contingency, the text of the narrative simultaneously finds [p. 30] its stage and can display the spectacle of its meaning,[26] by hiding this setting by the apparent intrusion of referential reality. The stage then becomes reality. Thus the theatrical enticement is created, the specular illusion in which the living reader-speaker enters.

The study of the toponyms initially addressed arises therefore from the interference of two problematic planes: on the one hand, the question of the proper name as a quasi-index of language and element of the code which necessarily refers to it; and on the other hand, the problem of the spatiality of the meaning in the narrative. The toponym is the proper name of a piece of space. How does it articulate a meaning in and by its referential insignificance as an element of a narrative? Such is the fundamental question which we would like to tackle in the analysis of the Passion narratives and the examination of which has suggested to us some hypotheses stated below.

Chapter II

THE PLACES OF THE NARRATIVE:
DEATH AND RESURRECTION OF THE TOPONYMS

To a certain degree the Passion narratives can be considered to be the story of the journeys of the hero[27] in his
movements from one place to another and itineraries carefully
consigned by the narrator. It is these journeys which we would
like to follow through the four texts which present them to
us.[28] The most apparent relationship, which the surface of the
text reveals, therefore does not belong to them personally, but
is created by the movements of Jesus or results from his voy-
ages. Initially we are eliminating the question, however pertinent on a general plane, of the choice of Jesus as an actor of
articulation or a relation of the places of the space. In effect, the narratives which we are studying are those of the
Passion of Jesus. It is Jesus who is found to be bestowed in
the text itself with the role or the foundation of a vector of
meaning[29] of the space. It is he who orients the space by his
movements between some poles which are often named, movements
which determine the places of this space in their names. Thus
some recurrences of names are noted which are landmarks in the
journeys of the hero by a referential pinpointing. But the
recurrences themselves draw attention, moreover, to the oscil-
lating character of these movements, while a cursive reading
leaves the contrary impression that Jesus "went up" to Jerusalem in order to die. These oscillations affect the space of a
more or less large amplitude as in extension and are not at all
isochrones from one text to another. It is appropriate therefore to enter into the analysis, on the one hand, by depicting
in the different variants[30] the journeys of the hero and their
toponymic points; and on the other hand, by locating the differences which are inscribed between [p. 32] them in order to
construct at the same time the syntax[31] of this space of meaning, and in a more ambitious way the syntax of the differences
of this space by which the meaning is established.

CONSTRUCTION OF THE TOPONYMIC NETWORK

JOURNEY I

In a preceding study, which has been corroborated by other
works, the "beginning" of the Passion narrative has been deter-

mined to be the messianic entrance into Jerusalem. We will not repeat here the methodological problems provoked by this determination, nor the reasons which have led to the placing of it as a boundary of the narrative.[32] Therefore let us set up as a postulate the messianic entrance as the starting point of the itinerary of the hero in the narrative which interests us. Henceforth the places are determined in the following way in the four texts:

Matthew	Mount of Olives[33]	(determined geographically by two other names: Jerusalem and Bethphage) (Mt. 21:1)
Mark	near the Mount of Olives	(determined by three names: Jerusalem, Bethphage, and Bethany) (Mk. 11:1)
Luke	near the Mount of Olives	(determined by three names: Jerusalem, Bethphage, and Bethany)
John	Bethany	(determined by only one name: Jerusalem)

This starting point is marked in the four texts considered by the joyous demonstrations of the crowd. The people cut off tree branches, and while scattering them on the ground the acclamations resound: "Hosanna to the Son of David! Blessed is he who comes in the name of the Lord!" (Mt. 21:9). "Blessed be the Kingdom to come! Blessed be He, the King in the name of the Lord!..." However this atmosphere of joy is already found in Luke and John to be troubled by a threat: "Teacher, rebuke your disciples," [Lk. 19:39] some Pharisees ask in Luke. And in this same text, Jesus himself completely changes the meaning of this royal entrance by his lamentations on Jerusalem (Lk. 19:41-44). In John (12:19) the same thing is heard, the discordant note [p. 33] of the reflections of the Pharisees: "You see that you can do nothing; look, the world has gone after him."

Then the second movement of the journey of Jesus begins, a movement also marked by a toponym in three texts, while in the last (John), the place is blotted out by a discourse (12:23f.) and by a movement of withdrawal (12:36).

Matthew	Jerusalem
Mark	Jerusalem Temple
Luke	Temple

The entrance into Jerusalem is qualified by a questioning of identity in Matthew ("Who is this?", someone asks, "And the crowds said: 'This the prophet Jesus from Nazareth of Galilee'", Mt. 21:10-11), by a simple glance in Mark ("when he had looked round at everything", Mk. 11:11), and by the episode of the expulsion of the merchants from the temple in Luke 19:45-46 ("And he entered the temple and began to drive out those who sold..."). The discourse of Jesus which is found in John is complex, but it has the characteristic of being the moment of a divine designation. To the trouble and the agony which Jesus manifests, a heavenly voice responds: "I have glorified it, and I will glorify it again" [Jn. 12:28], but as in Matthew, it is also the moment of a questioning of identity: "Who is this Son of man?" [Jn. 12:34].

The third stage is then completed, but only in Matthew. It is a stage marked by the episode of the expulsion of the vendors and the merchants, but also by some healings and some critical reactions by the chief priests and scribes to the acclamations of the children (Mt. 21-15-16). The four texts are then found again to note a departure of Jesus, a departure which emphasizes one toponym in the three Synoptics. It will also be noted that Luke focuses on the Temple, without any other explicit indication of local movement, all the critical, even provoking, teaching of Jesus with respect to the chief priests, scribes, Pharisees, Sadducees, but also the large discourse on the destruction of Jerusalem and the Temple and on the eschatological return.

Matthew	Bethany	
Mark	Bethany	
Luke	Mount of Olives	[p. 34]

The Spacings

At the end of this first description, one sees some characteristic differences are noted in the toponymic and topographic organization of the displacements of Jesus:

1. The text of Matthew includes four main headings, Luke includes two, and Mark's appears to be intermediary since it groups Jerusalem and the Temple into a single local unit. The simple binary organization of space in Luke is opposed to that which is ternary and redundant from Matthew, Mark being an intermediary variant.

2. In the three Synoptics the point of beginning is the Mount of Olives and the point of ending is the Temple. But again Luke is opposed to the two others by fixing the point of return of Jesus at the Mount of Olives, which is the starting point chosen by John. In other words, Jesus in Luke is never in Jerusalem, but either on the Mount of Olives (the point of departure and point of arrival) or in the Temple.

Therefore the formula can be written down:

(Mount of Olives vs. Temple)

as characteristic of Luke, while the text of Matthew will be defined by the two redundant formulas:

(Mount of Olives vs. Jerusalem vs. Temple)
(Temple vs. city vs. Bethany)

in which "Temple" is opposed equally to the "Mount of Olives" and to "Bethany", and each time through the mediation of "Jerusalem" and the "city".

In John on the other hand a binary articulation of space is found:

(Bethany vs. Jerusalem)

and, at this level of the narrative, there is a double disappearance of two toponymic elements figuring in the Synoptics: the Mount of Olives and the Temple.

Actors

If we now characterize the three topical points of Matthew by the relationships between the different actors which are [p. 35] revealed,[34] it is remarkable that the Mount of Olives is qualified by the conjunction of the people and the hero, the Temple by the disjunction of the merchants, the chief priests, and the scribes and the hero and finally "Jerusalem" is characterized as the place of the question of identity, the place of the neutral;[35] so the formula is:

(Mount of Olives vs. Jerusalem vs. Temple)
      C   O   D

In Luke, on the other hand, the two poles of the binary spatial relationship concentrate some semantic conjunctional *and* disjunctual elements: on the Mount of Olives the lamentations over Jerusalem are combined with the acclamations signifying the recognition of the King [*Toi*?] by the people; and the critical and trick questions of the Pharisees, chief priests, and Sadducees are blended in the Temple with the expulsion of the vendors and the enthusiastic attention of the people (19:48; 20:45; 21:38). The discourse announcing the destruction of the temple (21:6) and Jerusalem is ended with the return of the Son of Man on a cloud with power and great glory (21:25-28). The Mount of Olives and the Temple constitute therefore some compound places where some contrary semantic elements are united, even if they do not originate from the same semantic level. Henceforth we can write:

(Mount of Olives vs. Temple)
      C/D   C/D

As for Mark, the corresponding narrative segment could be described in the following toponymic articulation:

(Mount of Olives vs. Jerusalem-Temple // Temple vs. Bethany)
    C   O

a formulation which reveals the semantically unfinished character of the displacement in this variant.

In John the signifier opposition is different: (Bethany vs. Jerusalem). As in Luke it is qualified at each of its poles in a compound way. At Bethany the critical negative remarks of the Pharisees are blended with the acclamations of recognition of the King of Israel. The divine mark [p. 36] of "glorification" is articulated in the mortal agony which contains the discourse to the God-fearing Greeks (Jn. 12:27). It is a qualifying mark of the hero before the text (12:28) and the affirmation of triumph (v. 32).[36] The same remark will be made concerning the question about the identity of the Son of

Man. Therefore this will be written down:

(Bethany vs. Jerusalem)

C/D   C/D

a formula which is nothing else than Luke's toponymically and
topographically displaced. We separate from this analysis of
John an essential semantic articulation which we will tackle
later, which determines the place of Bethany, and the conclusion of which is a correlative of the episode of the qualifying mark of v. 28: the Resurrection of Lazarus (at Bethany)
vs. Anointing of Jesus (at Bethany) vs. the Point of departure and the royal entrance (at Bethany).[37]

We can regroup these analyses into the following table:

TEXTS	*Places:*	BETHANY	MOUNT OF OLIVES	JERUSALEM	TEMPLE
Luke			C/D		C/D
John		C/D		C/D	
Matthew			C	O	D
Mark			C		O

   Let us emphasize one last point concerning the process
which has allowed us to obtain the conjunctional or disjunctional determinations, the compound or neutral of the space of
displacement of the hero, thanks to which the space is articulated in places of the meaning in the text. This process is
that of the meeting, at these points of space, of the hero considered as a vector of orientation with other actors: the
people (or nation), Pharisees, scribes, chief priests, Sadducees, vendors, merchants, and finally the disciples. In fact,
we have only taken into consideration actions appearing in a
specified place in relation to the hero who is displaced and
who to some extent defines it as a place by his displacement.[38]
Conjunction or disjunction are understood therefore from the
relationship between the hero and an X whose semantic content
we connot take into consideration again. [p. 37]

JOURNEY II

The second displacement of Jesus is carried out therefore between Bethany and the Temple in Matthew and Mark only because Luke has concentrated all the qualifications of the two localized poles in the first displacement. It is necessary, however, to note that Luke's large sequence[39] "Mount of Olives--Temple--Mount of Olives" encloses, but in the form of a summary, the secondary oscillations which we find in Mark and Matthew. Although it could be that the opposition between the Mount of Olives and the Temple which is a characteristic of Luke constitutes the final stage of one transformation[40] of which the text of Mark would deliver the first state. The complex characteristics of the two poles of the relationship would indicate it sufficiently by an opposition to the articulation unfinished--inchoative--of the space of the meaning in Mark. This hypothesis is not insignificant because if it is confirmed it would give us the syntactic rules of transformation of the toponyms in some of the texts which we will consider.

Intermediary Space

Therefore let us examine the text of Mark. As in the preceding sequence, the telescoping of the places of arrival, Jerusalem and the temple, will be noted (Mk. 11:15), "And they came to Jerusalem. And he entered the temple...." The starting point is Bethany and the space between Bethany and Jerusalem--Temple is marked by the episode of the barren fig-tree, while the place of arrival is qualified as a compound term at the same time by the expulsion of the vendors from the Temple (Mk. 11:15-17), and by the opposition of the chief priests and the scribes, but also by the joy of the people to his teaching (Mk. 11:18). Therefore this formula can be presented:

(Bethany vs. Jerusalem-Temple)

But the opposition between the two places is negatively marked by the curse hurled at the fig-tree.

(Bethany vs. Jerusalem-Temple)
O   D = (fig-tree) D/C

We are also presented at this point of the narrative with the passage to a [p. 38] ternary sequence, but whose third term has the peculiar trait of not being toponymically marked: the barren fig-tree qualifying the *space between* Bethany (an unmarked term since nothing happens there) and Jerusalem--the Temple.[41] Finally, the point of return is not marked, "And when evening came they went out of the city" (Mk. 11:19).

In Matthew 21:18 it will be noted that the episode of the fig tree qualifies the movement to the city, and therefore the space between Bethany and Jerusalem. But Jerusalem is not named (considered as a toponym), the place of arrival of the displacement of Jesus being the Temple where Jesus gives a parabolic teaching which provokes the anger of the Pharisees, Sadducees, and scribes, but also as a counterpart the interest of the people ("they held him to be a prophet", 21:46; 22:33). This teaching is closed with the curses hurled at the scribes and Pharisees and with the reprimand to Jerusalem, Mtt. 23:31-39. One can then write:

(Reentry into the city   vs.   Temple)

Place not marked   D = barren   C/D

fig tree

Ternarity

This organization is ternary, the topic opposition being constructed between two poles of which one is a place which is not named: "reentry into a city" but whose relationship is at the same time oriented and marked. It is oriented towards the Temple and negatively marked in the intermediary space between this outside of the city which implies the arrival at it and the Temple, by the curse on the fig tree which qualifies the space of displacement, the journey into its oriented spatiality.

This organization is doubled by a ternary articulation oriented in a sense contrary to that of the Temple to the Mount of Olives (Mt. 24:1-3): "Jesus left the temple....As he sat on the Mount of Olives...." It is at this place that the narrator places the large eschatological discourse in which it is simultaneously announced that the holy place will see the installation of the desolating sacrilege (Mt. 24:15f.), but also the triumphal arrival of the Son of Man (Mt. 21:29f. and 25:31-46). It will be noted that, here again, as "on the outward journey", the intermediary space of the journey is negatively qualified by the remark of Jesus [p. 39] about the destruction of the Temple (Mt. 24:1-2). This process can therefore be summarized in the following way:

(Temple vs. Mount of Olives)

O   D   C/D

By combining the two descriptive formulas of the going and the
return, the opposition (Temple vs. Mount of Olives) is found
in Matthew characterized in these two poles by a complex semantic content, a complete formula which is nothing else than
that of Luke.

Finally, we can very rapidly analyze a third additional
sequence in Mark which repeats the same articulations as
Matthew:

(outside of the city	vs.	Jerusalem-Temple)
O	D (= fig tree)	D/C
(Temple	vs.	Mount of Olives)
	D (= announcement of the destruction of the Temple	D/C (= eschatological discourse)

It is enough for us to refer back to what has preceded in
order to obtain a signifier organization of the space identical
to that of Matthew, an organization which again returns to the
formula which we have given for Luke.

Overdeterminations

However, attention will be drawn to an important difference: Luke concentrates in the Temple, not only some disjunctional functions like the expulsion of the vendors and the
growing opposition to the Pharisees, Scribes...but also the
eschatological discourse which, in Mark and Matthew, qualifies
the Mount of Olives in a remarkable way. Therefore we find in
Luke an "overdetermination" of the Temple in its opposition to
the Mount of Olives which in Luke is only the ambiguous starting point of the messianic entrance. On the other hand, in
Mark and Matthew, at the end of the transformation of the initial signifier relationship of the space when all is said and
done, it is the Mount of Olives which, if not overdetermined, at least, balances the semantic values which [p. 40]
the Temple holds. In effect, it is at the same time the starting point of the messianic entrance of Jesus into Jerusalem,
and the point of return of Jesus, before the narrative of his

death properly speaking, it is a place where he pronounces the great eschatological discourse, i.e. the announcement of the vengeance, the judgment, and the royal-prophetic return of the Son of Man.

Also in order to transcribe symbolically the signifier system of the toponyms in this preface to the Passion narrative at the end of the transformations of the system through the texts of the three Synoptics, we could point out the opposition:

(Mount of Olives: Temple: Matthew--Mark: Luke)

a result of the transformation of a ternary organization in which Jerusalem occupies an intermediary position (neutral or compound). What does the obliteration of Jerusalem on the eve of the Passion narrative, properly speaking, correspond to on the plane of the significations? Only a carrying out of the analysis will be able to teach us. The extrinsic position of the system of toponyms in John receives from it then only more of a signifier value:

(Bethany vs. Jerusalem)

It could be possible indeed in effect that in John everything is already said before the messianic entrance into Jerusalem, since Jesus has already gone four times to Jerusalem.[42]

But in the text itself which we are studying and according to the segmentation which we have considered, it is certain that in John the term overdetermined on the eve of the Passion is Bethany. It is in this privileged place that some of the essential values of the Passion narrative are found presented, *before* the messianic entrance. We will undertake this study later.[43]

JOURNEY III

The Obliteration of the Toponyms

The opposition of Matthew and Mark on the one hand, and Luke on the other, is continued in the following sequences of the displacements of Jesus and in the naming of the places which these displacements connect. In effect it is remarkable that the starting point of the final journey of Jesus to Jerusalem is Bethany [p. 41] where the anointing of Jesus by a wo-

man takes place as an anointing for death in Matthew and Mark:
"In pouring this ointment on my body she has done it to prepare me for burial" (Mt. 26:12). "She has anointed my body
beforehand for burying" (Mk. 14:8). Before the tests the hero
receives the mark which qualifies him to confront them, even
if this qualification refers less, in the language of Propp
and Greimas, to the primary test, the crucifixion, than the
test immediately following, that of the death and Resurrection.
From *Bethany*, Jesus thus marked goes to a *city* where the meal
takes place, and from there Jesus and his companions leave for
the *Mount of Olives* where the scene of his agony and the desertion by his disciples unfolds before his arrest. It is fitting
to emphasize here that, in each of the three Synoptics, but not
in John, the proper name of Jerusalem is not mentioned, but
only the common noun of "city". Thus in Matthew 26:18: "He
said, 'Go into the city to such a one....'" The same thing
is true in Mark 14:13, 16 and in Luke 22:10. Thus in the first
sequence of the Passion narrative properly speaking the obliteration of "Jerusalem" as a toponym is confirmed which had already begun at the end of the preceding sequence, at the time
of the large eschatological discourse.[44]

In Luke we note a significant difference. Jesus has been
left on the Mount of Olives (Olivet) in Lk. 21:37. But there
is no named and marked starting point of the displacement of
Jesus. Not only is Bethany not named, but the episode of the
"mortuary" anointing of Jesus is missing.[45] Thus in Matthew
and Mark we find a ternary organization of the space, but the
central place of which is no longer determined by its name:

(Bethany vs. the city vs. Mount of Olives)

While in Luke we observe a binary organization in which
one of the poles is equally toponymically obliterated:

(Mount of Olives vs. city)

After his arrest, Jesus carries out a new displacement
from the Mount of Olives to some places especially marked by
the names of persons, the home of Caiphas, the palace of Herod,
the home of the Chief Priest, the Council of the Elders of the
People, the Praetorium, and the home of Pilate. These places
where interrogations and trials unfold are in Jerusalem, or as
is the case [p. 42] for the Sanhedrin, in the Temple. But here
again neither the Temple nor Jerusalem are named.

Finally, once the condemnations are delivered, a new displacement is produced to the place of the skull, Golgotha, a

movement which draws to a close at the tomb hewn in the rock
for Joseph of Arimathea. It will be noted that the toponym of
the death of Jesus on the cross, Golgotha, is translated by all
the evangelists: "the place of the skull".[46] On the other
hand, John will not name the Mount of Olives, but he will designate the place of the arrest as a "garden across the Kidron
valley" (Jn. 18:1). A significantly similar designation will
designate the place of his death and burial in 19:41: "Now in
the place where he was crucified there was a garden, and in the
garden a new tomb." Thus it seems that the Passion narrative
presents us with a progressive obliteration of the toponyms in
the central sequences: Jerusalem, and then the Temple disappear. Whenever they exist, they are translated, e.g. Golgotha.
Finally it is not until the Mount of Olives in John that a toponym is not erased from the map of the narrative.

The most apparent signification of this obliteration of
the proper names, which varies from one text to another, appears to us to be the following: at these fundamental points
of the narrative, which are the tests where the moment of the
reversal of the narrative logic is articulated, it is necessary to give the greatest signifier potentialities to the
places of the space of the narrative. The places are then
named by the names of the actors of the drama and not by the
geographic referent; or rather they are translated into common
nouns in order to be able to enter more directly into one or
several signifier systems.

Thus for the toponyms "Jerusalem" or the "Temple", which
do not appear as such in the narrative, the nodal points of
articulation of the trial of Jesus, the homes of the actors,
Annas, Caiaphas, Pilate, Herod, or the Elders of the people
joined in a body, are found substituted. The advantage which
figurative Christian representation will draw from "Golgotha",
which is translated by the expression "place of the skull", is
well known. The same remark can be made about the episode of
the death of Judas in Matthew (Mt. 27:3-10) with the name
"Akeldama" ["Field of Blood", Acts 1:18-19], doubly translated
as citationally and historically defined in its function. But
this process never appears as clearly as in John: the double
annulment of the proper names "Mount of Olives" and "Golgotha"
either by broad geographic localization, or by translation,
[p. 43] permit him to construct some homomorphic spatial
schemas from the Mount of Olives and Golgotha: two gardens
with a hill in the center of them, where on one side the departure to death will be accomplished, and on the other side
its completion in the tomb which hollows the hill out even
more centrally.

If the four texts[47] are superimposed and reduced to their spatial organization marked in the toponyms or their substitutes, and if the space that the text articulates is constructed in this way, then more interesting equivalences appear between some elements of the upper half of the model and those of its lower half, as if the stages of the displacements to the condemnation to death, to the principal test and their named or substituted points, by a purely synchronic logical action, could lead us to recover the stages of the displacements to the death and burial.

Bethany	Mount of Olives	Jerusalem	Temple	Affirmation of the toponyms
Sepulchre	Golgotha or place of the skull	Jerusalem	Temple	Obliteration of the toponyms by substitution

The advantage of this schema is to make apparent the structural equivalence between the Mount of Olives and Golgotha, Bethany and the Sepulchre. It is an equivalence of which only John begins to clarify in the interplay of substituted nominations and overdeterminations of certain places. We will come back to this.

JOURNEY IV

Resurrection of the Names

The last phase of the displacements of Jesus occurs after the Burial. Its principal episodes are the resurrection and the ascension. As a matter of fact, the nature of the spatial articulation reveals a change in its process. The *appearances* of the hero are substituted for the *journeys*. His displacements enliven the space in the horizontality and bear a signifier direction following some irruptions locally pin-pointed according to a scheme of verticality which makes access to, even gives rise to the "meaning", or the place where they take place. In Matthew Jesus appears to his disciples "to Galilee, to the mountain to which Jesus had directed them" [p. 44] (Mt. 28:16). In Mark Jesus appears in an unspecified place to Mary

Magdalene (Mk. 16:9), then to two companions who were walking
on a road in the country (Mk. 16:12). Finally Jesus appears
to the Eleven themselves during which they had dinner. In the
second case, the absence of the dead body in the sepulchre is
significant of the resurrection, i.e. of a Living *elsewhere* in
an open space, the mountain in Galilee, the country, and the
road, or the unspecified place where the Eleven were having
dinner. This "elsewhere", which is difficult to name, is in
some way the counterpart of the absence of the hero at this
precise point of the space of the narrative, the tomb. But
there is also another compensation which appears here, since
the living elsewhere (in different unspecified places of space)
is substituted for the absent dead person there (in the sepulchre).[49]

Luke

On the other hand, Luke offers us a complete version of
the events which have followed the death of Jesus and especially the appearances of Jesus to the disciples. But these
appearances take place in some points of space carefully named
and specified, Emmaus, a village about sixty-stadia from Jerusalem (Lk. 24:13) to Jerusalem is named as such (Lk. 24:33-
36). The ascension of Jesus, his glorious manifestation, and
the exaltation of the "hero" takes place at Bethany (Lk. 24:
50); and finally the disciples return to Jerusalem with great
joy (Lk. 24:52) and are continually in the Temple praising God
(Lk. 24:53). It will be recalled here that Luke, unlike Matthew and to a lesser degree Mark, in the initial phases of the
Passion narrative has immediately eliminated a certain number
of toponyms in the setting forth of the displacements of
Christ, in favor of an antithetical opposition (Mount of
Olives vs. Temple) in which the Temple was, moreover, the
overdetermined place. Bethany has only appeared to be a secondary determination of the starting point of the messianic
entrance, and the episode of the mortuary anointing, whose
rich intra-textual significance explodes from Matthew to
John, has disappeared from his narrative.

It would seem therefore--and the toponymic abstract
proves it--that Luke moves *after* the central episodes of the
Passion narrative some toponymic elements which Matthew and
Mark [p. 45] place *before*, namely, the supper, the arrest, the
trial, the putting to death and the burial. If the mortuary
anointing at Bethany does not occur in Luke, on the other
hand, the ascension takes place. If Jerusalem as a place of
action never appears to be named from the beginning of the
narrative, it appears two times in chapter 24. It is to Jerusalem that the two disciples go to give the narrative of

the appearance at Emmaus. It is at Jerusalem that the proclamation of repentance in the name of Christ must begin (24:47). It is to Jerusalem that the disciples return with great joy. Finally the ensemble of the narrative draws to a close in the Temple (24:53). Matthew and Luke from this point of view occupy an inverse position which the schema below summarizes:

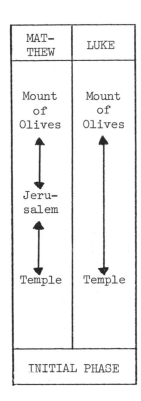

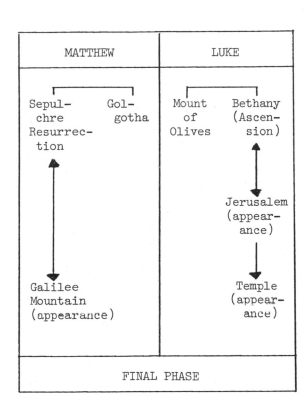

Finally it is necessary to introduce the information supplied by *Acts* 1:12 which describes the place of the ascension of Jesus on the *Mount of Olivet*. To the beginning of the messianic entrance, the Mount of Olives, geographically determined by Bethany (and Bethphage), a textual place of the beginning of the story, there corresponds the textual place of its conclusion, which is also a double, *Bethany* and the *Mount of Olives*. This duality is required in Luke by the necessity to compensate for the absence of the mortal qualification of the hero at the place Bethany, and by an eternal and glorious qualification. But it was also necessary that the Mount of Olivet

which, according to the same narrator, occupies in the first
sentences of the narrative, a position antithetical to the
Temple and which supports in the [p. 46] central phase with
its structural correspondent, the place of the skull, the importance of the negative functions (agony, desertion, and arrest on the one hand and crucifixion and death on the other),
receive a positive sanction by becoming the other place of the
Ascension.[49]

HYPOTHESES I AND II

Thus to the general hypothesis which we have alluded to
concerning toponyms and their substitutes, a collorary hypothesis is added which relates to the differential interplay of
the place names in the texts studies.[50] Let us reformulate in
complete clarity the general hypothesis: at the beginning of
the narrative in the inaugurative phases of the story the
proper place names are seized by the plot (the text) of the
narrative. If they receive a "semantic charge" from the displacements of the hero which integrates them into a signifier
system which is that of the text, at this point of its reading, they preserve however their referential indexing--ap-
parently at least--which has the advantage of "realizing" the
scene of the narrative, by giving it as a space of the world.
But for that very reason the toponyms do not come from a simple manipulation in the text, because despite their appurtenance to the system of the narrative, they designate and refer to some places of geographical and historical space.[51]
What therefore makes them participate in the large functional
inversion, in the transformations syntagmatic and paradigmatic
at the same time which display the narrative interplay of a
beginning and an end, of an initial negative situation and a
final positive situation through the multiple tests?[52]

It is necessary then to obliterate them as proper names,
to translate them, or to substitute for them some more generic
designations which will immediately submit without difficulty
to the injunctions of the general signifier system and will
permit a communication of the narrative, without viscosity,
"noise", or distortion.[53] "Jerusalem" becomes "the city"
where some points are defined which are only the positional
places of the actors of the narrative, the homes, or the
palaces of x, y, or z.... The Temple has disappeared from
the scene of the narrative. It is in an extrinsic-extra-
textual way that we know that the Council of the Elders of
the People in Luke met together in the Temple, and yet there
are some determinations that this toponym had not been em-
bellished beforehand. Golgotha expressly signifies the place

of the skull, and it is not [p. 47] until the Mount of Olives
in John that it will become "a garden on the other side of the
Kidron" [Jn. 18:1].

But once the Last Supper, Trial, Death, and Resurrection
are completed, i.e. once the functional inversions and the actantial transformations are realized in the text, then the same
toponyms reappear. But they are invested with a new signifier
system, just as the passage by the common nouns has permitted
it to be put into place. Thus we see, in the narrator who more
than any other has contributed to a weakening of the toponyms
of the Passion narrative around some antithetical places; thus
we see Luke names Jerusalem, the Temple, Bethany, and the Mount
of Olives in the final moments of the narrative.

This remark concerning Luke leads us to suggest a collorary hypothesis which simultaneously will contribute to color-
ing the general hypothesis and will also be a confirmation of
it. In effect, from one text to another and from one variant
to another, we see being produced in the nominations of the
places, their substitutions, and in their semantic content
(we mean by that the relationship that these direct or substituted nominations enter with some action of the hero who alone
permits them, since he himself displaces them or appears in
them) some differences which do not seem to be accidental to
us, the regular organization of which one can attempt to describe. Thus these differences and these systematic and coherent variances are themselves indirectly the proof that the
toponyms or their substitutes enter into a complex signifier
system, of which the general hypothesis has given us the law
of a more abstract formality than the particular signifier
systems which articulate it by their differences. [p. 48]

Chapter III

TOPONYMIC SYSTEMS AND SECONDARY TOPICS:
THE ENTRANCES OF JESUS
INTO THE CITY AND THE TEMPLE

Henceforth the problem is to introduce, with a much greater precision, the functional and actantial toponymic variants
within the general system of significance of the place names.[54]
This, by its very generality, is much too formal to permit us
to grasp the sense of the text, a sense which once again consists only of a difference between some secondary systems of
significance.[55] However the dimensions our study requires does
not permit us to discuss the totality of our texts. We will
set limits to our work on some segments of the narrative, and
we will present these studies as many independent fragments
that a complete general study in the scope of our work will
have to combine.

Our first work rests on the central segment of the Passion
narrative, that segment during which the proper names are obliterated and which for this fact offers very great interest
for the general articulation of the narrative. We have seen
that this central segment which includes the fundamental tests
of the narrative, from the trial to death, are begun in the
three Synoptics by an entrance of Jesus into the city, an entrance which is not only a prelude to the organization of the
"pascal" meal,[56] but during which the very name of Jerusalem
is found to disappear, in a particularly open way. We would
like to show that this entrance begins a second system of organization of the narrative space in the text, a system which
is, to a certain extent, superimposable on the "messianic" entrance into Jerusalem.[57] Consequently, the syntagmatic organization of the narrative which, in the textual diachrony, places
in [p. 49] a position behind the royal entrance into Jerusalem,
the arrival at the city for the meal, arising from a paradigmatic organization which achronically presents the spatial signifier systems in an extensive--comprehensive hierarchy. In
other words, the later episode 2 (arrival at the city) can be
folded back on the earlier episode 1 (entrance to Jerusalem)
in an achronic transformation of the spatial organization which
only preserves the most general relationships in it, but establishes an order between the two episodes which is a generator
of meaning.[58]

42

In the three variant texts it will be noted that the prep-
eration of the Passover poses a problem of place: *"Where will
you have us prepare for you* to eat the Passover?" (Mt. 26:17);
"Where will you have us go and prepare for you to eat the passover?" (Mk. 14:12), the disciples say in Matthew and Mark
(Peter and John in Luke 22:8-9). To eat the Passover together
is first of all *to know where* to eat it. The meal is inseparable from the place where it occurs, from the space which at
the same time makes it possible and which it establishes in a
place. The response of Jesus to the question about the place
of the meal is indirect: it consists of *sending some disciples, or Peter or John*, to the city where they will have to
meet a man carrying a jug of water (Mark and Luke), a man whom
they will have to follow to *his home* where he will enter. And
it is to the proprietor of the home that the question of the
place will be posed again, but on the part of Jesus: "Where
is *the room* where I am to eat the Passover with my disciples?"
(Mk. 14:14; cf. Lk. 22:11); and the master of the house will
carry up a large cask to an upper room furnished with cushions.
Only Matthew's texts presents a remarkable breakdown at this
point, since Jesus contents himself with requesting the hospitality for the Paschal meal by two disciples, in the city, with
"such a one" (Mt. 26:18).

But we note that the prelude to the messianic entrance into Jerusalem is organized according to an apparent schema:[59]
Jesus, arriving with his disciples at the Mount of Olives near
Bethphage and Bethany (Mt. 21:1), sends two of them: "Go into
the village opposite you, and immediately you will find an ass
tied, and a colt with her"; (Mt. 21:2): which no one has ever
ridden; (Mk. 11:2; Lk. 19:30): bring it to me; (Mt. 21:2):
untie them and bring them to me; (Mk. 11:2): bring it after
having untied it. To the owner [p. 50] you will respond that
"The Lord has need of it and will send it back here immediately..." (Mk. 11:3).

The entrance in two cases is prepared by two (or several)
messengers who must recognize a sign of entrance (the male
bearer of the jug of water, and the wild ass);[60] but the sign
announced by Jesus is at the same time a means of entrance
(the man leads the ass that will carry Jesus to the chosen
house). In the second case, a gift to Jesus will be required
to open a new space in its method, Jerusalem in one case, the
city in the other. He will not fill the cask; he will only go
into Jerusalem because "such a one" will have given to him the
means, a gift which is at the same time a foreseen and anticipated sign; an offering-sign of which he is sure by anticipa-

tion that he will not be refused:

	A	B	C	D
I	Jesus sends his disciples	to the village opposite	to find an ass (a she-ass)	means of entrance into Jerusalem
II	Jesus sends his disciples	to the city	to find a man (a bearer of a jug of water)	means of entrance into the city

And when subsequently Jesus will enter into the Temple, it is easy to see his structural equivalent in the upper room where the meal will be received.

This is therefore the second spatial signifier system which, at the time of the later entrance of Jesus into the city, doubles the first, and which the messianic entrance into Jerusalem establishes:[61]

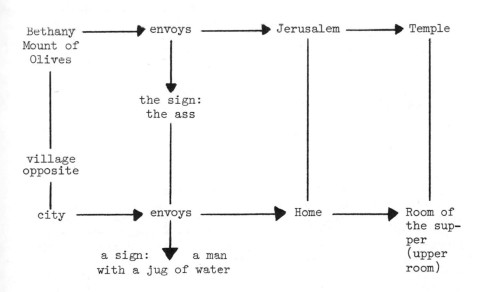

Henceforward it will be significant to note that the episode
which immediately follows the entrance into the Temple in [p.
51] the three synoptics is the expulsion of the vendors from
the Temple, as that which follows the installation in the home
of the meal is the announcement of the betrayal of Judas, that
is to say his expulsion, moral at least from the meal.[62]

The New Temple, the New Jerusalem

What reveals this superimposition of two successive episodes in a single achronic structure and the recovery of two
spatial organizations, is first of all the elucidation, by
this operatory interplay, of a meaning which, retrospectively,
explains to us the obliteration of the proper names in the
central segment: if from the last entrance of Jesus into the
"city", "Jerusalem" is the "home" where Jesus settles himself
with his disciples, and if this "Temple" is the "supper room"
where Jesus eats with them and celebrates the Passover, then
it is understood that the name of Jerusalem and that of the
Temple can no longer be uttered in their proper nomination.[63]
It is not, as a superficial reading would make us believe, the
generic term of a city which is to be substituted for that of
Jerusalem in particular. Jerusalem, in these fundamental moments where the narrative in its functions inverts itself
around its center, is the place where Jesus is. The Temple
is the place where the hero eats, i.e. sacrifices and is
sacrificed in a meal. The proper names are not only found
replaced by some common nouns, but they are focused again on
the only proper name which can exist as a person and a place,
which is by its very presence in the space, the place of this
space, i.e. the point where this space becomes meaning. Because at this point of space, the sense--the language in the
form of a unique proper name, "Jesus"--becomes a consumable
body--that is a thing sacrificed containing a sacred place and
a content of sacrifice.[64]

Metonymic Metaphor

If we now reflect on the processes by which this revealing transformation of a paradigmatic system of meaning is diachronically accomplished, we perceive in the work a kind of
transformation which we have already recognized in several
repetitions of the biblical texts. It is a metaphoric-metonymic transformation which permits us to conjugate the unfolding
of the narrative and the establishment of its coding.[65] In
effect, the house and [p. 52] the supper room constitute for
a hermeneutic of meaning, by a deciphering of the text, the
metaphors of Jerusalem and the Temple. And the "laminated"

["*feuilletée*"] structure by which we have described them constitutes a structure of characteristic orders of the symbolic
metaphoric function.[66] But it is remarkable that we cannot
consider the metaphor until we consider the allegory, or the
personification, i.e. until its literary conclusion.[67] In
effect his home is *in* Jerusalem. It is a home among other
homes of the city and in his home, likewise, the supper room:
a metonymic process, this time, by which one part is taken for
the whole. Nevertheless, this element is not only substituted
for the whole by pure contiguity, the home for the city, the
supper room for the home. It metaphorizes the whole in which
it takes place: inside of Jerusalem there is a home which is
"like" Jerusalem and in this home, a supper room which is
"like" the Temple is in Jerusalem, its center and its summary.
But this double process is connected by a double displacement
of Jesus in the space. He has entered into Jerusalem and into the Temple; and he has left them. Then again he has entered
into the city, into a home, and in this home, into a supper
room to celebrate the Passover; and this being done, the house
is "like" Jerusalem and the room "like" the Temple.

The repetition of displacements has permitted us to construct the metaphoric process; their diachronic succession in
the narrative articulates the metonymy in it.[68] Why? Because
a subject, the hero Jesus, appears to be a vector of meaning
in both cases. He is at the same time a dynamic element of
the space thanks to which the places are established. But he
is also all the space where the places are established, all
the space which is established as a place, which is concentrated in its heart, a concentrate of space. There is in the
city, a home; in the home, a supper room; and soon in the
center of this room, and in the center of the table, a piece
of bread and a glass of wine. Jesus is thus properly and
figuratively the operator of the twisting of the space around
himself as a topic organization of the text. He is a realized
metaphor of that of which the text speaks, but also a metonymic concentration of all the text which in a name becomes a
fragment of space.[69]

The text bears the marks of these movements of covering
up metaphoric-metonymic sites. The obliteration of the [p.
53] toponyms at a certain point of the narrative, the parallelism of two entrances of which the first, despite its air
of triumph and glory, is the unsuccessful double of the second,
which thanks to its obliteration will be glorifying. There are
still others that it is advisable to inventory.

THE INTERMEDIARY SPACE

As Hunger

In effect, between these two messianic-royal and paschal human-divine entrances, the texts of Matthew and Mark tell about another entrance which the analysis must reveal as an intermediary operation between the two spatial signifier systems in a position of recovery.[70] This is the journey between Bethany and the city[71] marked by the curse of the fig-tree. Without a doubt, this narrative segment does not contain any of the textual indices which have permitted us to put the other two entrances into correlation. Jesus especially in this case comes in person to recognize the fig-tree whose temporary barrenness becomes by his *parole* the sign of a mortal barrenness: a kind of parabolic miracle which wavers between the didactic symbolic discourse and the action employing a cipher with an edifying value. Moreover, Jesus draws from it a teaching about the power of faith, especially in prayer.

However, as for the ass's foal or the man bearing the jug of water, the sign of the fig tree must be a means of entrance into the city. "In the morning, as he was returning to the city, he was hungry" (Mt. 21:18). "On the following day, when they came from Bethany, he was hungry" (Mk. 11:12). As the ass's foal is a non-royal means of transport of the King of Israel, the man with the jug is a "picturesque" means of finding the point of arrival,[72] the home, the place of the sacrificial meal, the hoped-for-figs are a means of appeasing the hunger during the journey to the city. And the fig tree disappoints the hope paradoxically placed in it: "he found nothing but leaves, for it was not the season for figs" (Mk. 11: 13b). *Naturally*, the fig tree cannot give figs now. *Miraculously* and *parabolically* at the same time, the fig-tree will not *ever* give figs *again*. "May no one ever eat fruit from you again" (Mk. 11:14). Thus, whereas the middle-sign [*signe-moyen*] was at the same time foreseen and positive in the [p. 54] messianic and paschal entrances, the middle-sign is, in this "intermediary" entrance at the same time surprising and deceptive. It negatively marks the journey to the city as the space of the unappeased and forever unsatisfied hunger. And in our sense by Jesus, of the miracle of the "realized curse", as it often happens in the parable, the decipherment [*le décryptage*] only makes clearer one level of meaning, and again in an incomplete way.[73]

In order to give a naturalist analysis of the story, it would seem that Jesus who *believed* that the fig tree had some figs and who discovers that it only had leaves, because "it

was not the season for figs" (Mk. 11:13b), realizes his decep-
tion--*belief disappointed, faith deceived*--by striking the tree
with ultimate barrenness: negative power of faith, inverted
into the "moral" of the story with a positive force: "Whatever you ask in prayer, you will receive if you have faith"
(Mt. 21:22). However the second example, which is a comparison made by Jesus, is also negative: "Even if you say to this
mountain, 'Be taken up and cast into the sea', it will be done"
(Mt. 21:21; also Mk. 11:23). It is this negative aspect which
must be exploited in the interpretation of the text: the space
of the hunger. It is a space oriented towards the city.

The True Meal

The semantic advantage of the intermediary entrance is
then perceived. While the messianic entrance is marked by the
value of transport, the intermediary entrance introduces into
the space or the distance between Bethany, the Mount of Olives,
and Jerusalem, the signifiers of hunger and natural food: the
missing fruit from the tree whose absence comes to be finally
exhausted. Therefore since the miraculous power of faith does
not consist in covering a tree with out of season fruits, but
in making it die because it cannot naturally have them, it is
appropriate to substitute for this deceptor route to the city,
which follows the politically and socially ambiguous voyage of
the royal entrance on an ass, a "positive" route to a place
where the true meal will be received. Thus this displacement
of Jesus is parallel to two others already analyzed which frame
it in the narrative syntagmatic. Could it not have the function of "transforming" the apparently positive space, oriented
towards Jerusalem as a place of a royal arrival, into a vec-
torially negative space [p. 55] between Bethany and the city,
a space where it is not possible to be fed? In order to be
able afterwards to establish a positive space, but which is no
longer that which sets out the names of Jerusalem and the Temple, but the more common ones of the house and the supper room
in which the *true supper* will be consumed.

It will have been noted that this episode is missing in
Luke. Its presence in Matthew and Mark and the significance
which its analysis reveals, as an operation of transformation
between the messianic entrance and the paschal entrance which
is found in the three evangelists, confirms for us the structural hypothesis previously pointed out. In effect, the text
of Luke almost abruptly--let us say--describes a binary opposition

(Temple vs. Mount of Olives)

in the initial phase of the narrative--before the paschal en-
trance--with an overdetermination of the semantic values of
the Temple. Whereas the variants of Matthew and Mark as parts
of a ternary construction,

(Mount of Olives vs. Jerusalem vs. Temple)

lead, by gradual modifications, to an opposition of two elements similar to that of Luke. The additional narrative segment marked by the parabolic miracle of the barren fig tree,
is one of those modifications which is interested in negatively valorizing or practically annulling the intermediary space
oriented towards the city between Bethany, the Mount of Olives,
and Jerusalem which is not named.

Mark and the Temple Vendors

In this perspective, it is interesting to note that in
the syntagmatic organization of the narrative in Mark, the
episode of the withered, barren fig tree is cut in two. There
is first the word of cursing, and then its accomplishment. But
it is the narrative segment of the vendors chased from the Temple (Mk. 11:15-19) with its consequences, which interrupt it.
The vendors, buyers, and money-changers of silver are in the
Temple, as the absence of fruits is on the fig-tree: they are
negative signs of an indestructable nourishment. The double
citation from Isaiah and Jeremiah allows us to oppose the *house
of prayer* for all peoples to a den of robbers.[74] Therefore it
constitutes an important syntagmatic articulation of the transformation whose successive states we are trying to show: [p.
56] from the apparently positive toponymic space of the messianic entrance to the apparently negative or neutral substituted
space of the "paschal" entrance. Furthermore, the realization of the curse on the fig tree, which follows the expulsion
of the vendors from the Temple, has the function of preparing
for the effective obliteration of the name of the Temple,[75] and
of announcing the disappearance of the Temple in favor of the
house of prayer and the sacrificial supper room in this house.
We will come back to this on the function of the silver in this
text concerning Judas. Thus Mark's text, a variant in the syntagmatic order, makes apparent a secondary articulation of the
meaning on the toponymic-topographic level.[76] The position of
the narrative segment "vendors chased from the Temple" inside
of the larger segment of the curse miraculously cast on the
barren fig-tree opens, for both of these "micro-narratives",
a new difference productive of a meaning which neither of them
would have if they followed one another on the diachronic line
of the story.

The Eschatological Fig-Tree

Let us make one last remark about the problem of the entrances of Jesus and the correlative valorization of the space and places in their toponyms or their substitutes. One final confirmation of our hypotheses would be supplied by a fragment present in the three evangelists at the end of what it is fitting to call "the eschatological discourse". It is a question of the parable of the fig-tree which presents a remarkable parallelism with the miracle-parable which we analyzed.[77] "From the fig-tree, learn this comparison" (Mt. 24:32; Mk. 13:28). "And he told them a parable: 'Look at the fig tree, and all the trees...'" (Lk. 21:29). Now what does the simile of the fig-tree teach us? As soon as its branch becomes tender and it puts forth its leaves, as soon as it blooms, we know, by ourselves, at this sight, that henceforth the summer is near. The fruit season has its premonitory signs which permit us, by the spontaneous knowledge of the rhythms of nature, to anticipate its arrival and to forecast it. The buds and the leaves of the fig-tree are metaphors of the signs which will describe Jesus (Mt. 24:29; Mk. 13:24; Lk. 21:25...), cosmic announcer signs of his coming with all power and with all the glory of the Son of Man on the clouds. And the season for fruits, which buds and leaves announce, is a metaphor of the [p. 57] nearness of the Kingdom of God. Lk. 21:31: "So also, when you see (all) these things (taking place) you know that he (the kingdom of God) is near", "at the very gates" (cf. Mt. 24:33; Mk. 13:29). Thus the parable of the fig-tree in the eschatological *discourse inverts* the parabolic miracle of the fig-tree in the *narrative* of the entrances of Jesus. To the fig-tree forever barren because it was unable to give food out of season is opposed the budding fig-tree, an announcer of the season for fruits. To the tree which shows in the *"reality" of the narrative*, the negativity of the space oriented towards the city, is opposed the tree which shows in the *metaphor of the discourse* the nearness, the positivity of the space "in the doors", since "this space in the doors" is the Kingdom of God, which spawns the voyage on the clouds, the "vertical" journey of the Son of Man into the transcendance of the beyond.[78]

THE DEPARTURE FROM THE TEMPLE

As a conclusion to this point, we will confine ourselves to quoting the word of Jesus in Matthew 23:38ff.: it sets up as an enigmatic commentary, on this point of the text, the obliteration of the toponyms of Jerusalem and the Temple which will occur much later in the sequence of the narrative: "Be-

hold, your house is forsaken and desolate" (Mt. 23:38); a word
that the following verse comments on by extracting only one
single level of meaning: "For I tell you, you will not see
me again, until you say, 'Blessed is he who comes in the name
of the Lord'" (Mt. 23:39). And Matthew continues in chapter
24, "Jesus left the temple...", and while moving away announced to his disciples admiring the buildings of the Temple:
"there will not be left here one stone upon another, that will
not be thrown down" (Mk. 24:2). And from this moment of the
text, the names of Jerusalem and the Temple will be obliterated (even in Mk. 24:15-16). It is therefore the presence of
Jesus in some point of space which transforms it into an in-
habitable and uninhabitable place, into a house, and into a
supper room. It is this displacement (of Jesus) which takes
away from Jerusalem and the Temple the possibility of being
names and being named. It is a signifier displacement which
is a displacement in the textual space of the narrative by
which a new topic system is put into place by the subject,
until this same subject, who by his movement, and then by his
name, has established it, is constituted himself in a signifier element of this very space, in a place not only nameable
but consumable.[79] [p. 58]

Chapter IV

THE TOPONYMIC SYSTEMS AND SECONDARY TOPICS:
THE ENTRANCE PARABLES

We must make a second study entering again more deeply
into the organization of the textual space into its "places",
through the words which name them, themselves or by their substitutes. It is not a question here of analyzing the displacements of Jesus into the space which articulates it in toponymic
places, but the interior narratives in the narrative itself
which "mimes" in a second scene--that of the discourse inscribed in the text as a didactic discourse--the organization
of the space by the hero. This first degree narrative can be
considered to be an ensemble of orientations or directions
with the interplay of their inversions and their turning upside downs creating the meaning in the text.

TOPOGRAPHY AND TOPICS*

But moreover, the complex system of reflections and reciprocal representations in circularity, from the level of the
narrative to the level of the discourse which tells another
narrative in the narrative appears to us to be constitutive of
a new engendering[80] of the meaning. Its fundamental structure,
which all the narratives represent whatever their level in the
text may be, is a certain kind of organization of the space in
the text, i.e. of articulation of places, in the double sense
that this term can have in a geographic topography and a rhetorical topics.[81] The generation of the meaning therefore is
carried out from one level to another of a narrative, from the
narrative in the first degree to the narrative-discourse integrated into much larger narrative segments [p. 59] and arising
from different planes of the text.[82] As we have tried to show
previously for a single narrative isotopy, "Messianic entrance
--intermediary entrance marked by this parabolic miracle of the
withered fig-tree--paschal entrance", this engendering appears
in the form of reciprocally expressive or representative en-

---

*The title of this section in the Table of Contents is "Topo-
graphie et Topique"; in the text it is "Topographique et
Topique".

sembles, of functional structures or homologous qualificatives. The latter which function by displacements or from condensation according to some process of an antonymic or metaphoric type create the referential illusion of a "mundane" story which would be unfolded in the reality and which would offer with respect to the reader, the discrete spectacle of events appearing in their novelty at some point locatable on a map, in the very landscape of the world.[83] We have seen previously how the three "entrances" of Jesus demonstrate in the discourse of the narrator under three different, but connected, forms a single thesis; they proceed to some textual operations about which one can think that they have a real theological importance, although they only deal with some spatial relations, some points of this space and some movements in this space that the narrative has the fundamental goal of putting on stage.

The Second Scene

Now we discover in the staged-narrative a second scene, the former which erects the hero Jesus in his teaching in the Temple, in the form of some parabolic narratives the first of which we have analyzed, the withered fig-tree which is only present in Mark and Matthew. Now Jesus is in the Temple and teaches a people delighted to hear him, to the great anger of the Pharisees, Sadducees, and Scribes. Some trick questions are posed to him, the tax to Caesar, the resurrection of the dead, etc. But he also takes the initiative and relates some parables: coded narratives, ciphered stories[83] whose narrator in the second degree is Jesus. It is truly the evangelist who, as narrator of the first level, puts Jesus on stage, and takes care to give, if not the decipherment, at least the general theme of deciphering.[84] The number of these internal narratives in the first degree narrative varies from one text to another. While setting aside the narrative of the withered fig-tree already examined in its particular case, [p. 60] three of them are noted in Matthew, and one in Mark and Luke (at this point of the narrative-text).[85] The working hypothesis which we are proposing is the following: these parabolic narratives between the different variant texts and inside of each text are in the same relation with respect to the topic articulation of the space as the episodes or much larger narrative segments which frame them at another level of the text, in particular the entrances into Jerusalem.[86] It could indeed be possible that this may be a general rule for the relations between the parabolic narrative (a fragment of Jesus' discourse) and the narrative of the life and teaching of Jesus (therefore a discourse of the gospel narrator).[87] Here in the form of a table are these different narratives attributed to the different narrators:

Matthew	Mark	Luke
21:18-22 the withered fig-tree (parabolic miracle)	11:12-14 the withered fig-tree	
21:28-32 parable of the two sons	11:20-25 the withered fig-tree	
21:33-46 parable of the murderous vine-growers [wicked ten- ants]	12:1-12 parable of the murderous vine-growers [wicked ten- ants]	20:9-18 parable of the murderous vine-growers [wicked ten- ants]
22:1-14 parable of the marriage feast		

This table is only valid for this point of the syntagmatic line of the narrative. Elsewhere in Luke 14:15-24 the
parable of the marriage feast is found at a moment which does
not lack interest for our own study, since the parable is related to the heart of a supper theme which makes itself a consequence on the one hand of a lamentation on Jerusalem, Lk.
13:34-35, to that which we have found in Matthew in his prologue to the Passion narrative and on the other hand to a
particularly precise reflection by the hero on his voyage to
Jerusalem, Lk. 13:31-33 [p. 61]: "Nevertheless I must go on
my way today and tomorrow and the day following; for it cannot
be that a prophet should perish away from Jerusalem", Jesus
says in the response he asks the Pharisees to transmit to the
"fox" Herod: "Go and tell that fox, 'Behold, I cast out demons and perform cures today and tomorrow, and the third day
I finish my course (I am *consumed*)'"[88] (Lk. 13:32).

Thus it is remarkable--and we will never cease noting
it--that in Luke, the elements are found displaced which, in
the narrative syntagmatic, ought to ensure the positive or
negative mediations, between the Temple on the one hand, and

the exterior of the Temple, which is a matter of Galilee, Judea and their places of which the Temple is, in some way, the point of magnetization, or it is a matter of Jerusalem where Jesus is never found--in the text--but which is always viewed from a distance, which "is spoken" in the lamentation or the reprimand: thus in 19:41-44, as if the narrator wanted to construct for the inauguration of the Passion narrative, the abrupt opposition to two terms: (the Temple vs. the Mount of Olives [Bethany]) which will articulate all his narrative.

CITATION AND DOUBLE CODE

The Murderous Vine-Growers

The parable of the murderous vine-growers constitutes therefore the narrative element common to three variants in the *discourse* of the hero. It is with it that we will begin the analysis. As in the majority of parabolic narratives, it schematically includes two levels: the narrative properly speaking and its decoding by the narrator of the narrative. As is often the case, this decoding itself includes several elements which do not originate from the same textual isotopy. Thus in the parable which we are examining, the decoding is supplied by a citation of Psalm 118, which is itself coded. It is the relationship between these two codes which, by remaining implicit, come if not to constitute the deciphering of the parabolic narrative, at least to introduce an emergence of meaning particularly valuable for our purpose. However, Matthew will place in the mouth of his secondary narrator, a comment which will decipher the citation by extracting--as is almost always the case--only one signifier level. Luke [p. 62] on the other hand will give a new symbolic transposition of the citation, and Mark will let the reader draw the consequences of the juxtaposition of two codes.[89]

Luke

The sudden confrontation of the citation and the narrative, marked by the coding of the narrative, also gives the indication that the parabolic narrative is to be deciphered according to the equivalence of the vine, the place of the narrative and the Temple, and a work of the Lord. Therefore if the vine is the Temple,[90] it must be understood that the stone rejected by the builders is the owner of the vine's son who has been killed by the vine-growers and *thrown out of the vineyard*. But how can the rejected stone become the cornerstone or the capstone in the narrative? Where do we find the

equivalence? Some interpretive itineraries are outlined in
Mark and Luke. Matthew repeats them, completes them, and displaces them. Jesus, in Mark as in Matthew, specifies that a
watch-tower rises in the vineyard and a wine-press is dug out
(Mt. 21:33; Mk. 12:1). This wine-press allows one to crush
the grape of the vine and its fruit in order to extract the
wine. Now Luke in his symbolic commentary of the citation
from the Psalmist, states precisely: "Every one who falls on
that stone will be broken to pieces; but when it falls on any
one it will crush him" (Lk. 20:18). The capstone or cornerstone is an instrument of crushing or pounding like the wine
press, and the cornerstone represented, by a metonymic displacement, the avenging and punitive return of the master of
the vineyard: "He will come and destroy those tenants, and
give the vineyard to others" (Lk. 20:16). It is a metonymic
displacement, since these are not grapes which will be
"pressed", but the vine-growers, who will be crushed by the
fall of the cornerstone, i.e. by the destruction of the Temple
of which it was the masterpiece. It is a movement from high
to low, to a negative valorization which is the "transcendent"
reverse of the journey of the stone by the masons. One catches
here the double twisting that Luke causes the parabolic narrative to undergo by the interplay of the citation and his commentary by symbolic transposition.[91]

Matthew

On the other hand, Matthew indicates a different displacement in a proposition which can be considered to be the simultaneous decipherment and "the moral" for the parabolic narrative and the citation which is in it [p. 63]. "The kingdom of
God will be taken away from you and given to a nation producing
the fruits of it" (Mt. 21:43). If according to the citation,
the vineyard is the Temple, the stone rejected by the masons
will be the son of the owner *killed again outside of the vineyard*. But according to Matthew, it is not this point of the
narrative that the citation comments upon. The withdrawal of
the Kingdom is the renting of the vineyard to other vine-growers by its owner. And again it is the Temple taken away from
the people who visit it, who exploit it (cf. the vendors
chased from the Temple) in order to entrust it to another
people, who will make it produce its fruits, i.e. who will
crush them with the wine-press to extract wine from them.
Here again the wine-press represents the cornerstone (the son
of the owner) at first rejected, then at the top of the build-
ing or in the middle of the property, grinding the grape, but
thanks to which the grape of the vineyard produces its fruit,
the wine. The displacement performed by Matthew is opposite
to that of Luke. For Luke the grape is displaced by those who

pick it. It is the murderous vine-growers who will be crushed
in the wine-press of his vengeance, at the time of the eschato-
ological return. For Matthew the grape is displaced by those
who will give to the new vine-growers, or to a new people, the
possibility of extracting wine from it and causing the property
"to be returned". The wine-press, which is no longer the wine-
press of death but of life, is no longer the wine-press of destruction, but the wine-press of production.[92]

Mark

Mark, unlike Luke and Matthew, does not give any commentary on the quotation from the Old Testament. On the other
hand, like Matthew, but contrary to Luke, he describes the
three constituent "architectural" elements of the property:
the closure, separation of an *interior* and an *exterior* of the
vineyard; the wheel in *height* and the wine-press in *depth* ("he
will excavate a wine-press and build a wheel") which refers to
a dimension of "high-low" verticality. The wheel in the vineyard points to this architectural element of the citation
which is on high, at the summit, the capstone which controls
the whole edifice from above. A stone from above which is
also--we have seen--*the stone from below*, that of the wine-
press which at the same time crushes and produces the property, crushes the old grape vine-growers and is produced in the
fruits which it gives to the new vine-growers. [p. 64]

But the closure, the wheel, and the wine-press rigorously
articulate the space of the property in an "interior vs. exterior" and an "above vs. below" which comes to be covered by
the actors of the narrative.[93] The latter is constructed on a
movement of rejection and expulsion into the exteriority, of
the elements (the servants, then the son of the master) which
are introduced in the vineyard in the name of its owner: the
domain is de-valorized; the master cannot partake of the fruits
of the vineyard; the son of the owner is killed, a devaloriza-
tion which is at the same time exclusion since even the son is
killed or thrown to his death outside of the property. In
other words, the whole narrative is constructed on the redundant movement from the interior to the exterior, negatively
valorized. And its conclusion, particularly responsive to the
citation which is juxtaposed, by decoding it by the super im-
position of a secondary code, would mark the return of the
master according to the axis of the wheel and the wine-press,
of the capstone and of the millstone which crushes, according
to a *movement from above to below, at the same time negative
and positive*, since this movement is of a destruction of the
Temple and of the vine-growers, as far as *de*-production (of
fruits) by a new people. It is significant that this move-

ment of return receives its vection from the quotation of a
Psalm (118:22-23). That is to say from a textual place situated outside the narrative.

In other words, if the parabolic narrative reproduces--in
the negation, rejection, and expulsion--on the scene of the
discourse--the other scene of the narrative--the movements,
the displacements, and their articulations that the primary
narrative consigns between Bethany, the Mount of Olives (= the
exterior), and Jerusalem and/or the Temple (= the interior),
the positive or compound counterpart of these movements will
not be immediately found in the narrative itself, but in a new
discourse which will repeat in another "topic" the positive
and negative valorizations of the "interior vs. exterior" and
"high vs. low" spatial categories. We are trying to speak
about the eschatological discourse, which in many respects is
also a narrative, on a third scene, and about the quasi-impos-
sibility in the primary narrative which the hero runs into of
entering into Jerusalem and/or into the Temple and remaining
in it, dwelling in it, and taking possession of these places
as their owner or his representative.[94]

But it is indeed certain, in other respects, that if we
transport ourselves to the other end of the passion narrative,
into the segments which conclude it, we note that the displacements of the hero are [p. 65] then taken charge of by the semantic axis of the verticality articulated according to the
high and low. He is hoisted, and suspended at the summit of
the cross (the wheel). He finally ascends to heaven; movements
according to high and low which, in a characteristic way, unfold outside of the city and its Temple, at the place of the
skull (a summit) and in the garden which surrounds this place
(where the tomb is hewn); to Bethany or to the Mount of Olives
(where the Ascension will take place).[95] We can summarize in
a table the system of oriented spatial equivalences of this
(secondary) parabolic narrative and of the (primary) narrative
of the entrances of Jesus into the city and the Temple:

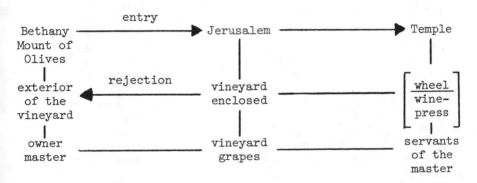

FRAMING PARABLES

We can in this case approach the study of two other parables of Matthew which frame that of the murderous vine-growers and which are only found in this variant. In the first, the place of the parabolic narrative is a vineyard; in the second, a ceremonial meal, a royal banquet for the son of a king, but in the second case, that which is in question—the "subject" of the narrative—it is a movement of arrival, a displacement, a journey valorized either by an order given and the virtues of obedience and of loyalty which attaches itself to the reception of the order by the rights and the duties of hospitality. It is therefore on this point that we will bring our analysis to bear.

The Two Sons or the Double Shackle

In the first narrative, two parallel and inverse positions are described [décrites], before the order of the Father to his two sons: "Go [p. 66] and work in the vineyard today", the refusal of the first which ends in obedience: "he repented and went", the acceptance of the second which remains verbal and which reverses itself into a refusal. "I go, Sir; but did not go" (Mt. 21:30). As in the Matthean version of the murderous vine-growers, the secondary narrator asks his hearers to draw the conclusion of the story by an alternative question.[96] "Which of the two did the will of his father?" Whatever the response may be, it condemns the one who makes it, either into an absurd ethical-religious formalism, if he responds "the second", a formalism which is correctly denounced by the example of the first son at the same time disobeying and repenting, or to stand aside if he responds "the first", with those who do not do the will of the Father. However, it will be noted that in the first case, the possible response is situated at the level of the narrative code. In the second case, it is at the level of its decoding, since it is a matter of understanding that the chief Priests and Elders of the People are represented by the second son who obeys in words and refuses in reality the order of the Father. Thus therefore a complete analysis of the parable would have to take into consideration these different positions of discourse of the real and symbolic, alternative and necessary, sender and receiver.[97]

But what interests us is the content of the order of the Father in the narrative: "Go and work in the vineyard." It is a matter of going into the property of the Father in order to reclaim it. The first son having refused in words, goes. The second, though going in words, refuses. He does not go

into the property. It is then that the decoding takes place:
the vineyard is the Kingdom of God, an access road, that of
justice has been opened by John. It has been neglected by the
Chief Priests and Elders of the People, followed by the publicans and the prostitutes. In other words, the Chief Priests
and Elders of the People formally surrender themselves (in
words) to the Kingdom of God, but have refused in fact to go
to work; unlike the publicans and prostitutes. The Entrance
or apparent arrival (in a certain form) which is in reality a
withdrawal, a breach [écart], withdrawal or apparent separation which is in fact an arrival, an entrance.

The missing intermediary element is furnished to us by the
following parable, that of the murderous vine-growers, already
analyzed: it is the Temple which then gives us the formula of
decoding; the Chief Priests and Elders are in the Temple like
the [p. 67] interlocutors--hearers of Jesus in the primary
narrative, at a time when the publicans and prostitutes are
not present. That means that Jerusalem is no longer in Jerusalem; the Temple is no longer the Temple; it is present elsewhere, "by the side of John, then by the side of Jesus".
There is where the Temple is.

But it is necessary to show that this interpretation concerning the topic of this parabolic narrative is only made
possible by the projection on its own articulation (Vineyard/
Kingdom of God + Father/Son × 2//God/Chief Priests, Elders of
the People × Publicans, prostitutes) of that of the most complex parable which follows it since between the vineyard and
the Kingdom of God, it lets in a "mediator" element, the Temple. But in turn, it is the construction in *double bind* and
all the primary context of the "emission" of this secondary
narrative (the hearers are the Chief Priests and the Elders of
the People in the Temple) which permit us to interpret the introduction of this element foreign to this parabolic narrative
and to give it the sense of a denomination, a starting point
of the transformation of which the fall of the cornerstone on
the grapes--vine-growers (Lk. 20:18 and Mt. 21:44 interpo-
lated), i.e. the "destruction" of the Temple, is one of the
points, one of the representations.[98]

The Wedding Banquet: Consummation and Rejection

The other framing parable is that of the wedding banquet,
which is at the same time the final form of the transformation.
Here again the "problem" of the parabolic narrative is that of
an arrival, of a going to the palace of the King, and precisely the royal banquet, the supper room. What is in question is,
beyond this journey to the supper, the entrance into the supper

room. We will not exhaustively analyze this very complex parable, but only its relations with the two preceding ones on the topical and dynamic plane.

The Father of parable (1), like of the owner in parable (2), is in a characteristic way, *outside of the vineyard*, implicitly in (1) since he gives the order to his sons to go to work in it. He is explicitly in (2), since it is told to us that he departed to go to a foreign land. In the parable of the wedding feast (3), the position of the Father-owner-King is reversed: he is not outside of the palace, even of the supper room, but *in* the Kingdom. The [p. 68] servants are not sent in order to gain access to the vineyard and take the portion of the fruit owed to the owner as in (2): the sons are not sent to work the vineyard and make it produce fruits, as in (1); the messengers of the King are sent to invite guests to the wedding. These are the guests who are *on the outside*, while the vine-grower-tenants of (2) were on the property. This initial opposition affects the rest of the narrative. The guests refuse to come into the palace, to the wedding, to take part in the supper while the vine-growers decide *to evict* the servants, and then the son of the King, *off the property*. Finally it is no longer a matter of *working* on the property (1), nor of *making* the vineyard *produce its fruits* (2), but of *eating*, of *consuming the fruits of the Kingdom*: "Behold, I have made ready my dinner, my oxen and my fat calves are killed, and everything is ready; come to the marriage feast", 22:4 (3). And from (1) and (2) to (3), one passes from the vineyard and its fruits (e.g. the potential wine, cf. the wine-press) to the animals--oxen and fat calves--a meat diet alimentation, in short from the grape, a *drinkable* thing (once it is pressed), to the flesh, an eatable thing (once it is cooked).

It is no doubt that henceforth from (1) to (3), the time of the announcement, the work, and the ripening is past. The time of accomplishment, and consummation comes, a passage from the exterior to the interior, from the fruits to the feeding, from the work to the supper. What confirms this first articulation of the parabolic narrative (3) is the presence in v. 7 of the episode of the vengeance of the King towards the guests, which is evidentally redundant with v. 41a of chapter 21 in parable (2): "They said to him, He will put those wretches (the vine-growers) to a miserable death", but while Mt. 21:41a is the concluding verse of the narrative, v. 7 from chapter 22 precisely marks the middle of the parabolic narrative (which includes 14 verses, i.e. Mt. 22:1-14). The second volet of parable (3) to which the first volet of parable (1) should correspond in the symbolic order--the Son who refuses to go to the vineyard, who afterwards repented, and went to it (Mt.

21:29)--is constituted by a second attempt of the King to find some guests: "Go therefore to the thoroughfares...", ἐπὶ τὰς διεξόδους τῶν ὁδῶν, a remarkable expression which dynamically indicates the journey from the outside to the inside; and from then on the wedding room was filled with guests. The movement of filling in "the inside by the outside" ends therefore at this [p. 69] point. However, a movement of expulsion from the inside to the outside immediately follows it, which is no longer the act of vine-growers, but of the King, no longer initial, but final. "'How did you *get in* here without a wedding garment?' And he was speechless. Then the King said to the attendants, 'Bind him hand and foot, and cast him into the *outer darkness*'" (Mt. 22:12-13). A royal sentence from parable (3) which is hardly different from that which describes the attitude of the vine-growers towards the Son of the Owner in parable (2): "And they took him, *and cast him out of the vineyard, and killed him*." Thus, in the same way that the vine-growers killed and threw *out* the--only--Son of the owner, likewise the King caused a *single* guest among those who had entered to be thrown *outside* into the *Darkness*.

Transformations

The parable of the marriage feast (3) simultaneously accomplishes the transformation begun by parables (1) and (2) from the work of the field to the meal of ceremonial consumption (the weddings) into the joy and the gratitude of the hospitality: it inverts them on the topic or topological dynamic plane, since to the movements of expulsion and rejection follow those of integration and reception. But parables (2) and (3) return again in order to organize at the end of the narrative, an expulsion, but with their agents reversed: that of the Son of the King by the vine-growers, that of the guest without a wedding garment by the servants of the King and with his order.

Therefore if parables (1) and (2) have made us understand that the vineyard is the temple, i.e. the Kingdom of God, but that the new Temple is no longer the Temple, but the place where the wine-press is found which, at the same time, crushes and produces, the place where that is situated which *at this moment* speaks in order to relate the parable which, whatever may be the response made to the alternative question, condemns the interlocutor, parable (3) we discover that this new Temple --wine-press is a room for a wedding meal. Therefore if the one who tells the parable is the wine-press of the vineyard, then he will also be the supper room where its weddings take place, and the food which is eaten there. No doubt, this final analysis of decoding exceeds the text which supports it, but it will be enough for us to put it into relation with our study of the "paschal" entrance and the conclusions which have led us to the operations of recovery by the latter of the messianic [p. 70] and intermediary entrances in order to perceive there the confirmations which would appear to be missing.[99]

THE REJECTION OR THE APPEARANCE OF THE TRAITOR*

But it will be asked, what structural interpretation can be given of this movement of rejection which closes the parable of the wedding feast? We have already alluded to a remark from Mark and the miracle-parable of the withered fig-tree, the expulsion of the merchants from the Temple: "My *house* is a house of prayer for *all peoples*", Mark writes, citing Isaiah 56:7. The Temple is the home of Jesus, although it may be, in the citation, that of God, by the ambiguity of the possessive which signals the very ambiguity of the secondary narrator subject of the parabolic narratives, though they may be discourse or "in action". But there are *some* merchants and *some* vendors; but there is only *one* guest without a wedding garment, who in parable (3) is the negative equivalent of the son of the owner of parable (2), just as the servants expelling him are the vendors in the prophetic-parabolic action. Who is this "singular" expelled from the dinner room, because he does not have the wedding garment and who must have some functional relationship with the merchants, vendors, and money changers? Structurally it is not Judas who has entered with the other disciples into the supper room (the Temple--the Kingdom...) and who has begun to eat with the others, who is the "vendor" of the one with whom he eats and who he eats, and who will leave the supper. "So after receiving the morsel, he immediately went out" (Jn. 13:30). "The King said to the attendants, 'Bind him hand and foot, and cast him into the *outer* darkness'" (Mt. 22:13).[100]

But, it will be objected, in the three Synoptics and especially in Matthew who is the only one to relate it, at this place of the narrative (the parable of the marriage feast in the terms which we have analyzed) Judas does not leave the supper room, Jesus, and the Eleven. Is not the appeal to the fourth variant for the demonstration, at the same time an error and a weakness? It can be thought so, although we initial-

---

*The term Marin is using here has the following meanings: "traitor", "villain" (in Propp's terminology), and also a "seller"!

ly decided to consider all four texts to be variants in a
position of reciprocal representation. So that one of the
variants can in this way furnish us a structural correlate of
which another of the variants is deprived. The total text and
its meaning is the differential interplay at the same time redundant [p. 71] and complementary of the four versions. But
only Matthew relates an episode to us which, although it is
staggered in the syntagmatic line of the narrative and dis-
torted from it at the same time, its meaning would offer us
the correlation sought. This is the matter of Judas' death.
The latter comes to the Temple *to attempt the exchange of
Jesus "in return" for thirty pieces of silver*. He comes to
buy Jesus back after having sold him and confronts the failure of his proposition of transaction. "And throwing the
pieces of silver in the temple, he departed; and he went out
and hanged himself." It is not at all the supper room as a
Temple which Judas withdraws from or is expelled; but from the
Temple as a place of a commercial transaction. It is this Temple which, from the episode of the vendors chased from its
courtyard, is "named" in order to be renamed "Jesus" as a
place and substance of consumption. This is an eminent mark
of the dereliction of the traitor, who is left even in his remorse with the name henceforth abandoned of the Temple as Temple. For if we follow closely the text of Matthew, in parable
(1), the son who accomplishes the will of the Father, accomplishes it with belated remorse in 21:29, 32. Does not Judas
in Mt. 27:3 also repent? Why therefore will he not enter into
the Kingdom? Simply because he believed again that the Temple
was the "Temple" at a time when it had ceased to be the Temple,
in order to become "this desolate house", this wedding room
"empty of guests" (Mt. 23:38; 22:1-3), or a toponym blotted
out by the signifier surface of the text. He had not understood that another temple has been substituted for it, a
house, a filled supper room, or a banquet prepared--Jesus'
word-body to be eaten. [p. 72]

Chapter V

THE TOPONYMIC SYSTEMS AND SECONDARY TOPICS: THE ESCHATOLOGICAL DISCOURSES

The last preparatory study to consider the "prologue" of the Passion narrative in relation to its narrative places should be based on "the eschatological discourses". In effect, the latter on the mode of the discourses articulate like the entrance parables, a space around names of privileged places, a space which is that of the discourse, but which is not without a relationship with that of the narrative. On the contrary, one of the working hypotheses which will have to guide us in the study of these texts will be to show that the form of structuration of the space in the eschatological discourses depends strictly on the position of the subject of discourse in the space of the narrative. It depends, after all, on its structuration in the form of a network of toponyms or of their substitutes diversely connected by the subject of the discourse. But it is quite obvious, otherwise, that a study of this type and of this particular point, does not exhaust the structural analysis of the eschatological discourses. We are studying them only in the perspective which has been ours initially. Methodologically we set apart from the text a single stratum of meaning; we deliberately chose to follow the citations of the topographic code into their toponymic and topic nominations.

POSITIONS OF THE SUBJECT OF DISCOURSE

The starting point of the analysis is offered to us by the variant texts of Matthew and Luke which show two contrasting positions of the subject of discourse in the space of the narrative, two different places [p. 73] truly "opposed" according to the first remarks made below. In Matthew, Jesus departs from the Temple after having pronounced the very remarkable phrase, "Behold, your house is forsaken and desolate....For I tell you, you will not see me again until you say, 'Blessed is he who comes in the name of the Lord'" (Mt. 23:38f.). Going out of the Temple in the narrative which is preceded in the narrative syntagmatic line by its announcement in the form of a discourse, but also by the announcement of a return (a quotation of Psalm 118, the same psalm which has furnished the essential coded citation of the "entrance parable" of the mur-

65

derous vine-growers). This departure of Jesus out of the Temple is then accompanied by the announcement of the destruction of the Temple. Also, once seated on the Mount of Olives, Jesus receives a threefold demand from the disciples: (1) When will the effective destruction of the Temple take place? (2) What will be the sign (σημεῖον) of your parousia, i.e. of your entrance and your return? (3) What will be the sign of the end (achievement and accomplishment of the aeon (συντέλεια τοῦ αἰῶνος)? [Cf. Lk. 21:5ff.]

Thus a departure from the Temple is opposed in the narrative to an entrance into the world, in the form of a discourse, marked in the first case by a destruction, and in the second case by an accomplishment, but being carried out for both of them in the discourse. Therefore, while separating for the moment the two levels of the narrative and the discourse, it could be written: to depart from the Temple is to destroy it, but it is at the same time to re-enter into the world in order to complete it. The centrifugal space of the narrative, the vectorial orientation of which is the obliteration of the central-Temple, reverses itself into the centripetal space of the discourse whose orientation is the establishment of a center: the Son of Man as King.

What is the case in Luke? There Jesus does not leave the Temple. It is in the Temple that his teaching is given. The Temple is the place of his discourse, and the Mount of Olives is the place where there is nothing to say, because it is a place of rest (Lk. 21:37-38). "And everyday he was *teaching in the temple*, but at night he went out and lodged on the Mount of Olivet. And early in the morning all the people came to him in the temple to hear him" (Lk. 21:37-38). To the people who admired the Temple (τινῶν λεγόντων περὶ τοῦ ἱεροῦ...) Jesus proclaimed its destruction: "everything that you contemplate...everything will be destroyed" (Lk. 21:5-6 paraphrased). Hence the twofold question which is posed about the Temple and which concerns only it: (1) "When will this (ταῦτα) [p. 74] be?"; (2) "What will be the sign (σημεῖον) when this is about to take place?" (Lk. 21:7). In other words, what is the premonitory sign of the destruction of the Temple?

Positions of Parole--*Object of* Parole

Speaking only about this point of departure, the position of the subject in the narrative coincides with the object of the discourse, the place of *parole* with the place of which it is speaking and that this very *parole* destroys. In other words, the subject of discourse in the narrative destroys its place of *parole* in the discourse as a referential object. And since the object of the discourse is rolled into one with the place of the subject which contains it (namely the Temple), it is henceforth no longer possible to speak of the Temple. The Temple can no longer be a referend [*référend*]--an object spoken about. It is gone totally in the direction of the one who speaks. The temple can no longer be a place of a non-referential *parole*, a position of *parole* beyond the world. It is what signifies that the one who speaks is henceforth his own place of *parole* in himself.[101]

This exceptional moment in which, thanks to the double interplay of the narrative and discourse, the obliteration of the referend [*référend*] of *parole* is realized and accomplishes the process of condensation of the referend [*référend*] and the subject does not exist in Matthew. In the latter, if one can say this, the homomorphic recovery is accomplished, but inversely oriented from the space of the narrative and from the space of the discourse which permits (by recovery and inversion) a kind of "*Aufhebung*" of the center, denied in its local and referential particularity that marks the toponym (the "Temple"), but preserved in its cosmological and eschatological universality: the Son of Man as a King gathering together the elect "from the four winds, from one end of heaven to the other" (Mt. 24:31). From this point of view, it was thus essential that the eschatological discourse be held on the Mount of Olives, i.e. *outside of the Temple*.

In Luke, on the other hand, the fact that this same discourse is given in the Temple permits and forces a kind of introjection of the referend [*référend*] in the subject of *parole* to be realized. It has become at the same time its own object and its own place of discourse. Also this could only be said *of Jerusalem* in order to destroy it, in a signifier opposition with *the eschatological return of the Son of Man*: "Jerusalem will be trodden down by the Gentiles, until the times of the Gentiles are fulfilled" (ἄχρι οὗ πληρωθῶσιν [p. 75] καιροὶ ἐθνῶν) Lk. 21:24: and when the Son of Man appears ..."when these things begin to take place, look up and raise your heads because your redemption is drawing near" (διότι ἐγγίζει ἡ ἀπωλύτρωσις ὑμῶν...Lk. 21:28). In other words, the return of the Son of Man, which is announced by a collection of cosmic signs, is first marked by a deliverance of a "Jerusalem" trodden down and destroyed by the gentiles.

The Day of the Son of Man: Utopia

This analysis of Luke could--in our viewpoint--be confirmed by the large discourse about the Kingdom of God and the

day of the Son of Man in 17:20-37.[102]   Luke in 17:11 indicates
that Jesus was making his way to Jerusalem, and he found himself on the border of Samaria and Galilee.   It was a remote
geographic point: but taken in an orientation towards the
center "Jerusalem", it was a frontier place between two re-
gions whose names have received a strong negative connotation
from the preceding narratives, Galilee (cf. Lk. 4:14-30), and
Samaria, a schismatic and foreign land from which Jesus is expelled (9:51-56).   In this space of the boundary which is, in
some way, outside of space and which at this point only has
meaning by the displacement which abandons it for the center,
"the subject of *parole*", Jesus, is to a certain extent *out of
place*.   Is this not what Jesus declares to the disciples, after
having been chased into this borough of Samaria: "The Son of
Man has *nowhere* to lay his head" (Lk. 9:55).   He has no place
and this absence of a place of rest (indeed of final rest) or
of familial taking-root is connected very directly to the Kingdom of God and to its proclamation.   Cf. the segment Lk. 9:57-
58 and the verses which follow it, in particular Lk. 9:59-62.

It is then that Jesus is *questioned by the Pharisees* about
the moment of arrival (πότε ἔρχεται) of the Kingdom of God.
Entirely by displacing the question from time to space, his
response indicates: 1) that the Kingdom of God is not visible
or foreseeable; 2) that it is ἐντός ὑμῶν, "in/among you", that
is to say, present in the midst of you (Lk. 17:21).   In other
words, the Kingdom of God is here, but outside of space, present outside of space, not connected to a "word" ["*dit*"] of
space and even less of time to a name.   In short it is a utopia, which is at the same time present and absent, a presence
which is "the other" of space.   But it is an element of discourse which occupies this [p. 76] position in the discourse,
which is there without being there; beyond discourse, but without which the discourse would not be uttered, to be precise of
the *parole* and of silence.   It is the subject of *parole*.   "Nor
will they say, 'Lo, here it is!' or 'There!' for behold, the
kingdom of God is in the midst of you" (Lk. 17:21).   It is
this very *parole* which expresses its obliteration and which
at the same time is affirmed as an absent presence, as the
other of this negation of the deictic which indicates a point
of space.   For that very reason it shows itself to be an unassignable subject.

But Jesus repeats this essential remark in its equivocity,
in the discourse to the disciples which follows his *response to
the Pharisees* (Lk. 7:22-37); but this repetition is in another
mode,[103] the eschatological mode, the "*genre* of the end of
time" whose object or content is then the Son of Man.   "The
days are coming when you will desire to see one of the days of
the Son of Man, and you will not see it.   And they will say to

you, 'Lo, there' or 'Lo, here!' Do not go, do not follow them" (Lk. 17:22-23). It is the same affirmation of invisibility of non-foreseeability, but as an object of desire (ἐπιθυμειν), unassignable *here* in *space*. And the development which follows then is a utopia, but an eschatological utopia of the Kingdom-of-God-among-you; the sudden flash of lightning which connects one border of heaven to another, the invasion from above of the rain of fire and sulphur, or of the flood, all catastrophic-cosmic forms which constitute an "other" of space-time, an eschatological figure of this reverse of the negation of space and place, by which, while being hidden, the very position of the subject of *parole*--of *this* subject of *parole* is designated.

Parole and Body

The final question which the disciples pose manifests a kind of incomprehension. It repeats, but in relation to space, the initial question that the Pharisees posed with respect to time: "πότε ἔρχεται ἡ βασιλεία τοῦ θεοῦ" the first ask; "Where? (ποῦ)" the second ask. In what moment of time? In what place of space? The "stereotyped" response which is made to the question, by connecting the utopia of the subject of *parole* to death and to the body, introduces a new direction of meaning that we have already seen appear, but on the symbolic-parabolic plane, that of the subject-body-language. "Where the body is [p. 77] there the eagles will be gathered together" (Lk. 17:37). Thus the obliteration of the place of *parole* as a toponym presents the subject of *parole* as a place of *parole* in which not only the one speaks, but those to whom he speaks are taken.[104] Such is the new place, the other of an appointed point, designated here (or there) in space, a *parole* which is uttered from an unassignable point and which in the last resort will be revealed to be in the place of the dead body--in the "place" that is to say "where", but also "in its place"-- being substituted for it, being changed into it and it back into it. We will come back to this in our conclusion to the semiotics of the traitor.

THE ARRIVAL AT THE CENTER

Everything is in some way already said in Lk. 17:20-37 but at a distance from the center and in a movement to the center. What the eschatological discourse in 21:5-38 "adds" in relation to what has preceded it on the boundaries of Galilee and Samaria is that henceforth Jesus is at the center of the center in the Temple at Jerusalem. It is necessary therefore once again to repeat the operation already accomplished in discourse and at a distance from this place, being constituted as a subject of discourse, as a utopian place of *parole*, that is to say not only as a day of the Son of Man and Kingdom of God, but again as a Temple. In order to do that, it was necessary to be *in the Temple*. He must speak in the very place which by negation as an object of discourse must disappear from the discourse in order to become a place of *parole*, i.e. the subject which utters its obliteration.

Narrative and Discourse: the Temple

One last point can then be taken up in Luke, before returning to the variant text of Matthew. We have noted at the time of the putting in place of the organization of the narrative space in Luke, that the narrative very quickly revealed a binary opposition between the Mount of Olives (Bethany), on the one hand, and the Temple on the other. And that in this way, except for Luke 19:28,[105] the name of the city is found omitted from Luke's text, unlike Matthew and to a lesser degree Mark. On the other hand, Jesus enters into the Temple only once during the narrative, even if at some points of the text [p. 78] a reiterative activity of displacement between the Temple and the exterior is indicated to us.[106]

In effect it will easily be understood that the narrative plainly performs successive and repeated displacements between two named places of space, plays a different role, and fills a different function than the summary or the condensation of these displacements in a single narrative. One will be convinced of this by reading Mark which is, from this point of view, the text presenting the most important variant with that of Luke. This opposition signifies in effect that the journey between the two places deserves being developed as a text only once. On the contrary in Mark, the dispersion all along several identical displacements, of successive events or episodes, gives to each between them a proper function in the syntagmatic line of the narrative, and thus will construct along this line, a change, will develop a transformation of which each displacement is in this way the representation in the narrative.

In other words, what is significant in Luke in opposition to Matthew or Mark is the initial and "static" inscription in the narrative of an opposition between the Mount of Olives and the Temple which, once and for all, eliminates the degrees and stages of which the toponym "Jerusalem" is the index. Its exclusion from the narrative therefore marks by its very absence the strength of the opposition that the textual singularity of

displacement between the Mount of Olives and the Temple emphasizes on its part.

But if the name of Jerusalem is obliterated in this way
from the *narrative*, it is remarkable that it reappears two
times in the *discourse*, once in the form of its generic substitute, "the city", in Lk. 19:41-44 and the second time and
doubly in the eschatological discourse in an explicit form in
21:20, 21 and 24. This compensation between the narrative obliteration and the discursive resurgence is not without interest. Because these two moments are precisely contemporaneous,
in the narrative and in the discourse, of the "overdetermination" and the "destruction" of the Temple.

It is at the moment in the narrative when the Temple
reaches the first plane, as a pole of opposition of the Mount
of Olives obliterating in this way "Jerusalem" as a named
place of space, that Jerusalem reappears as "the city", but
in the discourse, as the interlocutor of Jesus, the existence
which he addresses himself to in order to weep for it. You
will be destroyed, because, "Would that even today you knew
the things that make for peace! But now they are hid from
your eyes. [p. 79] ...because you did not know the time of
your visitation" (19:42-44). Ceasing to be a place of the
space of the narrative and named as such, Jerusalem accedes
to the discursive existence as a receiver of a message internal to the message itself. Jerusalem, to which Jesus addresses himself, not only does not respond, but even cannot respond, since if it did so, it would contradict the very message that was addressed to it. But conversely, it is at the
moment that the Temple is destroyed as a referend [*référend*]
of discourse in order to no longer be a place of *parole*, and
when it is identified with the very subject who utters the
discourse, that Jerusalem, as a toponym naming a place of
space, reappears as that about which the discourse speaks, as
the object of which the prophetic discourse announces destruction and captivity, a discourse held by a subject of which the
position of *parole* is a Temple, by obliteration of the Temple
by the prophetic *parole*.

We think that it is important to note that the announcement of the destruction of Jerusalem and the announcement of
the destruction of the Temple are not homologous because of
the *very place of the narrative* from where they are uttered.
In one case Jesus is *at a distance* from Jerusalem on the Mount
of Olives, and this lamentation is to a certain degree homologous of the eschatological discourse in Matthew, held, for him
as well, on the Mount of Olives. In the second case, Jesus is
in the Temple and the announcement of its destruction is *ipso
facto* its resolution in a pure place of *parole* and its trans-

fer to the subject who is connected to it.

Therefore in this way a point in this interplay of compensation between narrative and discourse, between a referend [référend] of discourse and place of parole, the hypothesis so difficult to conceive of a subject of discourse whose only possibility of acceding to the being in the narrative text is to be assigned a point of space that it can occupy only by pronouncing its obliteration;[107] of a subject capable of this movement, only because the text displays itself on the double level of narrative and discourse and more precisely of discourse which is pronounced from privileged points of the narrative.

MATTHEW

Returning to the variant text of Matthew in order to end this study reveals the existence in the text of a [p. 80] secondary system of discourse which, in the very interior of Jesus's discourse on the Mount of Olives facing the Temple and facing the world, is the "repetition" about the mode of parabolic micro-narratives whose function is twofold: on the one hand, to carry out by a paradoxical operation of coding the "prophetic" sense of the discourse which precedes them, and on the other hand to permit by the narrative developments occurring in the symbolic-parabolic level the articulation of the first part of the discourse (24:15-31)[108] in its second part (25:31-46).[109]

Totalization

Let us describe rapidly the structuration, in the discourse, of the space by the places after the initial segment that can be schematized in the following way:

NARRATIVE		DISCOURSE
from the Temple to the	departure of Jesus	destruction of the Temple
Mount of Olives	reentry of Jesus	fulfillment of the world

The two lines that the schema distinguishes thanks to the
threefold question of the disciples is continued in the following segments:

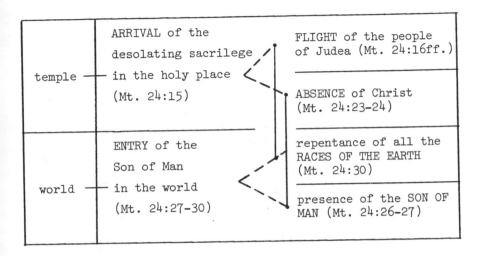

	ARRIVAL of the desolating sacrilege in the holy place (Mt. 24:15)	FLIGHT of the people of Judea (Mt. 24:16ff.)
temple		ABSENCE of Christ (Mt. 24:23-24)
world	ENTRY of the Son of Man in the world (Mt. 24:27-30)	repentance of all the RACES OF THE EARTH (Mt. 24:30)
		presence of the SON OF MAN (Mt. 24:26-27)

And the ensemble of the first part is completed with the
coming of the Son of Man on the clouds of heaven, with power
and great glory, and with the gathering of the elect which he
carries out from the four winds of the earth and from one end
of heaven to the other (Mt. 24:30ff.; 25:31). Therefore the
flight and the absence which marks the line of the Temple is
found reabsorbed in a totalization at the same time cosmic and
anthropological in the Son of the Heavenly-Man. This point is
even [p. 81] clearer in Mark, since the totalization affects
the very end of the earth and of the heavens, its astro-cosmic
opposite (Mk. 13:27).

The Separation, Function of the Parabolic Micro-Narratives

It is remarkable, by contrast, that the second part of the
eschatological discourse is the manifestation of a separation,
of a division starting from the first gathering: "before him
will be gathered all the nations, and he will separate them one
from another as a shepherd separates the sheep from the goats,
and he will place the sheep at his right hand but the goats at
the left" (Mt. 25:32-33). And at the same time, the Son of Man
becomes the King (ὁ βασιλεύς) (v. 34), who addressing himself
to the elect, will give them as an inheritance the Kingdom

which has been prepared for them from the foundation of the earth, while the others will go away to an eternal punishment (v. 46). The problem is therefore to pass from the gathering to the division, from the totalization to the separation. This is, it seems to us, the function of the intermediary symbolic-parabolic narratives which will construct a discontinuous space with discrete elements from a continuous and global space, a space with a binary structure, a construction which, we have noted from the beginning, is the specific topical problem of Matthew.[110]

These parabolic micro-narratives of mediation between the two discursive fragments are distributed in two volets of unequal importance: the first includes a short narrative explicitly qualified by a parable, that of the verdant fig-tree, the second is more complex since it includes two segments which are on the whole [plutôt] of comparisons, one an Old Testament [vétero-testamentaire] "story", evoking the days of Noah and the eve of the flood, the other "allegorical" opposing a master of a house, the thief, then three explicit parables of the servant, the ten virgins, and the talents of increasing abundance [longueur]. This division is not accidental. In effect, we have seen that the parable of the verdant fig-tree in Mark and Matthew was in a signifier correlation with the episode of the withered fig-tree, a parabolic miracle marking one of the entrances of Jesus in the narrative into Jerusalem. We are referring here to this analysis. But by virtue of a secondary correlation, one will note that the parable of the verdant fig-tree defines on the metaphoric mode a precursory sign, an announcement: "As soon as its branch becomes tender and puts forth its leaves [p. 82], you know that summer is near" (γινώσκετε ὅτι ἐγγὺς τὸ θέρος, Mt. 24:32). A knowledge of prevision is acquired. "Likewise, you also, when you see all that--that is to say the cosmic signs, but also the disaster in Judea, the false prophets and their signs--you know that it is near, at the doors." This knowledge however does not include any localization in time. "As for the date of this day and the hour, no one knows them...only the Father alone", v. 36. This lacuna, this absence of a point of reference in the duration can only establish an open, indefinite expectation of the event. The signs are not known which immediately precede it, which indicate its nearness. Temporal space continues, without the chronological articulation of a calendar that the progress of the maturation of the fig-tree interprets. But this ignorance of the day and the hour implies, by its opening, a vigilance, not only an expectation, but an attention to the signs.

Comparisons

It is in this way that one passes to the second volet, and first of all to the two "comparisons": the first alludes to Noah and the Day of the flood. It opposes the continuous time of the repetitive activities, "they ate, they drank, they bought, they sold, they planted, they built, but on the day when Lot went out from Sodom, fire and brimstone rained from heaven and destroyed them all..." (Lk. 17:29f.). Whether it is a question of an entrance or an exit, in both cases this movement is a movement of withdrawal from the world or from a city which articulates by a separation and rupture a simple continuity, that which marks the meals, the marriages, cultures, commerce, constructions.

The signifier importance of the episode of Lot evoked only by Luke will then be emphasized: *the departure of the just out of the city* was the signal announcing its destruction from above, just as the *entrance of Noah into* the cosmic Ark was the precursory signal of the destruction of the world from above. On the one hand, the double episode of Noah and Lot repeats in the discourse--by the [p. 83] parabolic narrative-- what the narrative and the discourse articulated in Matthew, according to the double line of Time and the World, but with some remarkable inversions and connections: it is by *departing* from the *Temple* that Jesus accomplishes (because it is a sign and a reality) and announces its destruction at the same time. It is by *entering* into the *Ark* that Noah announces the destruction of the *world*. But it is by announcing his *reentry into the world* (his return) that Jesus announces the *consummation* of the world, just as Lot departing from the *city* announces its *destruction*.

Schism

In other words, the Old Testament [*vétéro-testamentaire*] comparison, single in Matthew, double in Luke, inside of the discourse of Jesus and on the mode of a micro-narrative of reference, permits us to connect into the same totality the sacred history of the Jewish people, the present narrative of the acts and the speeches [*paroles*] of Jesus, and within this narrative, the cosmic eschatological discourse: this totality is defined then as a system of discourse levels (historic, parabolic, eschatological) in a narrative. These levels only combine to one another and to the narrative by the correspondence of the movements and the displacements between the places of the space which is thus invested with a similar and/ or contrary signifier function (such as the Temple and the Ark, or Jerusalem and Sodom, or the World and the Ark, etc.). The most general form which we can give to this function is that of a schism, a separation or a division in the heart of a continuity or a totality.

In effect if we try to decode the reference narratives by the indications of the eschatological discourse, it should be possible to note that the coming of the Son of Man is hidden [crypté] in the flood or the rain of fire whose function is to destroy. What would then be the corresponding symbolics of Noah and Lot who nevertheless, in the "historic" reference, are positively valorized? By really presenting the problem in this form, an allegorizing interpretation is carried out which substitutes, term for term, the symbolized and the symbolizer. It is not the Son of Man who is coded in the flood or the rain of fire, but his advent: his relation to the world and to all the races of the earth. This relation which is an entrance into the world and a gathering of the elect, is found [p. 84] hidden [cryptée] in the relationship of Noah and Lot to the flood and to the rain of fire, the story of Noah or Lot perceived as a dynamic relation in space and decoded as such makes the double contrary function appear in which each element of the relationship holds for itself an opposite (destruction and preservation, negation and position, disappearance and salvation, separation and gathering, flood or rain of fire, and Noah or Lot), but that, moreover, refers beyond the eschatological discourses, the entrances of Jesus into the city, and the Temple in order to establish his community there and his departure from the Temple and from the city in order to die there.

The brief comparison of the master of the house and of the thief is again more subtle in its construction: because the thief is indeed the Son of Man who enters into the World in order to fulfill it--by breaking through the walls of the house (Mt. 24:43)--by shaking the powers of the heavens (v. 29)--but the advice which is given after the fact to the Master of the house is to remain awake and not to permit one to penetrate the walls of his dwelling place. In reality, in order for the deciphering to be completed, it is necessary to carry out at the same time a displacement and a condensation, neither keeping nor stressing the thief as the destructive unexpected invasion, negative function of rupture of breaking open of the closed, but equally not keeping the advice of vigilance in order to keep intack the closure of the house, as the function of safeguarding, of collectedness. Thus the breaking open of the closed by the invasion of the exterior (negative function) and the preservation of the interior by rejection of the open (positive function) can be conjugated into the story of the their and the master of the house.

PARABLES

Return and Rejection: the Meal

From three large parables which follow, we will only re-
tain the essential articulation, in the spatiality of the narratives that develop them. The master in the parable of the
servant 24:45-51 returns to his home to find the faithful servant *giving food* to his people in time of need (ἐν καιρῷ). In
return, if the servant is evil, he will use the time of his
master's absence to begin to eat and to drink in the company
of drunkards and to beat the servants of the house. In the
first case, at the time of the *return* of the master, the servant will be installed in a ruling position. Instead of simply
giving [p. 85] the food, he will be *established* over all the
goods of the master (καταστάσις). On the contrary, if he has
been unfaithful and not very shrewd, he will be *removed* (διχο-
τομήσει αὐτόν), separated, expelled, and put out of the house.

In this first parable, two indications are to be remem-
bered: first of all, the movement of return of the Master
from the *outside to the inside, from the outside to his house*,
which will be followed, either by an elevation or an establishment on high of the servant if he has been good, or by a rejection, an *expulsion* if he has been evil; afterwards the semantic
content articulated on this spatial organization is that of the
feeding and the meal. The master returns in order to ascertain
if his servant, representative, and delegate, gives food to eat
in time of need: the return of the master is, in some way,
contemporary with a meal.

Immediately, the first parable gives us the beginnings of
two axes of interpretation that the narrator attempts to make
apparent in these micro-narratives: a return preceded by a
departure and a meal accompanied by a rejection, by an expulsion. In other words, two double movements of opposite meaning articulate one another by a gift of food. The point of
arrival of the movement of return is a banquet, a wedding-
party room, a place where one eats, but it is also the starting point of a movement of expulsion. Thus it is the act of
eating which simultaneously comes to establish a discontinuity,
entirely by affirming a continuity in the dynamic space of the
narrative, because it is in a relationship at the same time
with a return and an exclusion.

The Ten Maidens: Consummation, Exclusion, Marriage

The supplementary signifier relation which introduces the parable of the ten maidens in relationship to the previous one is the determination of the gift of food as a place--a marriage feast (25:10), therefore in a direct relationship to marriage. The ten *maidens* rush to meet the *bridegroom* and because of that they must *use up the oil* while waiting to participate in the marriage feast. The movements from then on are much more complex than in the first. A double movement of *departure* of the maidens, in 25:1 (ἐξῆλθον εἰς ὑπάντησιν τοῦ νυμφίου) and in 25:6 (ἐξερχεσθε εἰς ὑπραντήσιν αὐτοῦ) is articulated in its center by the sleepiness of *all* the maidens. But the foolish maidens will be [p. 86] forced to go to a merchant to buy oil, whereas the wise maidens will directly rejoin the husband and will enter with him into the wedding room. Thus the *departure to the husband* is finished in a *re-entry with him* into the henceforth closed place of the banquet. Hence the *exclusion* of the foolish maidens arriving too tardily. Here again the *place of the banquet* is indeed a *place of exclusion* after having been a place of *collectedness*, but because of the detour to the merchant of those who were not supplied with oil. At this point, the correspondence will be noted between on the one hand: 1) the wise servant who gives away food eventually to consume it next; 2) the disloyal servant who consumes the food instead of giving it at an opportune time; and on the other hand: 1) the foolish maidens who cannot consume the (lamp) oil because they are short of it and because the wise maidens do not give it to them, the moment not being timely; 2) the wise maidens who consume the wedding meal with the bridegroom and the foolish maidens who do not participate in the banquet. Thus the interplay of the displacements of departure and entrance, exclusion and reception which is found doubled, on the plane of exchanges, by the gift and the consumption of food permits us also to introduce it here from the discontinuity by safeguarding the continuity in the system of spatial localization.

The Talents: Consummation, Production

Finally the last parable will be able only to confirm this analysis with, however, some strong variant relationships. As in the preceding parables--but above all in the first--a man *departs*, and then he *returns*. The delegated servants who have received 5, 3 [2?], and 1 talent(s) on deposit account for them. The first two have made the *deposit* productive, since they have doubled it. The last one has *buried* his money in order to *preserve* it intact. Between the departure and the return of the master, there are two cases of discontinuity (not only of the food, but of the money). The sums are no longer the same; they have doubled. From the money a case of continuity has been produced. The talent entrusted to the last servant has been preserved. But the discontinuity is finished in the place of collectedness and joy by an entrance into the banquet of the matter, whereas the continuity of the deposit is terminated outside, in the darkness where the servant is. [p. 87]

Thus it is because the last servant has not produced anything that he cannot consume. It is because he has not "risked" discontinuity in the production that he is put in a state of discontinuity in the consummation.

The remark of the lazy servant about his master remains to be analyzed, "Reaping where you did not sow, and gathering where you did not winnow" (Mt. 25:24). It is without a doubt a stereotyped formulation of the harshness of the Master. But there is more, because the word of the servant marks an extreme case of productive discontinuity, since without sowing or winnowing, the master harvests and gathers. While the alert servants only double the sum which they have had on deposit, the master draws fruit from nothing. He extracts a profit from absolutely zero, in opposition to the bad servant who draws a zero profit from something entrusted to him. The servant will also be excluded from the house of the Master, while his companions will be received there. Also, according to the logic of the gift which we have analyzed elsewhere with regard to the parable of the sower, the talent will be taken back which had been entrusted to him, a talent which will be given to the one who already had ten. Because the gift is defined in the present case as a supplement to the having and the non-gift, the lack as a withdrawal in the lack, as a kind of negative supplement of the lack.

GATHERING AND JUDGEMENT

We perceive then on the symbolic-parabolic level how the micro-narratives introduced into the discourse of Jesus between the two large eschatological developments come to permit, by a change of isotopy, the articulation of an eschaton of gathering and totalization at the same time human and cosmic in an eschaton of judgement and of discriminating of separation. It was necessary that some narratives—and only some of the narratives were capable by their diachronic development of carrying out such a union—transform the totalization into separation. The functional categories that the narratives transformed into their successive episode however at the level of the discourse and in particular of the eschatological discourse had to be maintained and synchronically connected into a single structure. Here again the articulations of a continuous space by the displacements, the returns, and the [p. 88] departures, the receptions and the expulsions, which are constituents of places marked as supper rooms for weddings, or festival banquets, permitted us to conceive together, judgment and vengeance on the one hand, and reception and gathering on the other, a fulgurating immediacy of a presence and delays interminably extended by a waiting.

The parabolic narratives carry out in this way a paradoxical operation of coding of a discourse which, in itself, was delivered in plain language and this, in the end if not explains it, at least communicates it more completely. But the paradox was only apparent. Because the five "eschatological" parables were only capable of assuring the paradoxical conjunction of a delay and a presence, a future and an always present instant, by the passage from the discourse to some redundant narratives which, thanks to the transformations of the articulated space which is necessarily theirs, permitted us to conceive together what in itself is not easily conceivable.

Presence of the Traitor

But at the same time, and the multiplicity of the signifier strata of the parabolic narratives authorize this proliferation of correlations, this plural overture of the "emergences of meaning" [*"départs de sens"*], these narratives--like those which, in Matthew, constituted the entrance parables-- are constructed in correlation with the large narrative segment which comes to open, the *entrances* into the city, of Jesus to the house and the paschal supper room, the return for the banquet which will also only be able to take place in it perfectly by the exclusion of the one which will permit Jesus to die: Judas. The appearance of this other substance which is the money, besides the food of the feast and the *parole*, points in this direction.

As a conclusion, it may be permissable for us to recall, beyond the proliferation of our analyses, an index of this multiplication of the meaning inseparable from the biblical text and no doubt from every text, the initial problematic, our basic hypotheses, and the results which we have reached, in the form of tables which have no other goal than to indicate the fundamental connection in the toponym, of the spatiality and the meaning, which was the "subject" of our research:

General Methodological Tables

Problematic

TABLE A

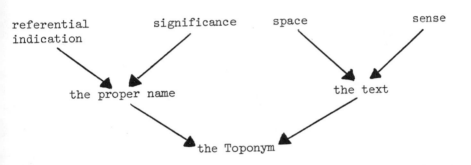

I   II

referential indication → the proper name ← significance

space → the text ← sense

the proper name → the Toponym ← the text

Note 1: It can be written more precisely, and by development inside of a narrative ensemble, in the following way:

TABLE B

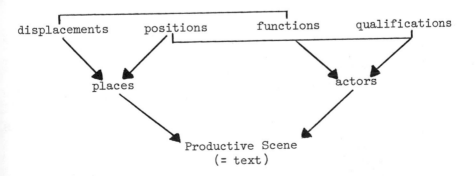

displacements → places ← positions

functions → actors ← qualifications

places → Productive Scene (= text) ← actors

General Hypothesis:

TABLE C

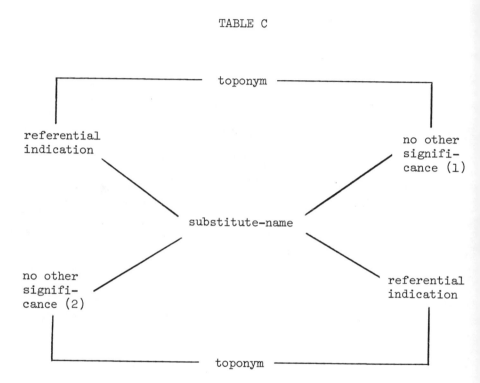

[p. 90]

Invested Tables: Narrative

TABLE D

Primary Transformations

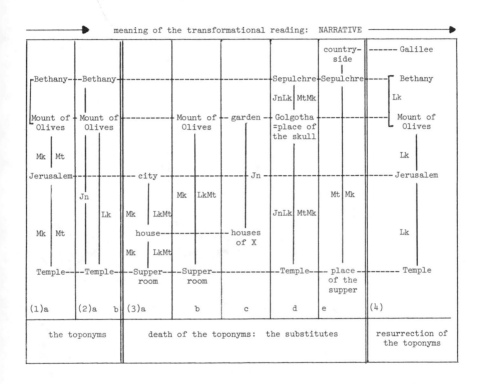

						country-side	Galilee
						Sepulchre	Sepulchre
						JnLk MtMk	
Bethany	Bethany				Sepulchre		Bethany
							Lk
Mount of Olives	Mount of Olives		Mount of Olives	garden	Golgotha =place of the skull		Mount of Olives
Mk Mt							Lk
Jerusalem		city		Jn			Jerusalem
	Jn		Mk LkMt			Mt Mk	
	Lk	Mk LkMt			JnLk MtMk		
Mk Mt		house		houses of X			Lk
		Mk LkMt					
Temple	Temple	Supper-room	Supper-room		Temple	place of the supper	Temple
(1)a	(2)a b	(3)a	b	c	d	e	(4)
the toponyms	death of the toponyms: the substitutes						resurrection of the toponyms

Note 2:   D is only the "invested" reading of C.

Note 3:   One should refer back to the tables included in the text in order to appreciate the significant differences between the variant texts, differences simply noted in table D (Mk, Mt, Lk, Jn). We limit ourselves here to describing the remarkable opposition of columns (1) Mt (Mk) and (2) Lk, and columns (e) Mt and Mk and (4) Lk.

Secondary Transformations

TABLE D(a)

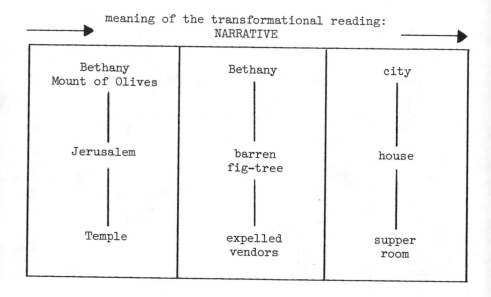

meaning of the transformational reading:
NARRATIVE

Bethany Mount of Olives	Bethany	city
Jerusalem	barren fig-tree	house
Temple	expelled vendors	supper room

Note 4: Table D(a) is superimposed on columns (1)a, (2)ab, (3)a [see Table D]. It belongs to the narrative or primary narrative level, but a secondary transformation is in it by displacement: one will note in effect that in (D), the city is the substitute name for Jerusalem, whereas in D(a), it is the house which "represents" Jerusalem. The intermediary column corresponds to the narrative of the miracle-parable of the withered fig-tree whose importance is not to be underestimated, because it articulates the primary narrative level (the first degree narrative), on the plane of the discourse and the narratives which are integrated (narratives of the second degree). We have shown it by its correlation with the parable of the verdant fig-tree.

Invested Tables = Narratives within the Discourse

     First it is a matter of three entrance parables. One
will note here again the remarkable correspondence of the
"parabolic" transformation with the table of the narrative
transformation D(a). [p. 92]

TABLE E

parable (2)

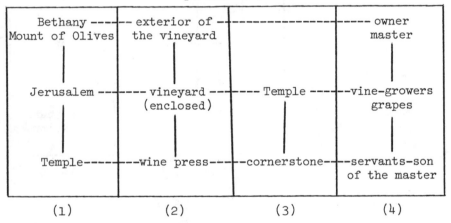

Bethany ---- exterior of -- ---------------- ---- owner			
Mount of Olives, the vineyard			master
Jerusalem -- ---- vineyard -- ---- Temple --- ---vine-growers			
(enclosed)			grapes
Temple---- ---wine press-- --cornerstone-- --servants-son			
			of the master
(1)	(2)	(3)	(4)

Note 5:   Table E jumps over an extra stage: thanks to the
          flexibility of the parabolic decoding in relation to
          the attribution of the signifieds to the signifiers,
          the transformation of places into actors is realized.
          Column (3) of this table exposes the essential struc-
          tural position of the citation of Psalm 118 with the
          value of the "Temple" which will allow us to articu-
          late between them columns (1) and (2) on the one hand
          and (4) on the other. (See our analysis in the text.)

          One will read the table which follows as the first
          "moment" of the preceding table:

TABLE E(a)

parable (1)

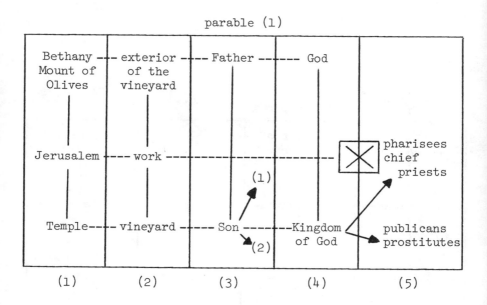

Note 6: Position x at the boundary of columns 4 and 5 is that non-assignable of the subject of discourse which relates the parable: we are [p. 93] forced to take it into consideration because column (5) which reveals the decipherment [*décryptage*] of columns (2) and (3) reveals to us the effective or potential receivers of the parable itself.

TABLE E(b)

parable (3)

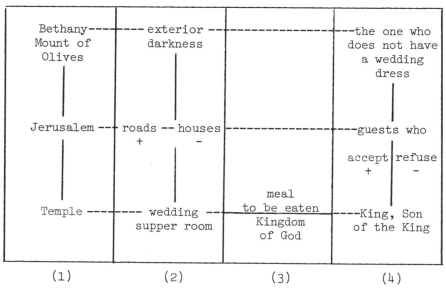

| (1) | (2) | (3) | (4) |

Note 7: We introduce column (3) which includes only one mention, but double in order to reveal in the table, the
beginning of decipherment [*décryptage*] of the parabolic narrative which is found in Mt. 22:2, a beginning which is at the same time an indicative of a
coded narrative in Matthew: "The Kingdom of Heaven
may be compared to a king who gave a marriage feast
for his son."

As far as the invested tables of the narratives integrated in the eschatological discourses are concerned,
we refer to the table included in the text p. 73.
[p. 94]

Second Part

SEMIOTICS OF THE TRAITOR

> *"It is in the chain of the sig-*
> *nifiers that the meaning dwells,*
> *but...none of the elements of*
> *the chain are composed of the*
> *signification of which it is*
> *capable at the very moment."*
> — Jacques Lacan

Chapter One

QUESTIONS AND HYPOTHESES

This study is not a continuation or a result of the study which preceded it. It forms an autonomous collection. But nevertheless, it is not foreign to Part I, because it is taken in a symmetrical and complementary problematic network to that of the places of the narrative in their names. In effect, the question which this work aims at, in its greatest generality, is that of the character in the narrative, and his structure in the perspective opened by the actantial model.[1]

THE NAME OF THE CHARACTER

Now we know that one of the privileged modes of appearance of the character in the narrative line is his proper name. It is the proper name which permits the reader to perform systematically--progressively and gradually his reading--the attributions of trial, functions, and qualifications to the subjects which support them, and subtend them, bring them to mind, or produce them.[2] The proper name is thus the index in the narrative, of a position of the subject, of a productive cause-to-be or ultimate origin--in the narrative--of the actions about which the reader reads successive appearances. And as in the case of toponyms, we perceive the power of the referential illusion that the proper name of the character introduces into the text, because as earlier with the place names, the names of the characters indicate in the text its exterior,[3] in the present case the subjects whose actions, in the world, in one time and in one [p. 98] determined place, are recited by the text, and whose characters are, by the names which are peculiar to them, doubles in the narrative.

Since this text which we read is given more as a "true" story, and not as a fiction, as a chronicle and an account of a time itself carefully entered under a reference number, here and there on the surface of the text, to some events of being, of places external to this very story, the network of the proper names is designated in a supplementary inductive function of a reality in the text. It is the composition of an archive,[4] a time, a group, and an individual, destined to the memory--in time--of groups which, rightly or wrongly, lead us to find their origin in this time, this group, this individual. But this archive is also destined to repeat it, in the recitation, indeed in the repetition, the gestures, actions, and *paroles* of this group, of this individual on the mode of the semiological discourse.[5] It is therefore not only a discourse in language, but a discourse in behaviors, rites, ceremonies, and positions, whose signs, between motivation and arbitrariness, refer to this narrative as to their origin; and in this narrative, to this subject, to these subjects, the names of which the narrative inscribes.[6]

Theological discourse has always been interested in the names of God, and more precisely Christology has traced out the network of names or titles which redouble in a proper-specific dimension the name of Jesus.[7] But it remains beyond or on this side of this network of names "Chief Priest", "Servant", "Son of Man", etc., the very name of Jesus in its double function, an indicial function, which is, as for every proper name, far from being explained, and a signifier function--symbolic of the text itself.[8] But the name of Jesus is not the only name and all the gospel narratives are marked with names of characters. They evoke some onomastic changes, as if sometimes a fixed system of appellations were being dealt with[9]--------(thus the name of Simon and his re-naming as Peter which is not free from recalling the operation of dis-investment and of a semantic re-investment of the toponyms which has been the fundamental hypothesis of the preceding study[10])--or the recurrences which do not appear to be accidental (thus in Acts the presence of Simon-Peter, before the test of the unclean, under the roof of Simon the tanner, the pure Jew who handles the unclean, etc...).[11] [p. 99] With the proper names, a double problem is presented: that of the character in the text and that of the subject of action and discourse in the referential relationship.

To a certain extent, the present work, defined in this way in the most general limits and in its most totalizing aim, retroactively conditions the previous study. In order to establish the signifier network of the places of the narrative in the text, we have not analyzed these places in the recurrence of their toponyms or their substitutes, thanks to the passages or the appearances, to the journeys or the presences of the "hero", of the principal character of the narrative considered in the form of a vector of meaning or an orientation of the space. Therefore it is the character ascribed to his name which, by its displacements, has specified the places in their names. The primary and secondary signifier investments, which have been able to be produced on what at first sight only appeared to be an index, have only been possible because these hero characters participate in some spheres of well-defined action,[12] in some functional and qualificative "places"--toπού. In other words, the character has had a meta-narrative function which we have not so far perceived, but which has conditioned our previous analyses: that of transferring some functions and qualifications, some narrative places into the places of the narrative, of the τοπού in which--at least as a working hypothesis--the functions and the qualifications of the narrative are classified (as, for example, to use the language of Propp or Greimas, opposition, struggle, test, etc.) in the *places* into which the story comes to be punctuated and comes to organize the space of the meaning into its different names.[13] The characters diligently insure this transference, drawing on the paradigms in order to distribute, along the syntagmatic line, the functions and qualifications which respectively insure the dynamic and the ontological determinations of the narrative, and that into some *topies* which the proper names designate. That is to say the importance of the character and the necessity of wondering if this metanarrative function, which "personally" belongs to it, i.e. considered as a character, did not require a return of the analysis, from the deep structures where so far it has begun with the success that is known about it, to the surface structures of the narrative. Perhaps more precisely, the deep structures should be on the very surface of the narrative, and not hidden by it, but manifested in some marks, [p. 100] whose network it would be a matter of establishing. And consequently, the task of the analysis should be to determine the rules of meta-narrative functioning of the character between paradigms and syntagms.

THE ACTANTIAL MODEL OF A. J. GREIMAS

It is known however that the strength of structural analysis has been in this domain--to dissolve under the proper name, what the presence individuated in the narrative lexiconized, the ontological subject of the process, while bringing about its dis-articulation in functions and qualifications and while establishing some ensembles determined by these functions and qualifications, the ensembles hierarchizable according to the principles which rule the limits by extension and comprehension.[14] It is equally known that from one text to another, these ensembles can be shared among several roles in several subjects, or diluted among them, etc.[15] It will only be noted that the actantial analysis is posterior to the qualificational or functional analysis, since it can only be carried out after the first has been performed. The actantial model is only after all an adaptation or an instrument of transition or transformation between the regular distribution of the functions along the narrative line and the question which poses--

on the surface of the text--the presence of characters. How
are the characters restored or reduced and, behind their nominal appearance, the "subjects" of the process, to the correlative oppositions of functions into the syntagmatic of the narrative, if not by the mediation of a model where some synchronic relationships are organized among classes of functions and
whose characters participate, while being established as such.

   It can only be asked if this operation does not only consist of repulsing, and the problem of the subject, and that of
the diachrony of the narrative: a narrative tells a story,
i.e. the successive upheaval, in the "time", of events whose
enchainment is irreversible. This is the first superficial
reading of the narrative in general. But another can be produced from it, quite superficial, according to which a narrative tells a story constituted by the actions of subjects (or
characters) some the opposite of others, stable subjects which
traverse the story, identical to themselves,[16] sources producing different actions [p. 101] which are the successive and
irreversible events of the first reading. The identity of the
subjects producing actions are articulated in the irreversible
succession of the events which these actions are or of which
they are the causes. The story in the narrative is the story
of this meeting of the plane of the identical (subjects--char-
acters) and the plane of the successive (the events).

   Now what is the actantial model, if not the paradigmatic
mending of the narrative. Or on the contrary, what is the
chronic [chronique] organization of the functions in the syntagmatic, if not the projection on the narrative line of actantial paradigms. The intermediary elements which allow this
repetition or this projection are constituted, on the one hand,
by the logical possibility which has allowed the structural an-
alyst to write down the chronic* relation of succession: $A \rightarrow B$
as a relation of implication: $A \rightarrow$ non-A (hence the importance
of the establishment of the correlations which "structure" the
temporality of the narrative); and at the same time, the possibility of rewriting the relationship: $A \rightarrow$ non-A as a relationship of disjunction: A vs. non-A which is from then on independent of the narrative temporality. One passes therefore
from the chrony [chronie]* to the diachrony and from the diachrony to the synchrony.[17] Henceforth the functions can be
structured a second time, not by the correlations of the syntagmatic, but by some opposite relationships, in the larger
sense of the term, between classes of functions.[18] These re-

---

*chronic--i.e. temporal or referring to time.
*chrony--i.e. temporal or referring to time.

lationships will describe the actants of the model, whose division will correspond to the roles. The latter, in their turn, can be individuals and figures in subject-characters.[19]

The Test-Struggle

But there is a very remarkable point of the narrative in its diachrony, where the place of articulation between the actantial structure and the narrative structure is shown. This is the test. The test-struggle has the characteristic of not being correlated with any other narrative segment or of belonging to all, to the extent to which it syntagmatically connects the rupture of the contract and the communication and the re-establishment of the communication and of the contract and where it transforms the structure of the narrative into its first phase

$$\frac{a}{\text{non-a}} \simeq \frac{c}{\text{non-c}}$$

in a structure of a second phase   [p. 102]

$$\frac{a}{\text{non-a}} \simeq \frac{c}{\text{non-c}} \quad ,$$

the negative into the positive. It includes this eminent sign of being devoid of a functional correlation. It is a central point by which the structurality of the narrative is produced. In other words, it is the place in the center of the structure where there is no structure, but where the structure originates. It is in short the place of the subject, in the double sense of the subject of the narrative and of the subject-character.[20]

Now it is at this privileged point that the actantial model is localized in all its dimensions: there is a passage from the rupture of the contract to the re-establishment of the contract or axis of the communication: sender----receiver, by the struggle where the helper-opponent axis is displayed which is completed by the result of the text, which is an axis of the object and of the subject. What can we say except that the actantial model functions at this central point of the narrative as a subject of structurality? It would not be useful to affirm that structural analysis has made us pass from an unconscious anthropomorphic ontology of the narrative to a conscious abstract and formal structurality of the narrative, if there exists in this very structurality as its blind point, the place where a subject produces a narrative, and where the structure itself is established around this point which structural analysis assigns, but where it cannot introduce the structure and where the actantial model is "concentrated" in all its power, i.e. the relation of the subject to the object through the double relationship of sender and receiver on the one hand and of the helper and the opponent on the other.[21]

We can formulate then our working hypothesis to its full extension. We assume the functional analysis done, and its results conform to the Proppian model formalized by A. J. Greimas, according to the schema of the contract and of the tests whose functions are distributed in a certain order along the syntagmatic line. We will assume that the construction of the narrative units of the Passion Narrative complies with the most general formula established for the folktale by A. J. Greimas, and that this Narrative is that of the tests of the hero in order to establish a new contract, in order to fulfill the Law in the New Covenant, and that in the present case, the object of its quest is "itself in another form", between the sender, "God", and the receiver, "a universal type of Community",[22] which will itself be established through the oppositions. [p. 103]

Problem

That being assumed, the problem which will be our subject is the following: what is the epistemological nature, the methodological value, and the transformational power of the central point of the functional model, the passage-mediation between $\overline{A}$, $\overline{C}$ and C, A, or F: the test-struggle where the inversion of the diachronic schema is performed, where is expressed, figuratively and anthropomorphically, the "versus" of the large synchronic correlation constitutive of the narrative form itself? What designates the sign of this correlation? If the test-struggle is the negative operation with a correlation of the negative operation without a correlation of the negative relational elements of the model and their replacement by some positive correlations, the only point which is neither positive nor negative, and/or positive and negative, simultaneously neutral and compound, then the question which we pose to ourselves concerns the place of this point in the narrative, the marks of its structural production in the text. In other words, it is a question of the narrative dynamic and of the punctual mark of its irreversibility.[23]

Certainly we understand well how structurally the passage
from the negative to the positive is accomplished: by the
presence of a narrative element in the actantial model, as in
the narrative structure, which, because it is positive and
negative on the one hand, and neither positive nor negative
on the other, can function as an intersection and "shifter" in
the exchange of functional signs and qualificative values.[24]
But this element is, not only the operator of the transformation, but the transformation itself of which the place can
only be marked *in the structure* as an empty place, since it is
the only non-relational element. Therefore it is "un-struc-
turable" because it is structured with everything, for the
good reason that it is the producer of the relationships which
constitute it. This element, we think, is the villain (or the
traitor) in the narrative which interests us: a figure of the
absence of necessity in the functioning of the structural model, the only figure of the freedom which the structures can
permit. It is, completely negative, the contradiction itself.[25] We think that this figure can only appear from now
on in the narrative as a figure--a proper name, superficially,
since that of which it is the figure is the pure transformation of the functional schema [p. 104] of negative into positive, since its figure is the central structural absence by
which the structure is organized, the very source, in its
character of the syntagmatic organization of the narrative,
and of the actantial model. What it figures is the empty
place that the correlations straddle and starting from which
the total structure opens itself into its different homologi-
cal correspondences.[26]

It is necessary indeed to perceive the most general methodological consequences of this hypothesis, in what we called
above the return of the structure to the "manifestation".
Thus it is on the very surface of the narrative text, which
should indicate--but figuratively--the narrative point where
the structure finds its relational equilibrium, where it is
produced as a structure. That means that superficially--as an
event and in the same contingency that the proper name already
draws attention to what the structural necessities can display
appears--the achrony of their network. At this point, the extreme superficiality coincides, in the separation [*écart*] of
the figure, with extreme depth: the one that comes back to
state that the opposition of the surface and the depth is not
a pertinent metaphor since the depth is on the surface.* Perhaps it is necessary to substitute for it the notion of a figurative separation, a kind of metonymic catachresis by which

---

à la surface may also mean "superficial".

the place of the structure is filled in, but by a transfer of correlative elements which only one "character" can conjugate.[27] Thus it is by the figure and the vertical separation that the figuring enters with an absence and that has only a "semantic" value by the narrative manifested in which the figure is inserted in metonymic contiguity, that the deep narrative structure is organized and the actantial model is focalized.[28]

THE CHARACTER OF THE TRAITOR

Henceforth it is fitting to state precisely this very general hypothesis with the case of the particular narratives that we are studying: the traitor *in the narrative* is less a dissimulator than a "Donor", ὁ προδότης, ὁ παραδίδους, the Greek text points out to us.[29] Judas Iscariot is the one who *delivers* Jesus and--let us note--who delivers him absolutely, who *transmits* the object and provokes the transmission of the object. He is the character and, specifically, the very place of the exchange. Also we are not able to link the traitor and [p. 105] the "functions of the villainy*" according to the categories of Being and Appearing.[30] The traitor is neither a hypocrite nor an imposter in the narratives which we are studying: for the obvious reason that appears in an intervention of the narrator in the narrative; when Judas is named for the first time--we will return to this point--the narrator indicates, at this point of the narrative where he *must* be named, that he *will be* the "deliverer", the "giver" (or "donor") of Jesus. It is a retrospective mark which has the value of a title or a naming of the figure: "Judas--the donor". Thereby and in one word, the transformation of the proper into the quasi-common is begun by an inverted antonomasia: "Judas" as a traitor [*judas*], because ὁ προδότης is already, in advance, by a retrospection of the narrative itself the proper name of this individual named "Judas".[31]

But there is another reason--less immediate--which confirms this same point: Judas is the traitor whose treason is announced before it can be carried out, but whose treason is denounced after it can exist; a situation which implies a powerful paradox whose structural significance is remarkable, we will see, because either a treason is discovered, but then it is accomplished; or else the treason is denounced, but it has not yet occurred. By discovering, the villainy is re-

---

traîtrise means both "treachery" and "villainy".

vealed, but after the fact. By denouncing it as anticipated.[32] Now in the case of Judas, an inversion of pairs appears. The treachery is discovered before accomplishment by the one who must be betrayed, and the traitor is denounced, after his treachery, close to those with whom he has concluded the treason contract. We will note, at the time of the minute analysis of the texts, that this inversion is more complex and that it sets into motion the quadri-variant system which is our object of study.[33] But the general rule of functional distribution is indeed the one which we pointed out. Therefore if the traitor is not the deceiver who appears to be what he is not (and is not what he appears to be), what is the categorical constitution of the traitor? The inversion in the distribution of the narrative functions related to the treason indicates, it seems to us, the operational necessity of the traitor. Let us summarize it in this formula which is a secondary working hypothesis: *it is necessary that the traitor exist in order to make what is necessary accidental and aleatory.*[34]

In this hypothesis, which it will be a matter of confirming or disproving [p. 106] by the analysis, the place of the achronic structure and the plane of the chronic or dia-chronic narrative are connected to one another. In the manifest behavior of the traitor and the position of the functions of the treason the structural necessity of the non-structurality of the traitor is designated. Let us state this point precisely: a very cursive reading of the texts makes apparent the death of Jesus at the intersection of two series of events or intentions--the transcendent series: will of the Father, plan of God for humanity in order to carry out its Redemption by the Incarnation and the Passion of His Son. It is this series that the different "creeds" of the universal community, which is a result of this story, proclaim in the recitation of the very story which constitutes it: "God became man--suffered under Pontius Pilate--was dead--was buried--was raised from the dead the third day, etc.". But there is also the immanent, historical, or factual series, which is that of the acts and behaviors of the actors of the story, and of their encounters, the increasing opposition of the Pharisees, Sadducees, and Scribes who found the unexpected opportunity to put into concrete form by the arrest of Jesus what had been vainly sought until then, the "treason" of Judas which begins the series of enchained events: trial, judgments, condemnations, putting to death, etc.... Therefore the treason follows at the precise point where the divine plan begins its realization and accomplishment. The death of God is a necessary condition for the triumph of God over death in the Resurrection. It permits its realization. It is at the intersection of two series.[35]

What is there to say? One of the problems that the gospel narratives pose is the following: how does one make God die?[36] Now, it is necessary that God die in order for man to live. It is necessary that the Eternal die in order for the mortal (man) to live eternally. But God cannot die. Therefore it is necessary for someone to permit this death, to make it possible without contradicting or compromising either the will or the very being of God. It is this insoluble problem that God and the traitor come to resolve together, to the greatest advantage of the "peoples" who will be simultaneously the instruments of this death and its beneficiaries. The death of God is necessary and impossible. Therefore it is necessary that someone make this necessity possible. How? By the aleatory act of treachery. The traitor is necessary in order to make this necessary possible by the contingency of his act, in which [p. 107] his very existence is summarized. At this precise point of the narrative, at this place of the text, the two series, transcendent and immanent, cross and exchange their modalities: since the necessity of the first is a question of God and His eternal will which can only repudiate itself in its development, colliding with its own impossibility of realization, exchange its necessity against the characteristic contingency of the elements of the other series (it is a matter of men, history, events) and at the same time become possible, but it is then--at this point of the narrative--the element of the factual series which is a bearer of the necessity of the transcendent series.

The traitor thus permits the joining of the signifier and the signified at only this point of the narrative. Its necessity is the necessity of a narrative logic which must resolve an insoluble problem: it is therefore a necessity of the signifier. But it is also the very necessity of one of the elements of an insoluble problem, that of the transcendent series: a necessity of the signified.[37] The marks are numerous in the system of the four variant-narratives of the unmotivation of the treason which is, in the textuality of the text, the site of an absolute necessity in the narrative significance down to its explicit return in the transcendent series, but inverted into its contrary. The non-God Judas betrays Jesus because the spirit of Satan has entered into him, while the only information concerning Judas before his treason arises manifestly from the contingent, historical factual series: his "economic" protest at the time of the anointing at Bethany (Jn.).

These are therefore our working hypotheses in their greatest methodological generality: by the reference that they imply to a theoretical questioning of the structural model of the narrative and its innate and productive center and in their particular adaptation to the textuality of the objects that we are given ourselves and which are perhaps privileged.

THE MODEL OF LÉVI-STRAUSS

One last point must again be approached before ending the preliminaries of the analysis. The position of our corollary hypothesis is connected very closely with the procedures that Claude Lévi-Strauss considers to be characteristic of the [p. 108] mythical mind. Myth, a logical instrument for overcoming fundamental antinomies, comes from the determination of two contradictory terms in a progressive mediation.[38] "The problem...is removed to the extent to which a couple of extreme poles is replaced by a less distant opposition."[39] (Life vs. death) is transformed into (Vegetable kingdom vs. Animal kingdom) and the latter into (vegetable food vs. animal food), and when the mediator himself is considered from the viewpoint of an animal being fed with carrion, then, intermediary between raptores and herbivores, it dissolves into its mythical being, the ultimate opposition to the extent to which it is neither raptore nor herbivore, but also the one and the other. Are we not introducing a model of this kind into our analysis? And at the same time, have we only examined the functional narrative model and the actantial model of the folktales in order to fall back on that which structural anthropology gives to the myth according to C. Lévi-Strauss?

It is true that the determination of the contradictory terms of the narrative that we are studying (Eternal vs. Mortal) furnishes a fundamental antinomy that the narrative has the goal of removing by a progressive mediation.[40] It is equally true that the instrument of the "solution" will be indeed a mediator and as such, a double--Jesus at the same time Man and God, a Messiah whose character figures in the series of mediating functions which Lévi-Strauss proposed in his famous article. With the trickster, the bi-sexual being, or the dioscuri, the variants of the myth of Zuni emergence presents a *messiah* endowed with the same ambiguity as that which we meet in our texts.[41] That the mediation may be connected to a duality of mythical personages, and that this duality permits the dissolution of the initial contradiction by repetition and difference of the same opposition in the succession of the episodes of the narrative, we are indeed persuaded.

But it could also be true that the structure of the mediator character, as we have determined it briefly above for our narrative, may itself be a *reduction* of the narrative elements concerning it, into the ambiguous simplicity of a personage who, bearing in himself the fundamental contradiction, is in himself the *resolution* for that very reason, *ipso facto*, by the tests which permit him to deploy successively the relationships which are, structurally connected in him. From then on, what is in question is not the duality of the mediator, [p. 109] who is after all only the structural projection of a passage and a transformation of opposites, the one into the other: it is the passage, the transformation itself, in other words, the narrative manifested which allows the mediator to mediate [*médier*] the contradiction by exposing its structure. This exposition which is in the articulation of the being of the personage and of the syntagmatic distribution of the functions has a proper dynamic which is revealed by the non-correlated character of the test-struggle in the distributional scheme of the functions and it is this dynamic in which it is necessary to find the inner workings of the narrative.

Whence the character of the traitor who is in addition to the structural organization, and of the characters in the actantial model, in particular of that of the mediator, and of the functions in the functional scheme. It is grafted--if one can say that--on that of the hero-subject at the precise moment of the narrative development when the negative "signs" of the functions are inverted into positive signs--but in an unmotivated, contingent way so that in the mediator and by the mediator the mediation is performed. The traitor, a character in additional structural is the chance of the operation of mediation in the duality of the mediator: catalyst of operation to the extent to which he exchanges the modalities at the same time in the signifier and the signified. In the signifier: by it, the narrative in its central necessary moment--by which there is a narrative properly speaking--assumes an accidental and contingent character; in the signified: since by it, the hero subject who is double can display his duality in an accidental way, thanks to the accidental incitement and as outside of the traitor who will carry out in this way the exchange of the contrary poles of the fundamental antimony (Eternal vs. Mortal) by exchanging their signs and values.

In order for us to understand it correctly, we can perfectly apply to our narrative in its structure the canonical formula of the myth established by Lévi-Strauss for the mediator process:[42]

$$Fx\ (a): Fy\ (b) \simeq Fx\ (b): Fa\text{-}1(y)$$

which was invested in our narrative in the following way:

Death (Man): Life (God) ≃ Death (God): NON-Man (Life)

We perceive how b (God) is connected on the first side of
the formula to a positive function y (Life, and we [p. 110]
understand, Eternal life), but also how it is capable of receiving the negative function x (Death). The mediator is
there in its contradictory and intermediary function. And it
is that which appears on the second side of the formula Fx (b)
which is the segment of the death of God, correlated: (1) with
the contradictory of a (but in a functional position), and (2)
with the function y (Life) (but in a final position). And one
will recognize in it the formulas of the New Covenant, and the
New Man, a function of the eternal life. But it is an indication which supports the equation in the particular interpretation which we are giving to it: the last term introduces a
dissymmetry into the formula. It is not the man who has access to the Eternal life; it is his negation which is the function of this Life. As Meletinsky excellently states it, "It is
not only a question of an annulment of the initial state, but
of an *additional* acquisition (italics ours), of a new state
which is the result of a kind of development in a spiral."[43]
It is this supplement which indicates the formula, but which
it does not explain and which is inexplicable in the formula
itself, because it interprets only the law of the permutation
group of the variants of the myth. Certainly this interpretation is fundamental, because it puts into evidence within the
group, not only the structural law of the myth, but its addition which is inscribed in the structure and by which the
structure itself is constituted in a mediator process. But
this addition remains to be explained, and by it and in it,
the process of exchange of which the dynamic of the narrative
consists as mediation and turning upside down. This addition
is "recovered" in the formula of a structural law. It does
not give its explanation; it interprets it. In the myth, but
at the level of its narrative, an "otherness of the myth" is
revealed in this way which integrates it, but which is irreducible to it. It is an addition by which the myth can be
narrated, and therefore effectuated;[44] which is not necessary
to the structure, and yet without which the structure would
not function as such: the event or the story, the contingency
or the risk. An addition which can be introduced in our text
thanks to this initial addition: the figure of the traitor.

Chapter II

THE THREE TEMPTATIONS
OR THE PROBLEM OF THE
NEUTRALIZATION OF THE SIGNIFIER

Perhaps it is better again to postpone the beginning of
the analysis, than to define the position and the mode of
manifestation of the sender-subject in the narrative that we
are studying. Perhaps it has already begun? In effect, the
traitor, we have said, is the "exchanger", the "donor", or the
one who in the narrative--signifier and signified--carries out
the modalizing transfers of the functions. Very well. Again
it is necessary to recognize what will sustain the exchange,
what will be the nature, and the consistence and the value of
the signs exchanged, in order to determine as well the moment
as the content of the exchange itself? But in the general
organization of the narrative, the question of the exchange
performed by the traitor poses the very question of the sender "God". There are, we know, two transcendent and factual
convergent series, and our problem is to determine the content
and the significance of their intersection, or the narrative
figure of their chiasmus. Now, the "transcendent series" is
that of the sender, father, and mandator who sends his son to
men so that they recognized him in the Good News which he
brings to them: humaneness, the sender of an object that the
subject--hero himself brings. There is therefore indeed a
message to be transmitted, some discourses and some *paroles*
to be given, and the axis of the sender and receiver is that
of the words, the language, and the signs of the *parole*.[45]
[p. 112]

PAROLES--FORCE--BODY

But these signs, by which the sender is presented in the
narrative as a message borne by the hero, can only be recognized in turn as signs of the sender, if the hero who bears
them in fact shatters the truth in the eyes of those who are
opposed to it, and if these signs not only form a message in
language, but a power by which the message is given to the
understanding as a strength with power: miracles and wonders
by which the subject-hero appears to be the true bearer of the
true message against those who refuse it. The axis of opposition and help to the subject-hero is modalized in power, and

the signs are, in their very verbality, a beneficent power of identification. The words are the forces. The *parole* is a power.[46]

But by designating himself as the powerful bearer of a message, the hero-subject gives himself as this message, a source of strength and life. The object is the subject hero, and the one who is sent by the sender is rolled into one with the one whom he sends. The axis of the subject and the object correspond well, according to the actantial model of Greimas, with the modality of the willing, but in a new sense: the subject-hero does not depart in quest of an object in order to appropriate it for himself, or to become a receiver, "to marry the princess and have many children". The subject is made to be an object, in order to give the object, because after all, it is indeed he that his Father has sent to men so that they will appropriate him, assimilate him, and in short consume him as *parole*, a source of power and life, as a *parole*-body. This is then the ultimate sign, the body by which the sender God designates himself in the narrative and that he transmits to men. The *parole* is a power of life, i.e. a consumable body, a food.[47] Henceforth, we can construct the actantial model by investing it into the narrative: [p. 113]

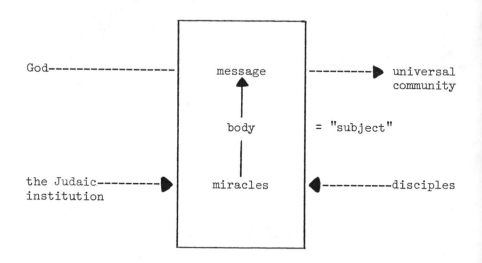

The Signifier Subject

The subject, in the actantial sense of the term, is then, as the schema shows, a subject constantly displaced, since it is a bearer of the message, therefore a subject of linguistic transmission, or object. But it can only transmit it if it is a possessor of a strong instrument of recognition, just as much with respect to those who follow it as for those who are opposed to it, and which, at the same time, because it is a possessor of such a power, can *be* made to become the very object which bore it, the message, by giving to the message, a body, a body which will be consumed by the receivers, a body that they will assimilate and in which they will be assimilated and thereby the subject will become the receiver, a universal communal body. It is necessary to reflect on this displacement which, after all, prohibits us from investing the subject actant in our narrative in an univocal and punctual form, since it shatters, according to the three modalities and according to the three axes of the actantial model; and because it is constituted by the intermediary space defined projectively by three forms of exchange: *paroles*, forces, body. In effect it should be possible to construct a three dimensional model, of which each dimension would be the place of realization of a modality of transmission. The space defined by the projections of each of the three schemas on the other two would be called the "subject", a kind of mediant volume, a compound place of the system of their transformations.[49]

In other words, and abandoning the geometric metaphors, the "subject" is constituted by the interferences of three series of signifiers whose univocal signified it cannot be, since each refers to it as a signified, and refers to it indirectly [p. 114] considered as a name designating the other two series. However, the three series of signifiers, paroles --forces--body, do not uniformly dominate the narrative in a striking way, especially the last which enters on stage simultaneously with the traitor. It would no doubt be an important working hypothesis for analysis of the gospel narrative to study the distribution or the economy of the signifier along the narrative line, according to these three series, which are themselves constitutives of the axis of transcendence. It can then be asked if the narrative does not present in all its primary segments an episode which precisely defines the relationship to the "subject" of the *paroles*--forces--body, in the sequence of the text, and which is at the same time a relationship to the traitor. This is a matter of the triple temptation in the desert in Matthew and Luke. This surface narrative segment offers us the "negative" paradigm of three signifier ensembles by which God transmits himself to men: a paradigm on the syntagmatic line since it is a question of an episode of the narrative which offers some principles of organization and classification of the segments which will follow. In effect, it is some relations between some elements and not these elements themselves which are in question. The elements are in-

deed--from this point of view--signifiers defined by the dia-
critical separation [écart] which is instituted between them.
But this paradigm is negative, since it furnishes these principles in the form of a triple rejection by the subject of
the propositions from the Non-God, the devil, or the tempter.
Therefore a narrative will be necessary in order to make positively clearer or really "to fill" the classifying frames that
the episode furnishes empty.[50]

Hunger-Parole

The first temptation is that of hunger: "If you are the
son of God, command that these stones be changed into bread,"
the tempter says, and he replied: "It is written: 'Man does
not live by bread alone, but by every *parole* which comes from
the mouth of God.'" The *parole* which comes from the mouth of
God is put into relation with the bread, the consumable body
which enters into the mouth of man, both of which supply life
according to the Deuteronomic citation.[51] The schism, which
includes the response to the diabolic proposition, of the *parole* of God and the bread-food of man, is thus the *negative*
significance of the divine sonship of the subject, the negative mark that the subject is the [p. 115] signifier of the
Father. This negative signifier mark will be transformed into a positive significance, and therefore into a positive mark
of the paternal significance of the subject, when, by an act
of the same power, the *parole* leaving the mouth of the God-man
will be transformed into the body-bread of this same God-man
which enters into the mouth of man. Thus the constitutive relationship of the significance of the message and the body-
food is found introduced.

Body-Force

The second temptation in Matthew (the third in Luke [Lk.
4:9-13]) negatively establishes the relationship of the body
and the power, but in the sacred space of the temple. "Then
the devil took him to the holy city, and placed him on the
pinnacle of the temple, and said to him, 'If you are the Son
of God, throw yourself down; for it is written, "He will give
his angels charge of you, and on their hands they will bear
you up, lest you strike your foot against a stone."' Jesus
said to him, 'Again it is written, "You shall not tempt the
Lord your God."'"[52] The diabolic proposition consists of
questioning the body of Jesus, starting from the holy place,
so that the body, being thrown down in this way, would manifest the power, the force of the Father, in His own place, the
Temple, and thereby reveal the subject, there again, as the

signifier of the Father. The response of the subject is a refusal of this form of signifier manifestation, by which the
manifestation is in some way necessitated by the way in which
the signifier relationship is presented. It is necessary that
the corner-stone or capstone of the Temple be thrown down. It
is necessary that Jesus, not only be hurled down from the summit of the Temple, but again that he carry with him the capstone and that no angel support him; in order that the relation between the body of the subject and the force of the
Father be shown as significant, in order that the Temple be
destroyed and a new Temple be rebuilt by this very destruction.[53]

Force-Parole

The third temptation in Matthew [the second in Luke] reveals the relation of the force to the *parole*: "Again the
devil took him to a very high mountain, and showed him all the
kingdoms of the world and the glory of them; and he said to
him, 'All these I will give you, if you will fall down and
worship me.' Then Jesus said to him, 'Begone [p. 116] Satan!
for it is written, You shall worship the Lord you God and Him
only shall you serve.'"[54] In this last temptation of the
devil, and in the response which he receives, again the signifier relationship of the paradigm is negatively introduced
by a disjunction of the *parole* of praise and adoration (which
belongs simultaneously to language and to behavior[55]) and of
the obtaining of the power in the realizations which show him,
"the kingdoms of the world and the glory of them". The *parole*
of adoration is a necessary condition for the possession of the
power, to reveal thereby the signifier character of the subject, in his relation of sonship to God. But that is no longer the question in this last stage, since the contrary, the
adoration must be addressed to the Non-God, and it would be a
denunciation of this sonship. Henceforth, the re-erected or
positive relation will consist in *connecting* the possession of
the power to the *parole* of adoration addressed to the Father
and at the same time to identify in the perfection, this possession in this *parole*: being powerful will consist therefore
in perfectly doing the will of the Father found in the *parole*
of adoration.

Grid of Signifiers

The three temptations constitute therefore, on the border
of the narrative the paradigmatic grid which rules the economy
of the signifiers of the sender in this same narrative, according to the three modalizations of communication, power, and

will; or more precisely according to the three articulations
of *paroles*, forces, and body.[56] But it is fundamental to
note, and we will not cease noting it, that this paradigmatic
grid is negative. The lines of significance which are introduced by it into the narrative are only indicated negatively
and doubly: 1/ because each line or series signifies only by
its difference with the other two, the *parole* in relation to
the body, the body in relation to the force, the force in relation to the *parole*; 2/ because the three signifier series
are opened empty by three semantic disjunctions which, in the
narrative, place at an irreducible distance, the *paroles*, the
body, the forces, for the obvious reason that the one who proposes them is the non-God, the non-Father, the devil, the
sender reversed from the transcendent order. Also by a transformational interaction the articulation of which it should be
easy to outline, it will be understood that if the "sign" of
the [p. 117] sender is inverted, in this same order, and if
the mandator is the Father, the living God, then the disjunction, by which the signifier series are to be opened, will be
inverted in its turn in conjunction. In order that finally
parole, force, and body be identified at one point and one
unique place of the narrative.[57] The schema below symbolically interprets this inversion in the epistemological space of
transformation:

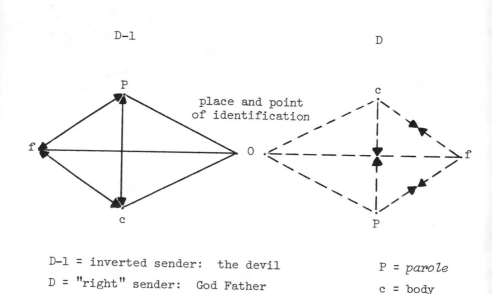

D-1 = inverted sender: the devil
D = "right" sender: God Father
⬤──────▶ : disjunction
----▶◀---- : conjunction

P = *parole*
c = body
f = force

Note: the plan[e] (pfc) D is the "explanatory" projection of the point O of identification of p, f, c. If one
wanted to make it take into consideration the syntagmatic
narrative line, it would be necessary to recover the plan[e]
(p, f, c) D-1 by the inverted plan[e] (p, f, c) D and show
that the three signifier series begin three series of transformation of the disjunction in conjunction, perfectly realized by the identification at point O.

THE MORTAL POINT OF THE NEUTRAL

But if this is the structural schema of the distribution
of the signifiers in the narrative--we mean the signifiers of
the sender to/in the subject-hero, object, receiver--it does
not follow at all that it explains, or makes perceptive, the
reason for the dynamic passage by the negation to regain the
positive modalizations of the narrative functions. In other
words, the structural schema perfectly describes for us the
terminus *a quo*, the terminus *ad quem*, and the interplay of
inversion by which the narrative passes from one to [p. 118]
the other. But what it does not explain is the point of negative departure, nor the "narrative force" of inversion, except by the end which must be positive.[58] It does not explain,
after all, the truth of the second temptation, which is central
in Matthew and conclusive in Luke, and which is perhaps the
fundamental temptation. In effect, this truth is the following: it is necessary that Jesus, a stone at the top of the
Temple, be thrown down, that the Temple be destroyed, and that
he be broken in this fall in order to be revealed in his significance of Son of God. The inversion is only in the signifier, since the Temple is Jesus, and the fall of Jesus down is
in fact his mortal elevation on the cross. Thus it is because
there will be no guardian angels of the Son in his fall that
the Son will be affirmed a Son of God. This is the truth that
the diabolic temptation parodies.

But the "negative" interplay of the signifier relations
in the Temptations between *paroles*, forces, and body does not
include and cannot include, as its positive, this mortal paradoxical point in which the negative ceases to be negative without being positive, but which is the very condition of the
emergence of the positive.[59] Point O of the identification
must be not only the perfect conjunction of the *parole*, force,
and body, but also the zero point of the death, of the annulment of the serial signifiers of the *parole*, the force, and
body. Therefore it is necessary to understand point O of the
structural schema not only as the point of identifying conjunc-

tion of three signifier series, but also, *and in addition*, as
the point where they are annuled in order to be able to be exchanged into their positive contraries: the neutral point of
the exchange, the pure passage. Now the subject-hero cannot
very well accomplish in this neutralization what he necessarily ought and wants to do, in order to reveal his character of
divine signifier. He cannot accomplish it, we have seen, for
the reason that the three signifier lines by which he is manifested, *parole*, force, body, *would be insignificant* and at the
same time he would cease to be, *for an instant*, i.e. *always*
the signifier of God. Also the neutralization at the same
time *necessary and additional* which must occur at the "center"
of the structure, as the other of the identification of three
signifier series, is itself the work of this character, who is
a necessary and supplementary figure in the narrative, the
traitor *Judas*.

We understand then why Judas simultaneously betrays [p.
119] in an unmotivated way--it is here his supplementary char-
acter--and why he is the instrument of the non-God, the devil,
in the "sphere of action" of the subject-hero; and this is here
his necessary character in the signified. In another terminology, Judas, an instrument of the negative possessed by the
tempter, works negatively and prolongs the negative interplay
of the signifier opened by the three temptations. But the
negative ceases to be negative by betraying in an unmotivated
way. It is the neutral event which creates an irruption in
order to neutralize the signifier and permit its accession to
the signified.[60] "Then Satan entered into Judas called Iscariot, who was one of the number of the Twelve; he went away
and conferred with the chief priests and captains how he might
betray him to them" (Lk. 22:3-4). John is again more explicit
in his confrontation between the two senders, negative and
positive, in the figure of the traitor and the hero-subject:
"And during supper, when the devil had already put it into the
heart of Judas Iscariot, Simon's son, to betray him, Jesus,
knowing that the Father had given all things into his hands,
and that he had come from God and was going to God, rose from
supper, laid aside his garments..." (Jn. 13:2-4).

VARIANTS

Let us make two remarks again before drawing some conclusions from this first approach to the problem of the traitor.
The three temptations in the desert appear only in Matthew and
Luke. In Mark the episode is noted in two verses immediately
after the sonship mark by which Jesus is constituted into a
signifier of the God-Father, at the time of the baptism: "And

when he came up out of the water, immediately he saw the heavens opened and the Spirit descending upon him like a dove; and
a voice came from heaven, 'Thou art my beloved Son; with thee
I am well pleased'" (Mk. 1:10-11). The Spirit immediately
drove him out into the wilderness. "And he was in the wilderness forty days, tempted by Satan" (Mk. 1:12-13). This episode disappears in John. These variants are interesting because Mark will present the treason of Judas as purely unmotivated, or as the upheaval of an unforeseeable event, "Then
Judas Iscariot, who was one of the twelve, went to the chief
priests in order to betray him to them" (Mk. 14:10), just like
Matthew, but unlike Luke and John who causes his step to result from a diabolic enterprise. [p 120]

The Johannine Variant

As for John, if the three temptations do not appear, the
signifier series are begun, on the one hand, thanks to the
testimony of John about the sign of sonship (Jn. 1:31-34), and
on the other hand, thanks to the wedding at Cana and the episode which immediately follows them, the expulsion of the merchants from the Temple. In the first episode, the body is
blood, but it is a sign, the wine, the first of the signs of
Jesus (Jn. 2:1-12 and especially 9-11). The force is completely positive and made clearer in a double reference to the
praise of God, to the body, and to the sanctuary, and at the
same time the *parole* begins as a body being defined retrospectively as force (Jn. 2:16-22 and especially Jn. 2:21-22). This text from
John is remarkable in many respects, from the form of expression of this variant in general, which is presented quite often
as a narrative which includes its own deciphering, and as a
narration endowed with an explicit metalinguistic degree which
furnishes to it one of the codes in the message itself.[61] But
it is remarkable also for our purposes.

In effect, on the one hand we find, in addition to the
negative episode of the temptations which has arranged them in
the inauguration of the narrative, the three signifier series,
paroles, forces, body, explicitly connected--as in the tempta-
tions--but in a way which is at the same time direct, coded,
and decoded--at the Temple and at his death: "The Jews then
said to him, 'What signs have you to show us for doing this?'
Jesus answered them, 'Destroy this temple and in three days I
will raise it up.' The Jews then said, 'It has taken forty-
six years to build this temple, and will you raise it up in
three days?' But he spoke of the temple of his body" (Jn. 2:
18-21). It is a metaphor of the enigma whose deciphering occurs in the sequence of the story, *after the fact*, in order to

constitute the *parole* in a prophetic sign.[62]

But on the other hand, in the syntagmatic contiguity of the narrative, the act of exchange of the signifiers is found prepared which will only find its effective correlate much later in the reading. All the dialogue which we have cited is a continuation in effect of the expulsion of the merchants from the Temple. Is it not a metaphoric destruction of the real Temple as a place of trade where is carried out [p. 121] each day, at the mercy of transactions of the moneychangers and the vendors of pigeons, the transformation of the holy sign of the Father and his House, into a "profane" sign, into a house of trade? But before the real Temple is rebuilt into the body of the subject-hero and in order that it may be done in this way, a commercial exchange or transaction will be necessary, in the Temple itself, the body of Jesus in exchange for the money.

Therefore it can be said that the three episodes--"Wedding at Cana", "Expulsion of the merchants from the Temple", "Dialogue with the Jews"--constitute in John: 1) the "positive" syntagmatic projection of what we have called the focal point of conjunction--identification in Matthew and Luke; 2) the paradigmatic projection in the positive plan[e] D of the three temptations of Matthew and Luke, the schema below symbolically interprets this transformation:

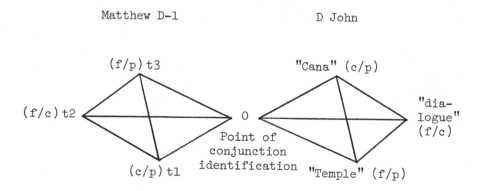

Matthew D-1   D John

(f/p) t3   "Cana" (c/p)

(f/c) t2   0   "dia-
                  Point of   logue"
                  conjunction   (f/c)
(c/p) t1   identification   "Temple" (f/p)

Note: We are using the same symbols as in the preceding schema. However, it is necessary to supply further information concerning the disjunctional or conjunctual relations in the plan[e] D (f, c, p). "Cana" realizes a remarkable conjunction of the body and the *parole*; but it is only metaphoric, since this sign, while being a signifier of the divine sonship of Jesus (a signifier of its proper significance), is also the

mark of the *parole* as power of transformation (of the water into wine), a metaphor of the transformation of the *parole* itself into blood in the wine. On the other hand, "Temple" (or
let us say the expulsion of the merchants from the Temple) is
a disjunctive relation between the force of Jesus which chases
the merchants and the *parole* of prayer and of praise of which
the Temple is the place. And at the same time, this relation
of disjunction between the force and the *parole* is a direct
homologue, although transformed, of the third temptation in
Matthew which subordinates the possession of the glory and the
power of the kingdoms of the world (therefore profane glory and
power) [p. 122] to the worship of the Non-God. But it is an
inverted and metaphoric homologue of the treason "contract" of
Judas where the conjunctional relation is revealed between a
participant in the sphere of action or the significance of the
hero and the temple as a place of commercial transaction. The
third relation correlated in Matthew and John may be the second temptation, and the "dialogue of the Jews and Jesus" about
the destruction of the Temple; and its reconstruction in three
days. It does not present any particular problem. Rather it
appears to us to confirm our metonymic interpretation of the
second temptation:[63] to be thrown down from the top of the
Temple is to throw the stone of the Temple down; it is to destroy the Temple. This is an interpretation that the text of
John confirms by giving it its second element in the decoded
enigma: "the Temple will be rebuilt in three days"; and what
our analyses of the toponyms of the Passion narrative have led
up to, especially that of the parable of the murderous vine-
growers.[64]

Luke-Matthew

The second note concerns the syntagmatic order of the
temptations in Matthew and Luke and the interest that this
difference can present appears clearly in the series of preceding remarks made concerning John. It can, in effect, be
thought that the third temptation in Luke (or the second in
Matthew), because it concludes the debate with the Non-God,
the inverted sender, begins and introduces in total clarity
the transformations of the narrative which should be achieved
by the metaphoric destruction of the Temple (or of the Jewish
Law) and by its real fulfillment in the consumable body. Food
becomes constitutive of the universal community by the ceremonial recitation of the same narrative by which it was fulfilled.[65] In Matthew, on the other hand, the conclusive temptation is that of the rupture of the signifier and of its inversion into a covenant with the Non-God, i.e. into the possession of profane power. It opens another signifier inter-

play which we have seen appear in John, on the syntagmatic line, with the succession: 1/ "Expulsion of the merchants from the Temple"; 2/ "Dialogue about the Temple as a metaphor of the body." It would signify that the Non-God who belongs to the sacred transcendent sphere is in reality the index of the profane "immanent" sphere, that of power and [p. 123] political glory, of material riches, etc. And it is indeed the figure of the traitor named "Judas"[66] who will function later in the narrative as a transmitter or intermediary donor between these two spheres.

Therefore, in this way we can, following the first marking [jalonnement], formulate one of the elements of our working hypothesis. The sender in this narrative (i.e. in the four variants connected into the same narrative system) only appears in its signifier which, in the narrative manifestation, is named "Jesus"; and Jesus can only be indicated as a signifier of the Father by *being* such a signifier, i.e. by an interplay of signs distributed according to three series: *paroles*, forces, and body.[67] The fundamental narrative problem, which we have alluded to from the beginning, will be to define in the following way: how "Jesus", a signifier of the Father, could be exchanged in his triple serial significance for his signified: God; and how in this exchange an eternal universal community will be established? But, let us repeat, only the traitor will permit this operation by neutralizing the signifiers of the "subject", and by annulling into a neutral the signifier "subject". [p. 124]

Chapter III

AN ATTEMPT TO PROVE THE HYPOTHESIS:
THE SIGNIFIER NETWORK IN THE SYSTEM OF THE TEXT

MATTHEW'S READING: THE QUESTION OF THE NAME

The hypothesis being presented, in order to confirm it, let us collect on the surface of the text in an almost uniquely citational form, the signifiers issued in sequence from the distribution grid of the temptations or from the three episodes in John. We quickly perceive ourselves that one of the first questions that the text furnishes, and which traverses it through and through, concerns the identity of Jesus with his name: thus Mt. 1:21-25, which signals the two signifiers by which the nominal identity of Jesus is found split up into a remarkable ambivalence: "All this took place to fulfill what the Lord had spoken by the prophet: 'Behold a virgin shall conceive and bear a son, and his name shall be called Emmanuel' (which means, God with us)...but [Joseph] knew her not until she had borne a son; and he called his name Jesus." And this ambiguity in his name is found continued in his place of birth which is Bethlehem, according to the star, a cosmic signifier and the Scriptures on the one hand, and Nazareth on the other, which is equivalent to a new name for him, "Nazarene", also announced for him by the prophets (Mt. 2:23).

The question of his identity is then developed according to the three series indicated: on the plan[e] of the *paroles* (Mt. 7:28-29). "And when Jesus finished these sayings [discourses] the crowds were astonished at his teaching, for he taught them as one who had authority, and not as their scribes"; to which corresponds on the plan[e] of the forces, Mt. 8:27: "And the men marveled, saying, 'What sort of man is this, that even winds and sea obey him?'" [p. 125]

The first interventions of the Pharisees will then consist of inverting the sign of the signifying series, by distributing them on the plan[e] from which they have been excluded from the beginning, that of the Non-God, D-1. Thus Mt. 9:32-34: "As they were going away, behold, a dumb demoniac was brought to him. And when the demon had been cast out the dumb man spoke; and the crowds marveled, saying, 'Never was anything like this seen in Israel.' But the Pharisees said, 'He casts out demons by the prince of demons.'"

117

Again the identity of Jesus is questioned by John, the same one who at the time of the baptism had been the one to give the sonship mark: "Are you he who is to come, or shall we look for another?" The response of Jesus is remarkable, because it is a response by signifiers. Jesus defines his identity by the "signs" which signify him and not by a naming of being. "And Jesus answered them, 'Go tell John what you hear and see: the blind receive their sight and the lame walk, lepers are cleansed and the deaf hear, and the dead are raised up, and the poor have the good news preached to them. And blessed is he who takes no offense at me" (Mt. 11:3-6). The response made according to the signifiers of the *parole* (Good News), and of the force (the miracles), says serially who "Jesus" is, not in a statement of significance, in his being a signifier of the Father (Mt. 11:25-29).

The signifiers of the body appear in Mt. 12:1-8 in the remarkable relationship that we have already met in the temptations, between the hunger, the food and the Temple as a presence here and now: "his disciples were hungry, and they began to pluck the ears of grain and to eat. But when the Pharisees saw it, they said to him, 'Look, your disciples are doing what is not lawful to do on the sabbath.'"..."I tell you, something greater than the temple is here....For the Son of man is *Lord* of the sabbath" (Mt. 12:1-8).

And the end of Matthew 12 combines the three signifier series starting with a new question of identity (12:23): "And all the people were amazed, and said, 'Can this be the Son of David?'" The response of the Pharisees is here again according to D-1: "It is only by Be-el´zebul, the Prince of demons that this man casts out demons" (Mt. 12:24). And Jesus, in turn, will indicate his own being by a triple metonymy in the signifiers of force (Mt. 12:25-29),[68] [p. 126] *paroles* (Mt. 12:32-37),[69] and finally body, in response to the request for a sign by the Pharisees (Mt. 12:38-40), a request which is remarkably homologous with the second temptation (in Matthew).[70] The sign is given by Jesus, but prophetically, by anticipation and in a coded form, with the sign of Jonah.

This metonymy of being in the signifiers signifies in its turn the true kinship which is no longer according to being but according to the signifiers: Mt. 12:46-50.[71] This point is important, because the biological kinship, according to the blood, determines, by a precise system of relations, the being in the immanence. But the transcendent significance is only signified by the signifiers which redouble it, without the signified being able to be properly connected to any of them.

Hence the two questions of identity: that of the people

of Nazareth (Mt. 13:54-56): "Where did this man get this wisdom and these mighty works? Is not this the carpenter's son? Is not his mother called Mary? And are not his brothers James and Joseph and Simon and Judas? And are not all his sisters with us? Where did this man get all this?" And then that of Herod the tetrarch (Mt. 14:2): "This (man) is John the Baptist." And the response of Jesus is carried out according to the signifiers of the *body*--this is the multiplication of the loaves of bread (Mt. 14:15-21)--of *force*--this is his walking on the sea and the healings by contact with his body or clothes (14:22-36)--and of the *parole*--and this is the discussion about the Pharisaic traditions which are concluded by the teaching about clean and unclean in Mt. 15:10-20. It will be noted that this conclusive teaching is the inversion of one element from the first temptation: "Man shall not live by bread alone, but by every word [*parole*] that proceeds from the mouth of God", Jesus had responded to the diabolic proposition by separating the bread (body) and the word [*parole*], the consumption by *in*gestion of food and the utterance by verbal *ex*pression. Here the food--the body (and it is necessary to remember that in the syntagmatic order, the miracle of the multiplication of the loaves of bread has just been read), that which enters by the mouth does not defile man, while it is that which comes out of man, the *parole*, which has the trace of the unclean. But in the comment which Jesus gives about it (15:17-20), there is another difference which is found described: the food cannot defile [p. 127] the body because it is evacuated, while the *parole* is a sign of the thoughts of the heart.

The same series of signifiers is found repeated--*paroles*, forces (Mt. 15:21-31), body (15:32-39)--but they are unceasingly more strictly woven to one another, as if, bit by bit, the signifiers arranged on the different lines were focused on a single point. Thus the signifiers of the body, the force, and the *parole* by the interplay of the "real" and the metaphor in the dialogue with the Canaanite woman (15:25-28)[72] of the *parole* of praise and the miraculous force in 15:31.[73] Likewise the question of a cosmic sign originating from the opponent is found repeated to which Jesus responds by the prophetic evocation of his own significance, *hic et nunc*, coded in the sign of Jonah (Mt. 16:1-4).[74]

The Question of the Name Again

We arrive then in our reading of Matthew at a new question of identity, but it is that which Jesus himself poses to his disciples in one of his names. The problem of the correct being, the question always suspended, "who is this 'I' of the 'subject'?", no longer comes from others (Pharisees, inhabi-

tants of Nazareth, Herod, etc.) but from the subject himself.[75]
However, the subject does not ask "Who am I?", but asks what
"the other" says about one of his names, as he defines it. To
the saying of the people, "who is the Son of Man?", the subject
poses the question of his identity, but as from another and in
the "milieu" of the other. And when the disciples have enumer-
ated a series of equivalents, John the Baptist, Elijah, Jeremiah, or some one of the prophets, only then the subject poses
the question of his own being to which Peter responds: "You
are the Christ, the Son of the living God" (Mt. 16:16), i.e.
not only the signifier of the Father by sonship, but Christ, a
name by which Peter proclaims the messiahship of Jesus. It is
Peter who proclaims the signified of this signifier in a decla-
ration that the subject attributes to the Sender: "For flesh
and blood has not revealed this to you, but my Father who is
in heaven" (Mt. 16:17). In other words, "Your *parole* is not
connected to the signifier 'body', but to the signified itself
that 'I, Jesus' signify, the Father." And perhaps, it is not
without importance to note, at this point of the development
of reading, that Simon, in his own name, comes to be doubly
designated: on the one hand, in [p. 128] the narrative statement [*l'énoncé*] of his relation of sonship to Jonah, the same
name which has marked twice prophetically and in anticipation,
the conjunction of the signifiers "*paroles*" and "body" in death
and life (as resurrection); and on the other hand in the substitution for the name of Simon, that of Peter or Cephas, itself a common, metaphoric name of the future function of Simon-
Peter in the universal community.[76]

Simon-Peter = Satan

In other words, at the very moment when Simon-Peter states
in a proclamatory discourse the signified of the signifier of
the subject, the same subject transforms it into a series of
nominal signifiers which designate it in a past and anticipa-
tive prophetic reference and in the narrative statement
[*l'énoncé*] of a (founding) function in the community which
Jesus has come to establish, a community which will be Jesus
himself. Just as if the operation of exchange of signifiers
for the signified had been missing at this point of the narrative, as if this exchange could not, nor had to, be made into
parole, into discourse, but into an act on the primary surface
of the narrative.[77] It is perceived clearly at the same time
in verse 20: "Then he strictly charged the disciples to tell
no one that he was the Christ" (Mt. 16:20); and also in the
verses which follow 21-23. The exchange of signifiers and of
the signified is missing because it must be carried out in his
death and precisely by the neutralization of the signifier
himself--(the three days of Jonah in the belly of the whale)--

in order that the signified may be recovered at the end of the account.

And the instrument of this exchange whose finality Simon perceives by a revelation from the Father will not be Peter: "Peter took him and began to rebuke him, saying, 'God forbid, Lord! This shall never happen to you'" (Mt. 16:22). It is then remarkable that the response of Jesus may have been the same response that he made to the Non-God in the third temptation according to Matthew. Even better, Peter has become for a brief instant, the Non-God himself, Satan. "But he turned and said to Peter, 'Get behind me, Satan! You are a hindrance to me; for you are not on the side of God, but of men!'" (Mt. 16:23). Having placed the exchange of signifiers and signifieds into the pure *parole*, Peter is not only de-nominated and thrown out of the present situation into the past (Jonah) and into the future (the Church community), [p. 129] but he is again compared to the Non-God, when he refuses the information that this exchange cannot be simply of *paroles*, but of force, and the body all together. As Satan had proposed the breaking of the relation of significance with the Father for the possession of material, political power, perhaps the entrance of Jesus into the profane immanence, so Peter defines the messiahship that he had by affirmed inspiration, as his immediate proclamation in a discourse of faith. It is at the very moment when Peter speaks the *signified according to God* that he becomes a *parole of the Non-God*, because he was only made "*to speak*" and he only perceives this signified in a "speaking".

The Exchange of Signifiers

This point is important, because on the contrary, we understand that when Judas *will make* the exchange of the *signifiers according to the Non-God*, when he will be the very action of the Non-God, only then will the affirmation of Peter, and behind it, that of the Scripture be fulfilled. At the same time the signified will be established *here, now,* and forever. Peter is connected to Judas in the narrative; the proclaimer (helper) to the traitor, as the "speaking" and the "doing", as the signifier-signified on the one hand and the signifier-signifier on the other, and their relation is very precisely that of a "doing--saying", of a *parole* which must obtain its value of "performative" act in order to have access to its truth of *parole*.[78] This relation will reappear in the opposition between the two episodes which are rigorously correlated of the treason of Judas and the denial of Peter. The real treason being, if one can say so, the indirect truth of denial, the possibility offered to the negative *parole* to become an act in order to find its truth, its

its positivity. We will return to this.[79]

The repetition of the same episode will be found with the
Transfiguration in 17:1-8, a direct revelation here again of
the signified of the subject, and equally marked by an intervention of Peter aiming at a profane installation of the transcendent which bluntly interrupts the characteristic fulgura-
tion of the Deity: the bright Cloud, the Voice affirming Jesus' divine Sonship.[80] And as in the preceding series, this
exchange of signifiers and the signified is separated by the
"subject", in the name of death and suffering. And in expectation of the resurrection.[81] The questions concerning [p.
130] John the Baptist and Elijah, the healing of the demoniac
and the Temple dues, three segments articulated in a new announcement of the death and suffering, connecting the signifier series of the *paroles*, forces, and body to a zero point
of the annulment of the signifier, an essential condition of
the arrival or the possession of the signified.

Peter--Judas

Therefore, it is necessary that the character, or the
event, which will realize the exchange missing between these
signifiers, and the signified that they designate, intervene
at one point of the text, and very precisely, at the "moment"
on the syntagmatic line closest to the point of conjunction
and identification of the signifiers (*Paroles*, forces, body).
How? By the substitutive annulment of the signifiers which
will leave the productive force of the signified to be discovered in the very interior of the text.[82] In one sense it
would be perfectly correct to perceive in the opposition of
"Peter" and "Judas" the anthropomorphic surface figure of the
actantial act of the helper and the opponent with the presence
of the Father, the living God behind each of them (who inspires
the *paroles* of designation of the signified) and of the Non-God
of death, Satan (who inspires the act of treachery). But this
articulation does not take account at all of the passage of
Peter to the other pole of the opposition, Peter appearing as
a false traitor who does not succeed in performing the annulment that the traitor Judas will perform; but who affirms the
truth of the signifier, the messiahship of the subject. It no
longer takes account of the positivity of Judas which will permit this annulment, a condition, not of the affirmation, but of
the advent-possession of the signified. The opponent will have
a helping function, and the helper a function of opposition.[83]

We propose to take the problem from another aspect, and to
note that the only means that the narrative as discourse and as
text has of *practically* realizing the transformation of the neg-

ative into the positive, of the alienation into integration, is
by carrying out in the text itself the "central" annulment of
the signifiers by being given as the report of an unforeseeable
and unique event which interferes *in addition* with the narrative logic in order to give it its dynamic. It is at this
level, in [p. 131] this articulated mixing of contingence and
necessity, that could be grasped what could be called a textual
practice,[84] let us say a unique and contingent textual element
which renders the operating theory from it and by which it
structures the text. This element in the text is the report
of an event, or of an act of a character. It is a purely surface figure which does not refer to anything else, if not to
the central point of the structure. It is not enough to perform the substitution of the signifier and the signified in
order that the meaning be produced. A kind of "blank" is also
needed in the signifier series where the signifier is annulled
in an outside of the text from which the signified can be established in the text. This would only be because all the signifiers, lacking correlation before the central event-point,
obtain it from one or more; and in this way the meaning is
produced.

MARK'S VARIANT: THE DEMONIAC PROCLAMATION

We have marked out the signifier series into some of their
moments through one of the variants of the gospel narrative, up
to the drawing near of their points of conjunction and identification. This signaling [*basilage*] ought to be constituted in
a network, by an identical work carried out on the three other
constitutive variants of our corpus. We cannot undertake this
in the dimensions of this work. Let us only indicate in Mark,
which like John does not possess the distribution grid of the
signifiers constituted by the three temptations, the starting
points of these three open series in the system of our text.

We shall take into consideration the large fragment immediately following the indication of the temptation in the
desert, that is Mk. 1:14-15 where the question of identity
which is posed at the same time by the demon of Capernaum and
the inhabitants of the city is found connected to an element
of the *parole* (Mk. 1:14-15 and Mk. 1:21-22)[85] and to the miraculous force-power (Mk. 1:26, also 1:29-34 or 1:39-43).[86]
To this question the demon himself responds by *speaking* the
signified: "What have you to do with us, Jesus of Nazareth?
Have you come to destroy us? I know who you are, the Holy One
of God" (Mk. 1:24f.); while the inhabitants remain uncertain:
"And they were all amazed, so that they questioned among themselves, saying, 'What is this? A new teaching! With authori-

ty he commands even the unclean spirits, and they obey him'"
(Mk. 1:27). [p. 132] The episode of the demon which is also
found in Luke (4:31-37); and in Matthew (8:24) can be correlated into the system of the text with the temptations in the
desert, but also with the episode of Peter-as-"Satan" after
the revelation of the identity of Jesus by Matthew in 16:23,
and by Mark in 8:27-33. And it is remarkable that Jesus, entirely by dominating the demons with his force, refuses to be
identified by them. The signified--the Father, the living God
--cannot and must not be spoken before the moment when the signifiers of the signifier subject can be substituted: "But he
forbade the demons from speaking because they knew who he was"
(Mk. 1:34). And the importance of the miracles of expulsion
of demons will be noted up to the end of chapter 1, as if the
collection of the affirmations of the subject into his signs
were being displayed on plan[e] D-1 of the damned [*sacré*] Non-
God, Satan. The *parole* of the "subject" is connected to his
power, given both to denials and disjunctions on the plane of
the damned Non-God: "And he went from there through all Galilee *preaching* in their synagogues and *expelling the demons*."
It is not even the desert, even the withdrawal of the "subject" into a space separated from men--(and a place of the inaugural tests which has permitted the signs to be distributed)
--that may appear insistently in this large fragment: "That
morning, well before daybreak, he went out, departed, and went
from there to a solitary place and there he prayed...and he
was drawn outside, into the desert...."

Finally, the signifier series of the feeding, of the body
in its double relation to the power and to the *parole* appears
in Mk. 2:15-17 with the meal of repentance and of calling the
sinners, in the discussion about fasting in Mk. 2:18-22 and
the episode which we have met in Matthew of the stolen ears
of grain the day of the Sabbath.

We can therefore suggest that the different segments of
the initial narrative fragment in the Markan variant function
like the three temptations in Matthew and Luke, and like the
first segments from the Johannine narrative already analyzed,
in order to distribute the signifiers, by which the subject is
displaced and is signified, along the syntagmatic line of the
narration to the point where they will have to be reabsorbed
in an exchange from which they will receive meaning. [p. 133]

LUKE'S VARIANT OR THE PROBLEM OF THE DOUBLE

Luke's variant presents some other problems which do not
directly concern our purpose, except at one inaugural point.

It will have been noted that the definition of the signifiance
[*sic*] of the subject, or in the terms of the actantial model,
that the mandate of the subject-hero given by the sender, is
provided in the meeting with John: the first text of the subject who receives his mark[87] in the dawn [*aurore*] of the narrative, the baptism by water, by the one who preceded him, announced him, and who will come a second time in the course of
the narrative to verify the initial mark of which he had been
the instrument: "Who are you?"..."Are you he who is to come,
or shall we look for another?" And we have seen that Jesus'
response is an indirect response by signs. He does not say
who he is, but states everything which signifies him, and at
the same time, everything which he signifies, i.e. the divine
sonship which John was already aware of. But it is known that
one of the characteristics of Luke's variant is to construct,
in the form of two parallel and corresponding segments, *two
subjects* or *two heros* whose destinies are intertwined up to
the moment in the narrative when one is erased and the other
takes over, a moment which is actually that of the baptism of
Jesus.[88] We will not emphasize these correspondences, but we
will limit ourselves to alluding to two points: the first concerns the end of John which it is fitting to put into a relationship with that of his "double and substitute", Jesus. The
second, which conditions the first, refers to this initial
duality and its signification.

John Betrayed

We note first that the variant which develops parallel to
that of Jesus, the biography of John, is the only one not to be
introduced into the text--the narrative of his end--as if it
performed a kind of compensation intended to balance the dis-
tributions of the narrative functions and eventually to break
a surface homology, and therefore to conceal a relationship of
meaning that delivers us in return the other variants of Mark
and Matthew. In both of them the narrative of the execution of
John the Baptist is a continuation by a characteristic inversion of the temporal line of the narrative[89] of the question of
Herod concerning the identity of Jesus: [p. 134] "This (man)
is John the Baptist, he has been raised from the dead, that is
why these powers are at work in him" (Mt. 14:2). "Some (besides Herod) said, 'John the baptizer has been raised from the
dead; that is why these powers are at work in him'...But when
Herod heard of it he said, 'John whom I beheaded has been
raised'" (Mk. 6:14, 16).

Now we read in both gospels that the death of John was the
result of a "treachery" by the daughter of Herodias who "wanted
to kill him" (Mk. 6:19). She did not succeed "for Herod feared

John, knowing that he was a righteous and holy man and kept him
safe. When he heard him, he was much perplexed; and yet he
heard him gladly" (Mk. 6:20). In Matthew the relationship is
less favorable, because the reason Herod did not kill John was
because he feared the people who considered John to be a prophet (Mt. 14:5). But it does not follow at all that Herod
agrees, by an oath, to grant to the daughter of Herodias, Salome (according to Josephus), anything that she might ask.
The following is known: the beheading of John, the presenta-
tion of the prophet's head on a platter, and his burial by his
disciples. It is possible to rearrange in some way these successive segments in order to find the same order of the story
of Jesus in its factual nakedness [nudité]. There is even a
resurrection of the Baptist which appears in the remark of
Herod, but *under the corporal species of Jesus.*

And it is at this point--in the sphere of the discourse,
and not of the narrative,[90] that the parallels of "John" and
"Jesus" are reunited. John being annulled, if that can be
said, in Jesus. By defining the analysis further, it is perceived that the villainy is shared with regard to the death of
John by Herod and Salome. In effect, the promise made by Herod
to give Salome whatever she might ask, constitutes the first
function of the villainy, that of a contract, the second being
to honor the contract by ordering the execution. But it is
noted that this contract is a contract of passive villainy, to
the extent to which the active traitor is Salome here, since
it is she who, "conjoined to Herod", obtains from him an act
contrary to his will, a "disjoined"[91] act. It will have been
noted that Judas also concludes the contract of villainy with
the Pharisees and Priests. But once the contract is honored,
he repents of it, regrets it, and attempts, by returning [p.
135] the pieces of silver, to denounce it when it is completed.
Judas is, for Jesus, successively an active and passive traitor, just as the treachery concerning John was successively
passive and active by Herod and Salome.

Thus the same story is told twice in the system of the
text between Luke on the one hand, and Mark and Matthew on the
other, with the same point. In order to cause the death, the
abrupt intervention of the traitor who obtains by surprise
what appeared to be difficult, even impossible, to obtain according to the logic of motivations which is also partially
the narrative logic.[92] But there is a fundamental difference
between the two, the examination of which introduces us to the
second problem which the beginning of Luke poses: the duality
of the subject-hero. The execution of John, as we have seen,
is a continuation in the narrative syntagmatic, of the questioning of Herod concerning the identity of Jesus: "Jesus is
John, but John resurrected." It is from this equivalence that

the narrator relates the execution of John which alone can explain the anxious remark of Herod. It is because John is dead that Jesus finds an identity in the remark of Herod. His resurrection "in discourse" is a repetition in continuity in the narrative, of the hero-being doubly assumed until now. It is because the hero is resurrected only in discourse in a kind of metaphoric equivalence; it is because the resurrection of the hero is a "missing" resurrection; and it is because it is in language and not in deed, as the double, that it is necessary that it be begun again, repeated, recited, and the point of connection between the false and true resurrection, is equally the remark of Herod by which the false resurrection is identified with the living subject himself, until he dies thanks to the other traitor, Judas.

Duality of the Subject

Thus the value of the duality of the subject in the system of the text is perceived. This duality is at the same time metaphoric and metonymic.[93] It is correct to say that John is a metaphor of Jesus, Salome-Herod of Judas, and Herod again of Pilate (and the full implications of the variant segment from Luke is understood: "Jesus before Herod" Lk. 23:8-12, is inserted between the two trials before Pilate) and Herodias, of the Priests and the leader of the Guards. [p. 136] But it is just as true to affirm that this metaphor is displayed in a metonymic contiguity, that it is situated on the line of the narrative *before* that of which it is the metaphor; and that its significance, the narrative episode in a metaphoric position, will be found transferred onto its "phor" [*phore*][94] by the point of contiguity that constitutes the remark of Herod who resurrects John in Jesus and assures the displacement of the signifier into the signifier of the subject, inside of his metaphoric duality: a duality of subject, certainly, but also an internal movement of this duality by which the displacement of the serial signifier is found secured from one variant to another up to the point where it must "in truth" be exchanged and annulled. But is it not John himself who proclaims: "...but he who is mightier than I is coming, the thong of whose sandals I am not worthy to untie..." (Lk. 3:16)...."He must increase, but I must decrease. He who comes from above is above all" (Jn. 3:30-31)?

THE JOHANNINE VARIANT AS METANARRATION

The Johannine variant introduces into the ensemble of these articulations some very important distortions from which

we suggest an explanatory hypothesis drawn from the very contexture of the text. According to John, in effect, the narrative is expressed only in the form of the beginning of a commentary discourse which is related to a metanarration whose
every function has systematically revealed the secondary, even
tertiary, signifieds of the primary signifiers of the narrative.

We have seen an example of this by examining the segment
"Wedding at Cana"--"Expulsion of the Merchants from the Temple"--"Dialogue with the Pharisees"....But very frequently the
metanarration occurs in the narration itself in order to produce some meaning effects of a metalinguistic nature. Hence
the creation inside of the narrative of the distortions which
we have alluded to in its linearity. From this point of view,
the meeting with the first disciples is significant, since provoked apparently by a remark of John about Jesus, the messiahship of Jesus and his divine sonship is immediately expressed:
"Behold the Lamb of God", John says (Jn. 1:36). The two disciples heard him say this and they followed Jesus....What do
you seek?...'Rabbi [which means Teacher], where [p. 137] are
you staying?'--Come and see. They came and saw where he was
staying, and they stayed with him that day..." (Jn. 1:37-39).
But Andrew, the brother of Simon-Peter, who is one of those
who had followed Jesus, declares at daybreak to Simon: "We
have found the Messiah!" (Jn. 1:40-41). And some lines further on, the same effect of immediate recognition of the signified is produced by the remark of Nathanael, consecutive it
is true, to the prophetic sign given by Jesus: "Rabbi, you
are the Son of God! You are the King of Israel!" (Jn. 1:49).
There is another example of this at the end of the "Wedding at
Cana" episode (Jn. 2:11): "This, the first of his signs, Jesus did at Cana in Galilee." It is here a part of the signifier. "He manifested his glory; and his disciples believed in
him" (Jn. 2:11). Such is, immediately determined, that of the
signified, because the δόξα has a precise signification here
of presence *hic et nunc* of the transcendence.[95]

In other words, perhaps the Johannine variant could be
schematized within the system of the narrative by showing how
each narrative signifier is accompanied and thus overhung by
its signified in a metanarrative position, when this is not by
the commentary of this signified. While in the synoptic variants the signifiers, as we have seen, are arranged in a serial
form on the narrative surface which, at the same time, the
necessary exigency of a passage to the signified, of an exchange, will authorize from it the taking charge of it by the
narrative.[96] What is the case in John?

The Discourse of the Subject

In fact, even if he makes his own commentary intervene in the narrative which he narrates, it will be necessary to distinguish with the narrator himself two planes of discourse in his text—the narrative-discourse and the discourse which doubles it and punctuates the significance in it—either in the form of a discourse by the "subject" commenting on the event of which he is the narrative subject, or in the form of prospective or retrospective notes, reflections, or interventions, of the narrator which, to be sure, exist in three other variants but are particularly important here. The narrator is conscious of this rule of reading since he attributes it to the "subject" of the narrative in Jn. 2:23-25: "Now when he was in Jerusalem at the Passover feast, many believed *in his name when they saw* his signs [p. 138] which he did." This is the primary level of the narrative in its signifier organization, and the "subject" appears here as a name producing signifiers. But the narrator continues: "But Jesus did not trust himself to them, because he knew all men and needed no one to bear witness of man; for he himself knew what was in man" (Jn. 2:24-25). The "subject" is not only a name (a signifier) which is signified by other signifiers; it knows and it understands absolutely everything: self-sufficiency, fullness of the signified of which these same signifiers are the manifestation; like the fixing of the signified in the signifier in the introduction of the conversation with Nicodemus: "Rabbi we know that you are a teacher come from God; for no one can do these signs that you do, unless God is with him" (Jn. 3:2).

Johannine Paradigms

But by a gesture opposed to our own commentary, at no place better than in the Johannine variant, the signifiers are not designated of which we have established the distributional grid with the three temptations, but they are located, or shown by the signified that the narrator develops in his commentary: *Paroles*—food and body—forces and regenerated powers, source of life. In other words, what the synoptic variants linearly expose for us in the syntagmatic succession of the narrative in the form of a progressive serial focalization of signifiers, the Johannine variant paradigmatically constitutes by constructing step by step on each narrative segment one or more codes of reading and meta-reading which fit it.[97] But an important consequence follows from this principle of interpretation; namely that this paradigmatic construction in a position of narrative metalanguage will react on the narrative itself, in order to modify the ordinate unfolding in it—we have seen an example of this in the syntagmatic position of the expulsion

of the merchants from the Temple--or in order to suppress certain segments which are no longer necessary in a narrative
manifestation since they play a part in the text, but as a
code (in a position of metalanguage).

The Paradigm of the Traitor

We are going to give an example essential for our [p. 139]
purposes. It will have been noted that the intervention of the
traitor in the three Synoptic variants is produced at the moment of the focalization of three signifier series at the point
of conjunction--identification, i.e. at the time of the eucharistic meal in which all the elements of signifiance are found
connected: community--meal or ingestion of food--*parole* of
praise and repentance--productive power of a sign--finally
body as *parole* become a prospective constituent of the universal temporal and eschatological community. Now it is to be
noted that there is no eucharistic meal in the narrative in
John, as a narrated event which centers the signifiers of all
the earlier narratives, because the eucharist in John belongs
to the code, and the latter is "meta-narratively" set forth in
the discourse at Capernaum in Jn. 6:26-63, at the same time in
its articulations and the rules of its use, notably for the
connection of the signifiers to their signifieds[98] (see especially on this last point Jn. 6:26-27).[99] And it is interesting to note that if the code thus given narratively intervenes
in several repetitions,[100] essentially in order to mark some
disjunctions in the "sphere of action" of the subject, the
traitor belongs to the code. He is introduced in the fundamental paradigm where the *parole*, the force, and the body are
connected. Thus Jesus declares in response to the complaints
of the disciples: "It is the spirit that gives life, the flesh
is of no avail;[101] the words that I have spoken to you are
spirit and life" (Jn. 6:63). The *parole* spoken by Jesus is a
living-bread-body. It is spiritual flesh descended from heav-
en and regenerative of the world (cf. Jn. 6:63 and 6:51). And
Jesus concludes, "But there are some of you that do not believe..." (Jn. 6:64). And it is then that the traitor intervenes, but as a commentary of the metanarration: "Jesus knew
from the first...who it was that should betray him" (Jn. 6:64).
And some lines further on, it is Peter who *precisely repeats
the words of the demon* at Capernaum (in Mark): "You are the
Holy One of God" (Jn. 6:69). Jesus responds: "Have I not
chosen you (the Twelve) and yet one of you is a demon", a response that John comments upon by reintroducing a new ambivalence between Peter and Judas by the interplay of the homonyms:
"He spoke of Judas, son of Simon Iscariot, for he, one of the
twelve, was to betray him" (Jn. 6:71).

Thus in John the traitor belongs to the two planes of the text, narrative and metanarrative, but he is not dependent in the same way [p. 140] nor at the same moment on the syntagmatic line. By virtue of the narrative, Judas will appear in Jn. 12:4 at the time of the Bethany anointing in order to catalyze around the mortal annulment, the ensemble of the signifier relations which we have already referred to, and then he will appear at the time of the last supper in chapter 13. In the metanarrative section, the traitor shows himself to be an element of the code previously presented, at first in Jn. 2:24-25; 5:38; and then 5:42-43,[102] an ensemble which defines those who do not believe and whom Jesus cannot trust, except by being signified by some signs; and then in Jn. 6:64 and 6:67-71[103] in which, in this ensemble, the singular, the unique individual who must deliver God is distinguished. Also the traitor in the code is an instrument of the damned Non-God, "one of you is a *demon*" or in Jn. 13:2: "when the devil had already put into the heart of Judas Iscariot, Simon's son, to betray him..."; while in the narrative, his motivations are of a profane, or implicitly profane order. So in Jn. 12:4-6 an opposition of Judas to Jesus appears for reasons of an economic order. From this point of view, the code and narrative will coincide in Jn. 13:27[104] and then indeed, at this point of the text, the "focalizer" scheme is found which has guided us in our analysis of the Synoptic variants.

We can henceforth conclude our analysis in a network into the system of the text, with three propositions which we will consider henceforth to be established (at least as postulates):

1. The signified "God" is revealed in the text by the "subject", "Jesus", who is defined in this way as the signifier of the Father.

2. The subject, one of whose names is Jesus, responds, in his turn, to the questioning of his being by three open series of signifiers that can be grouped on the axes of the *parole*, the power, and the body.

3. These three series lead to a point of identification and conjunction where the signifier which is henceforth unique will be able to be exchanged for the signified: the traitor is, at this point, the performer of the exchange by neutralization of the signifier.

Precisely how is this exchange and neutralization to be carried out? It is that which we are going to try to determine by the analysis of certain segments of the text. [p. 141]

Chapter IV

JUDAS ISCARIOT AND THE ANOINTING AT BETHANY: FIRST NEUTRALIZING EXCHANGE

Judas the Zealot

We evoke Judas only as a reminder, because we have already earlier dealt with the "naming" of Judas Iscariot in the list of the Twelve (Mt. 10:4--Mk. 3:16-19--Lk. 6:15-16). Nevertheless, we can make two remarks about these lists, which will be shown no doubt to be useful for the organization of the meaning in the text. Judas Iscariot appears at the end of the list with the mention by the narrator in a retro-prospective [*retro-prospective*] value, "The one who must deliver him", which is integrated with his name and which designates the "property" of traitor in him: a reading mark which will permit us to remove every ambiguity later on. Judas is defined by his name as "the donor". But there is a supplementary indication which is furnished to us by the very order of the names in the list.[105] In Matthew, and in Mark also, Judas is connected by a καί to Simon the Zealot, and in Luke he is connected to another Judas, the son of James, and to Simon surnamed the Zealot. We will not emphasize the mention of the homonymy in Luke which always indicates an ambivalence in the text in the significance of the figures.[106] But we will note, on the other hand, the connection between Judas and Simon the Zealot, which is the beginning of an *extra-textual* correlation.[107] It is known in effect that this term "Zealot" designated the members of the Jewish resistance to the Roman occupation, and there is the perhaps audacious interpretation which has been proposed of the word "Iscariot" having the same meaning.[108] Thus Judas will be like the Simon who he appears beside in the list, a political resistor, a man of Jewish independence, a nationalist idealist facing the [p. 142] foreign Romanity. We have shown in another work that one of the axes of transformation of the Passion narrative was constituted by the opposition of the Jews and the Romans, as that of national particularity and the non-national universality sought by the universal community.[109] From then on Judas Iscariot, like Jesus-Barabbas, will mark this axis in its negative part. The treachery of Judas, like the liberation of Barabbas, will constitute the negative moments permitting the turning upside down of the functions *on this axis* which indicates the neutrality of Pilate, then the positivity of the centurian at Golgotha while awaiting the fall of the Spirit on Cornelius, the centurion of Caesarea in *Acts*.

Judas and the Demon

The second remark about the appurtenance of Judas to the Twelve is a simple reminder. Matthew, Mark, and to a lesser degree Luke, indicate that the essential power of the Twelve is their authority over the demons. Thus in Mt. 10:1: "And he called to him his twelve disciples and gave them authority over unclean Spirits, to cast them out, and to heal every disease and every infirmity." Likewise in Mk. 3:14-15 where this power is connected to the *parole:* "And he appointed twelve, to be with him, and to be sent out to preach and have authority to cast out demons." As for Luke, the verses which immediately follow the list of the Twelve indicate in the narrative itself the connection of the *parole* and the power over the demons: (Lk. 6:18-19) "And all the crowd sought to touch him, for power came forth from him and healed them all." The Twelve partake of this *parole* and this force; and Judas therefore with them. In other words, on the helper-opponent axis of the actantial model and characterized by the modality of *power* in the sphere of action of the "subject", Judas, one of the Twelve, like the eleven others, holds power over the demons and the power of *parole*.

Hence the importance for the narrative transformations of two indications: one of the clearest characteristics of the demons whose exorcism is narrated to us is that they name Jesus by his signified, his messiahship. The power of Jesus, and therefore of the Twelve, over the demons amounts to compelling them to keep silent about the signified, only in order to reveal its signifier, its power, and its force. On the other hand, when Simon-Peter, the first on the [p. 143] list ("foremost" as Matthew writes) and Judas Iscariot, the last, are called "Satan" and "demon" by Jesus precisely for the naming of Jesus, and the revelation or realization of his signified, it will be understood that the helper begins here his transformation into his contrary, into the modality connected with the power and the *parole*, so that the treachery as a compound function is generated at this point of the narrative by the relation, inside of the helper actant, of two "actors", Simon-Peter and Judas. Another indication of this transformation into the narrative is supplied by the healing of the epileptic demoniac (Mt. 17:14-21; Mk. 9:14-29; Lk. 9:37-42) which reveals the powerlessness of the disciples before a demon, and therefore a weakening of the helper and the beginning of his inversion into his contrary.[110]

JUDAS AT BETHANY

These preliminary remarks being given, it will be noted that two variants occupy--as far as our study of the traitor is concerned--a peculiar position in the system of the text. Matthew and John offer in effect for reading two episodes where the traitor is revealed, in addition to the large central segment of the narrative formed by the treachery properly speaking, the last supper, and the arrest. In John, Judas appears in the episode which is so important for the general economy of the Passion narrative, the anointing at Bethany; and Matthew alone relates the death of Judas after the denunciation of his treason near the Chief Priests in the Temple. Strictly speaking, as far as the first episode which is narrated in Mark and Matthew is concerned, it can be assumed that Judas belongs to the group of disciples (Mt. 26:8) or those (Mk. 14:4) who are indignant with the squandering of the perfume poured on the head of Jesus.[111] Finally, it is known that Luke's variant does not include, at this point of the text, the segment "Anointing at Bethany". But on the other hand, in Lk. 7:36-50 the story of the pardoned sinful woman is found following an anointing, at the time of a meal with the Pharisee Simon. But the signifier axis of the narrative is here only the "touching" of the body of Jesus by the sinful woman. There is therefore a danger of impurity here; while in the other three variants, the relation of the anointing and the silver is added. We will choose therefore, as a vector text of our analysis, the most [p. 144] expansive variant, that of John which contains multiple correlations with earlier or later segments of the narrative, even if the variants of Matthew and Mark are brought in to determine the irreducible functions to which the traitor would be found connected.[112]

The narrative of the anointing at Bethany in John is remarkable in many respects, because around the signifier kernel that we found in two other variants, the narrative is organized around a double ensemble of correlations--on the one hand with the resurrection of Lazarus (Jn. 11:1-44) and its consequences (Jn. 11:45-54); on the other hand, with the preliminaries of the last supper or the washing of the feet in Jn. 13:1-20. In this double ensemble the traitor is indicated at the same time by the name of his figure, and by the functional or qualificative interplay that this figure introduces.

Let us recall the signifier kernel of this episode. By receiving at Bethany an anticipated funeral anointing, "Jesus", the subject, explicitly indicates his death to come. But he also indicates his resurrection. In effect, the Bethany anointing will be negatively marked in the narrative,

136

since the anointing of the corpse of Jesus by the women who
come to the tomb could not take place, and this failure will
be the mark of triumph by the subject.113 Thus the Bethany
anointing constitutes the segment of the narrative by which
this living hero is indicated to be dead, but also as non
dead, in his absence as a corpse in the tomb. It is a "compound" episode in which the "subject" superficially reverses
the order of the narrative functions and receives all the determinations which will later permit him to die *and* to triumph
over death, in short to die and not to die. That is the importance of this narrative segment for our purpose, because
this is indeed the "problem", or one of the problems, which
the narrative has to resolve--How the eternal God can die, he
who must live [*le?*] in order that the mortal live? And this
is indeed the "milieu" in which the traitor should, according
to our hypothesis, exercise his operatory force of transformation. We are also not surprised to see one of the variants in-
insert the name of Judas here.

The Resurrection of Lazarus (Jn. 11:1-44)

The first large ensemble of correlations which includes
the anointing at Bethany in John is constituted by the resurrection [p. 145] of Lazarus. The death of Lazarus is "for the
glory of God, so that the Son of God may be glorified by means
of it" (Jn. 11:4). The text indicates this even more "clearly"
again in Jn. 11:14-15: "Lazarus is dead; and for your sake I
am glad that I was not there, so that you may believe." And
finally in a magnificent way (but with a passage into the code
as always in John) in the dialogue with Martha in Jn. 11:25-
26: "Jesus said to her, 'I am the resurrection (and the life);
he who believes in me, though he die, yet shall he live. And
whoever lives and believes in me shall never die.'" The death
of Lazarus is therefore the occasion, almost provoked by Jesus
to be manifested as the glory of God, as his Son. Why? Because Jesus will resurrect him and will reveal in that way his
power over death; because he is in himself and by himself, resurrection.

In other words, before the central segment of the "arrest,
judgment, death, and resurrection of Jesus" narrative, the same
sequence is found specified with the secondary "subject", Lazarus: illness, death, and resurrection. The significance of
which is, as that which will follow, belief in the resurrection
of the dead (Jn. 11:24). We can even go much further again and
note that an anointing is evoked at the beginning of the narrative (to be sure, this anointing is that of Jesus by Mary, and
not that of Lazarus, but it does not follow that an anointing
is indicated in the enumeration of the functions on the narra-

tive line; that Jesus took *three days* in order to go from the place where he was found to Bethany where Lazarus is buried: the three days of the sign of Jonah, the three days of the burial of Jesus himself; and that *the women, Martha and Mary, went to the tomb from which the stone was rolled away*. But the corpse found there is "already alive", and Jesus calls the corpse *outside* in order to manifest the glory of God.[114] Finally, the resurrection of Lazarus introduces the death penalty made by the Pharisees and the Chief Priests and for eminently political reasons: "What are we to do? For *this man performs many signs*. If we let him go on thus, every one will believe in him, and the Romans will come and destroy both our holy place and our nation" (Jn. 11:47-48). The reasoning is clear. There is on the one hand the sacred signs which prove his messiahship or at least his prophetic character, and at the same time incite the crowds; and on the other, the Romans who hold the real force capable of destroying the Temple and the Jews as a nation (as a national community).

The resurrection of Lazarus--that is to say the iterative sequence [p. 146] of the death and resurrection of the "subject"--presents, on the line of the narrative, the double problem of the divine or sacred significance and the profane or political significance of the "subject-hero". By the same metaphoric-metonymic movement that we have already noted, "Lazarus" is an anticipatory metaphor of "Jesus"; but he is also an inductive element in the causal time and in the significance of the "central" element. He is the adjoining part in time and meaning with all of it. The semantic axis of death and life will then be marked in manifestation by the anointing at Bethany, and the semantic political axis of the national religious community and the universal Church will be marked by the messianic entrance.[115]

The Anointing Turned Upside Down

"I am the Resurrection" (Jn. 11:25), Jesus had said to Martha and he resurrected Lazarus. The power over death had first been given as a qualification of the being in a discourse and then related as an act [*faire*] in a narrative. The narration was unfolded, according to the modality of power, from the being (in discourse) to the sign (in act). And it is from this sign-act (at the level of the narrative) that the Jewish leaders decide on the death of Jesus in order to save the national community: "It is expedient for you that one man should die for the people, and that the whole nation should not perish" (Jn. 11:50). The anointing at Bethany will be unfolded from the sign (in act) to the being (in discourse). It is an inversion of the order which will be at the same time an inver-

sion of the poles of the axis of death and life, since the
sign-act will be an anointing of festivity (and of rejoicing),
and the qualification of the being in the discourse, a qualification of death: the anointing being interpreted as a mortuary anointing. The substance used is the perfume which is
also invested with an ambivalent signification. If we compare
John's narrative with Luke's which has already been cited (Lk.
7:37), we see that the anointing by Mary can be perceived as
an anointing which serves as a prelude to the festival meal--
that is particularly clear if we read the interpretation by
Jesus of the sinful woman's gesture.[116]--And is it not also a
festival meal which is offered to Jesus, the feast of the Resurrection of Lazarus, "Martha served--Lazarus was one of the
guests". The death, which by virtue of the force and the *parole* of Jesus has acceded to the state of non-death, is at the
[p. 147] very table of the living.[117] And the scent of the
perfume spread over the feet of Jesus filled the whole house
(Jn. 12:3), just as the tomb was filled with the odor of
"Lazarus's" corpse some time beforehand (Jn. 11:39).

It is then that the transforming operation takes place
which "Jesus" carries out and which is fundamental. The
anointing is not a festival anointing. It is a mortuary
anointing and the scent of the perfume is accomplished no
longer *in the sign*, but in favor of *the ambivalence of the
sign* and in the interpretative discourse, in the commentary
which Jesus gives deciphering it. However, this commentary
is a first level commentary, or a second degree discourse, as
the discourses of Jesus[118] often are. Because a metadiscourse
intervenes for the readers who recite the narrative, and who
are by the reading already reiterated endlessly in the community proclamation at the end of the narrative. There is a second commentary for which the mortuary anointing is a signifier
in reality of the resurrection of Jesus, since his corpse is
not in the tomb for anointing (has that not already been performed at Bethany?). But in its place there is the message of
the Angel announcing that Jesus is already somewhere else in
Galilee. The signifier is thus repeated; and at the end of
this double repetition the anointing indeed again becomes the
anointing of the feast of the resurrection, no longer of Lazarus alone, but of his metaphoric-metonymic double, Jesus, and
by implication of the recited-narrative.

The Monetary Sign

It is in this way that the traitor intervenes; but in ad-
dition--as it was seen in the reading of our analysis according to the structure of the narrative--since we have been able
to survey the structure fully in its transformational logic,

without making the traitor intervene. But Judas intervenes in
Jn. 12:4-6, and it is indeed his indignant interruption which
provokes the turning upside down of the "perfume" signifier,
from a perfume of festiveness and anointing of the joy of hospitality, into a perfume of death, into an ill-smelling mask
of the negative perfume of the corpse. Therefore what is this
addition, which is at the same time useless in the logical
structure of the narrative and necessary to its narrative unfolding, and which gives an unexpected dimension to the prophetic interpretation of the subject? "But Judas Iscariot,
one of his disciples (he who [p. 148] was to betray him),
said, 'Why was this ointment not sold* for three hundred denarii and given to the poor?' This he said, not that he cared
for the poor but because he was a thief, and as he had the money box, he used to take what was put into it" (Jn. 12:4-6).
*The addition which introduces the traitor is a signifier of
the monetary exchange.* The perfume, a sign of the festive and
resurrection anointing, is exchanged by Judas--at least by his
question, as an unreal project, neutralized by the question--
into *three hundred denarii*, into those empty signifiers which
are the pieces of silver, since they are said by Judas to be
given to the poor, and by the narrator to have been stolen by
the traitor. But in both cases, will they become food, wine,
bread, or arms for the Jewish resistance against the Romans,
etc.? We do not and cannot know.

The intervention of Judas realizes--but in discourse and
unreally (since the perfume is already poured out)--*the first
exchange of the signifier for another signifier, the silver
which annuls and neutralizes it in its significance.* It is an
exchange which has no value on the plane of the signifier, except as a pure exchange, an insertion of displacement of the
signifier into another signifier, whose entire significance is
reduced to being exchanged for "another thing". Now the signifier which is in question here is that of the resurrection
of "Lazarus" (from his non-death).[120] And the intervention of
Judas then provokes the turning upside down of its significance
into a contrary significance, that of non-life, "from the day
of the burial". The intervention of Judas thus marks the zero
degree of the turning upside down of the positive to the negative. It is not marked in the structure of the narrative, except in the form of an arrow of the contrary or implication and
that from which, after all, the structure can take place, because it restricts itself to recording the trail of the rela-

---

*The term used by Marin here also means "to betray". It is
unfortunate that there is no term in English meaning both to
sell and betray.

tional dynamic. This movement of turning upside down is so powerful that "Lazarus", the non-Death, is seriously in danger of being carried away by it: "So the chief priests planned to put Lazarus also to death, because on account of him many of the Jews were going away and believing in Jesus" (Jn. 12:10-11). The schema below attempts to express this unexpressable which is the addition of the traitor, as a neutralizing exchange: [p. 149]

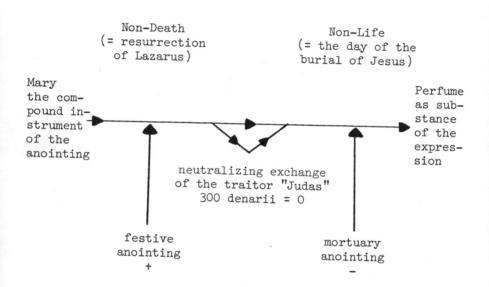

Non-Death
(= resurrection
of Lazarus)

Non-Life
(= the day of the
burial of Jesus)

Mary
the com-
pound in-
strument
of the
anointing

Perfume
as sub-
stance
of the
expres-
sion

neutralizing exchange
of the traitor "Judas"
300 denarii = 0

festive
anointing
+

mortuary
anointing
−

Remarks: We will make two remarks. The first is obvious. The anointing at Bethany at the time of a supper with the intervention of Judas which determines precisely the cost of "the verity of the perfume" at 300 denarii, is metaphoric of another supper, and another less productive verity, since it will only be a matter of thirty denarii. But the introduction of this metaphoric correlation is interesting for the production of the meaning, since if that which is sold for three hundred denarii is a sign of resurrection, that which will be sold for thirty denarii will be the resurrection itself ("I am the Resurrection," Jesus said to Martha). Moreover, it is not very important in this sense that the precise cost is fixed in John alone and constitutes what could be called an induced effect of a metalanguage or a code. Because the metaphor in the Johannine variant of the numerical relationship 300/30 is only produced by a comparison with Matthew, who alone states precisely the cost of the treason-transaction of Judas. Thus the metaphor is only produced in fact in the system of the text by the in-

terplay of two variants which operate in this way by a reciprocal cumulation of meaning.

The second remark concerns the substance and the instrument of the expression, the perfume and Mary, whose name is
found connected to the anointing of the body. The perfume is
a feminine substance, used by the women in our text, and it is
connected, although it is material, volatile, and atmospheric,
to contact with the body. There is here the beginning of a
classification of material qualities which must not be neglected.[121] We will limit ourselves to indicating some reference points. The healing of the women by touching the cloak
of Jesus, the anointing by the sinful woman, down to the *Noli
me tangere* [Jn. 20:17] after the Resurrection. What directly
concerns our purpose here is the transformation of the contact
with the body by the women in the anointing into the ingestion
of the body-food by the men in the meal and into the kiss [p.
150] of the hero by the traitor. We will come back to this in
our analysis of the supper and the arrest.[122]

The Washing of the Feet

The second large correlative ensemble of the anointing at
Bethany is another meal and another kind of anointing: the
washing of the disciples' feet by Jesus. It will have been
noted in effect that according to the three variants the perfume is poured by the woman either on his head (Mk. 14:3; Mt.
26:7) or on his feet (Lk. 7:38; Jn. 12:3). Now before the
last supper with his disciples, and in John alone, Jesus washes
the feet of his disciples; and that provokes an intervention by
Peter who asks for a total "anointing" of purification, after
having refused for the moment the action of Jesus: "Lord, do
you wash my feet?" Jesus responds to him: "What I am doing
you do not know now, but afterwards you will understand."--
"You shall never wash my feet," Peter says to him. Jesus answered him: "If I do not wash you, you have no part in me."--
"Lord," Simon-Peter said to him, "Not my feet only, but also
my hands and my head!" And Jesus responds by explaining the
sign (Jn. 13:6-9).

As in the meal at Bethany, we are dealing with a certain
kind of anointing, and as in the meal it provokes a reaction
which produces an interpretation. The large narrative functions are homologues: anointing--sign--intervention--dialogue
--primary interpretation of the sign. But all the actors
change. It is no longer Jesus who is anointed--but he is the
one who is anointing, and contrary to this the disciples are
no longer women (Mary), but men (Peter and the Eleven), who
receive the anointing instead of giving it. The intervention

provoking the interpretation is Peter's, and not Judas's. But in both cases it is a matter of an indignant protest. And so in both episodes the interpretation consists of turning upside down the meaning of the rite. It is not a matter of a feast and a death, but of purification and lordship, or more precisely of relationships within the community. And it is again the traitor who is in question, but as an object and not as a subject of discourse.

The Blazon of the Body

Like the anointing by Mary at Bethany, the washing of the feet is a ritual sign leading up to a festival meal. Here again we refer [p. 151] to Jesus's discourse with Simon the Pharisee in the episode of the anointing by a sinful woman (= Mary?). "Do you see this woman (he said to Simon)? I entered your house, you gave me no water for my feet, but she has wet my feet with her tears and wiped them with her hair. You gave me no kiss, but from the time I came in she has not stopped kissing my feet. You did not anoint my head with oil, but she has anointed my feet with ointment. Therefore I tell you, her sins which are many are forgiven, for she loved much...." We have cited this text at length (Lk. 7:44-47) not only for its anthropological interest,[123] but, because we think it permits us to draw up a ritual chart of the body of Jesus with a reparation of the signifier functions fitting each of its areas, which will correspond--as we have been aware in our preceding remarks--to specific narrative fragments:[124]

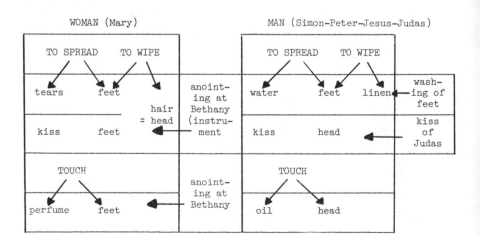

WOMAN (Mary)			MAN (Simon-Peter-Jesus-Judas)		
TO SPREAD	TO WIPE		TO SPREAD	TO WIPE	
tears	feet	anointing at Bethany (instrument)	water	feet	linen — washing of feet
	hair = head				
kiss	feet	←	kiss	head	← kiss of Judas
TOUCH		anointing at Bethany	TOUCH		
perfume	feet	←	oil	head	

In other words, as a prelude to the meal the body of Jesus becomes precisely a signifier in relation to the feet, which are reserved on the whole for the anointing and the feminine gestures, and in relation to the head which is reserved on the whole for the anointing and the masculine gestures. It will be understood how much the signifier body is determined here by the Last Supper vigil in which Jesus will participate as a *guest* and as *food*, no longer touched on the head and the feet *before* the meal by an *anointing*, intended at the same time to *purify* and to *honor*, but *during* the meal in a *manducation* intended simultaneously to *vivify* and to be *commemorated*. This is therefore the significance of the "washing of the feet" sign which introduces the last supper in John. [p. 152]

The Common Body

But this sign comes to be doubly *overdetermined* in him in the sacred transcendant sphere by God and the Non-God, by the Father and the Devil. The latter has instilled into Judas, the son of Simon, the plan to deliver him; the former has put everything into the hands of Jesus. And it is in this interference where the wills *hic et nunc* take over from the positive and negative wills of the transcendent sphere, where the transference starts from the side of Judas to the Chief Priests, from the side of Jesus to the Father. (Judas has the plan *to deliver him*, Jesus knows that it has *come from God* and that he will *return* to God.) It is at this moment therefore that Jesus rises from the table in order to wash the feet of the disciples: in order to proceed therefore with a rite of honoring the body (but of the disciples). What will be transmitted to the Chief Priests and Pharisees is Jesus, in order to be put to death in his body. The one who will return to God, having come from God, is Jesus, as a glorified body, resurrected and exalted to the Father, on the other side of death. But by an inversion of what is expected, it is not Jesus or his body which is the object of the ritual but the disciples, which signifies (going immediately to the end of the analysis) that in a certain way the disciples joined together around the table are the body of Jesus. The gestural signifier, by the double overdetermination which concerns it, indicates by anticipation the later movement of the ecclesial community as a universal body of Jesus. Just as the anointing at Bethany, beyond the interpretation of Jesus as a mortuary anointing, indicated the resurrection in depth. Thus it is the following stage which is signified here. But as far as that goes, it is necessary again for Judas to transfer Jesus' body to his enemies. Here is the schema: [p. 153]

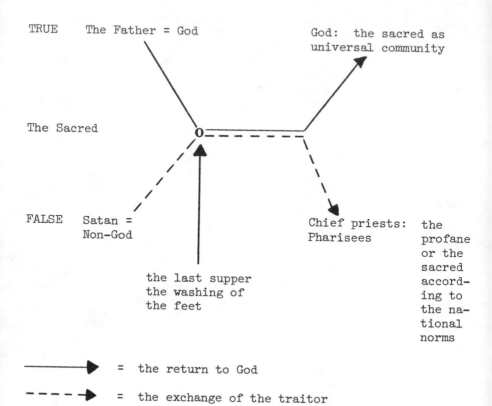

TRUE   The Father = God

God: the sacred as universal community

The Sacred

FALSE   Satan = Non-God

Chief priests: Pharisees

the profane or the sacred according to the national norms

the last supper
the washing of
the feet

―――――▶ = the return to God

‐ ‐ ‐ ‐ ▶ = the exchange of the traitor

SUBJECT--OBJECT--ADDITION

The washing of feet paradox is in some way the ambivalence of the active and the passive, the subject and the object.[125] The one who must be the object of the act of honor seems to have been Jesus. But it is the disciples who benefit from it. Hence the scandalous intervention of Peter who, before the resistance of Jesus, turns this ritual of honor into a ritual of total purification of which the disciples can effectively be the objects. What Peter demands--but in an unreal way since it has already been accomplished at the beginning of the narrative--is the baptism of repentance and purification by the immersion in water which John practiced (Jn. 1:26-34, but also Jn. 1:35, 40-41).[126] As Judas complained after the fact and unreally about the truth of the perfume, likewise Peter complains after the fact and unreally about the baptism of purification. And Peter's intervention provokes a reinterpretation of the significance of the sign by Jesus: "Since you are clean, you do not need a rite of purification." Moreover, this is not a rite as such, but a metaphor of the community brotherhood. "If I then, your Lord and Teacher, have washed your feet, you also ought to wash one another's feet. For I have given you an example...a servant is not greater than his master....I say to you, he who receives the one whom I send receives me; and he who receives me receives him who sent me" (Jn. 13:14-16). [p. 154] A community brotherhood which *is Jesus* as a (sent) signifier of the Sender Father, a life-giving body, spiritual bread for you.

But in addition, here again the intervention of Peter provokes the presence in depth of Judas, because the perfect community could not be realized in Jesus' life-giving body. If Jesus is delivered, condemned to death, and if the unclean, the donor, the son of the Devil is admitted to the table: "It is that the Scripture may be fulfilled, 'He who ate my bread had lifted his heel against me'" (Jn. 13:18) and this is why some verses earlier, Jesus had declared simultaneously: "You are all clean and the washing of the feet signifies a perfect community"; and "You are not all clean and the washing of feet cannot signify purification" (Jn. 13:10-11 paraphrased). Judas, a reverse negative of Peter, is indeed here again, in this correlation of the anointing at Bethany, the one by whom the truth of the signifier can not only be discovered, but realized.

The three episodes, "Resurrection of Lazarus", "Anointing at Bethany", and "Washing of the feet" are in a signifier correlation. It remains for us to construct the model which will articulate them and where we will see the place of the traitor appear empty.

THE CONSTRUCTION OF THE MODEL

This model is established by a semantic axis articulated by two poles: Death vs. Life. Let us suppose the semantic axis S articulates at the level of the form of the content in two contrary semes s1...s2 which "indicate" the existence of their contradictory terms s̄1...s̄2. We can henceforth construct the elementary structure of the signification:

146

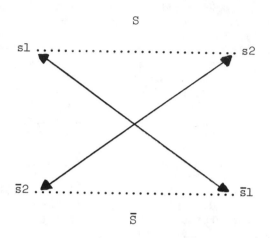

S

s1 .... s2

s̄2 .... s̄1

S̄

[p. 155]

or according to the investment characteristic of our textual system:

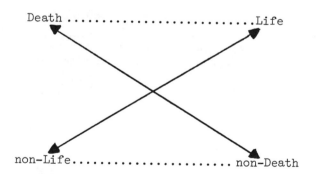

Death ....Life

non-Life........................ non-Death

or again $\dfrac{\text{Death}}{\text{non-Death}}$ $\simeq$ $\dfrac{\text{Life}}{\text{non-Life}}$

Either (1) the death (of Lazarus), its contradictory will be
his non-death (2) (the resurrection of Lazarus).
Or (3) the non-death (of Lazarus) will find its contrary (4)
the non-life (of Jesus).
Or (5) the non-Life ("national" ritual system of purification),
its contradictory will be the Life (6) (universal fraternal
community). In this way the passage from (1) to (6) is realized. There are two fundamental movements, the first by which
one passes from "Lazarus" to "Jesus" and which defines the
first large ensemble of homologous relations: (Anointing at
Bethany/Resurrection of Lazarus); the second by which one
passes from the (anticipated) Non-Life of Jesus to Non-Life as
a ritual of "pharisaic" purification and which defines the second large ensemble of homologous relations: (Anointing at
Bethany/Washing of feet).

Schema 1: s1 + $\bar{s}$1, Death vs. Non-Death, defines the constitutive relation of the narrative of Lazarus's resurrection
whose more particular investments could be: Death or absence
of Jesus in the space vs. Non-Death or presence of Jesus in the
space. The axis $\bar{S}$, Non-Death vs. Non-Life appears in the narrative of the anointing at Bethany, but according to the following particular investments: Non-Death or presence of Lazarus as a guest at the meal with its ritual consequences vs.
Non-Life or presence of Jesus as an anticipated *corpse*, an object of a ritual of (mortuary) anointing in a meal.

Schema 2: s2 + $\bar{s}$2: Life vs. Non-Life, which is constitutive in our sense of the washing of the feet narrative, can
then be invested in the following way: Non-Life or presence
of the disciples as an object of a ritual purification *already*
accomplished (baptism by water) vs. Life or living presence of
Jesus as a fraternal community. We have indeed passed from (1)
Death as a "spatial" absence of Jesus to (6) Life as a "human"
community presence of Jesus. [p. 156]

Axis $\bar{S}$: Non-Death vs. Non-Life or the neutral axis is the
semantic axis defining "the anointing at Bethany". This is the
axis of the contradictories $\bar{s}$1, $\bar{s}$2. The disjunction of the
contraries in the negative that the axis displays is *necessary*
in order to "resolve" the initial opposition of Death and Life
which constitutes the "problem" of the narrative. But it is
apparently the moment of the conjunction of the contact, and
of the most cordial anointing: that of the festive perfume
which Mary dries with her hair. The opposition would continue
therefore if Judas did not intervene by performing the real
disjunction. The perfume of the anointing is neither Life nor
Death. It is the very neutral, *the silver*: the three hundred
denarii. The Neutral, the neither Death nor Life of axis $\bar{S}$, is
indeed in the form of the invested content, the presence of the

resurrected Lazarus (the Non-Dead) as a guest and that of the living Jesus as a corpse (the Non-Living). But what permits the functioning of axis $\bar{S}$ is *in the manifestation* the operation of Judas who transforms the semantic vehicles of conjunction into pure disjunction.

The passage from axis $\bar{S}$ to schema 2: s2 + $\bar{s}$2 also presents a problem in the investment. $\bar{s}$2 has been defined as Non-Life by a formal assimilation with the particular investment of pole $\bar{s}$2 of axis $\bar{S}$. It is necessary to justify this. Just as Jesus (in axis $\bar{S}$) is the object of an *anticipated* mortuary ritual which consecrates him living as a corpse, so the disciples in schema 2 are the objects of an *accomplished* purification ritual which defines them as disciples of John, while they are already members of a Living-Jesus. In short, that defines them as non-living by a useless ritual purification. Hence the passage to the fraternal community in Jesus of which the ritual gesture of Jesus is the signifier. But like the contradiction Non-Life vs. Life, it would be traversed if the traitor Judas did not intervene as the negative of Peter's intervention--the ritual purification is useless, to be sure, because it is already accomplished, but also because there is one among the disciples who is not clean. It is because there is an unclean disciple that the ritual no longer has a course and the reception of Jesus as the host sent by the Living God is substituted as the food which gives Life, in order to establish the community. And Judas, far from receiving Jesus, gives him and expels him. (But for that very reason, he allows him to be truly received.) [p. 157]

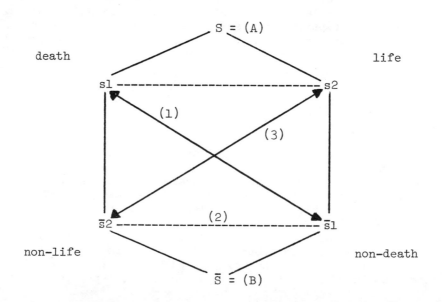

(A) = fundamental opposition or compound
        axis = S

(1) = resurrection of Lazarus

(2) = anointing at Bethany

(3) = washing of the feet

(B) = opposition of the contradictories
        or neutral axis = $\bar{S}$

The model can be translated into the following formula:

$$S = (s1 \rightarrow \bar{s}1) \Rightarrow (\bar{s}1 \rightarrow \bar{s}2) \Rightarrow (\bar{s}2 \rightarrow s2) = s1 + s2$$

which would be the diachronic formula of the three narratives
which follow one another on the surface of the text. [p. 158]

Chapter V

THE EUCHARISTIC MEAL AND
THE FUNDAMENTAL EXCHANGE

With the treachery, properly speaking, the last supper, and the arrest of the hero, we enter into an essential part of our semiotic analysis of the traitor. Because in these rigorously articulated segments, he is constantly manifested and presented as the anti-hero.[127] He is the one by whom the preparatory negative functions are produced in the series of large tests of the trial, the condemnation, and the putting to death.

THE PLACE OF THE FIGURE WITH ITS DIFFERENCES

But paradoxically, entirely by presenting the important problems through the system of the text, this part is what is, to a certain extent, the clearest for our purpose, because the anthropomorphic figure, who is animated and named a traitor, apparently stands out here. The conjunction of the circumstantial actants of the helper and the opponent, through the preceding narrative segments, is indicated in the reading in the form of narrative potentialities in the constant displacement of the subject through the three signifier series, *parole*, forces, and body. This conjunction, which ensures the narrative of its narrative "dynamic" in the test-struggle, receives a figure here into which some acts are inserted [*rapportés*].[128] Or in other words, a sphere of action coincides almost precisely with the author who participates in it.

Let us return our attention then to the system of the text in its variants, i.e. to the interplay of the differences which are [p. 159] manifested in the syntagmatic arrangement of the functions of the narrative. It is an interplay where the place of the treason is produced under the figure of Judas.[129] And recalling our working hypothesis, this place and this figure are a place and an operator of exchange of the signifiers in which the subject is summarized for other signifiers which neutralize them in order to permit them to be loaded with a signified that they manifested on their horizons, but which they will henceforth be able "to realize". The Living God will be able to die and mortal man to live in order to constitute together a universal living community.

151

"The anointing at Bethany" in the Johannine variant offers us the first form of this exchange, but in discourse and with a compound signifier of resurrection and death. The perfume, as an anointing substance for the body, was by the intervention of Judas, found exchanged (but in *paroles*) with the silver, which was an empty signifier since it was simultaneously a gift to the poor and money stolen by Judas.

Matthew's Variant: the Inversion of the Contract

Therefore our analysis will be pursued logically by a study of the passage of the exchange indicated, but missing in the exchange proposed as projected and carried out, namely the treason contract which we find in the Matthean variant (Mt. 26: 14-16). We note that the treason contract,[130] namely the "delivery" or "gift" of Jesus to the Chief Priests, or to the leaders of the religious and political community, versus the "gift" in hard cash to Judas, is here at the same time proposed and *honored by anticipation*. Jesus is not transmitted or given at this moment, but the thirty pieces of silver are deposited. This indication is unique in the system of the text. And however essential this *hapax* may be, it gives us the reason for another *hapax* figuring in the same variant: the death of Judas. Jesus has been delivered. The contract is then *completed*, but it is at this moment that the *contract* is *denounced* by Judas who returns to give the silver back, despite the refusal of the Chief Priests. He throws the silver into the Temple. But this silver is, in turn, expelled from the Temple, in the form of a purchase of a field, to become a burial place for strangers, which is called a "Field of Blood". The neutralizing signifier is then definitely expelled out of the political and religious community of Israel as a signifier [p. 160] of death *and* the body, in the form of a place inscribed and reserved for the corpses of strangers. In this way, therefore, it is because the contract has been anticipatively honored that it is retrospectively denounced. And it is by the double action of this anticipation and this retrospection: 1/ that Jesus as a body is given to the religious Community of Israel in order to be put to death outside of it (outside of Jerusalem and the Temple); 2/ that the signifier for which he has been given as a signifier makes a return to this community (into its place, the Temple) in order to be put outside of it as a place of death for strangers; 3/ that Jesus can then make a return as a resurrected body and constitutive of another community, which is the same but different, the universal-fraternal community.

This is the way in which the Matthean variant resolves the problem of the "real" exchange which had indicated the ex-

change "in *parole*" of the anointing at Bethany in the Johannine variant. By a double inversion in the diachronic succession of the moments of the contract[131] which marks out the
moments of the exchange of Jesus, a signifier body, for the
silver, an empty signifier.

John's Variant or the Enigma of the "Gift"

There is no treason contract in the Johannine variant.
Judas is nowhere shown meeting with the chief priests in order to propose to them the "gift" of Jesus for the silver.
But it is true that the anointing at Bethany has filled this
function, since the perfume, the anointing of the body (res-
urrected-corpse) of Jesus, had been exchanged for three hundred denarii. Nevertheless, this exchange which is maintained
at the level of the *parole* at the time of the anointing, will
have to be repeated by John, in a real way, but in an enigmatic or metaphoric formulation carefully decoded by the narrator: "Jesus said to him, 'What you are going to do, do quickly.' Now no one at the table understood why he said this (*parole*) to him. Some thought that, because Judas had the money
box, Jesus was telling him, 'Buy what we need for the feast';
or that he should give something to the poor" (Jn. 13:27-29).
All the functions of the treason contract figure here, but
they are obliquely explicit, while the "gift" of the traitor
is implicitly stated: "Do what you have to do." That is to
say, "*Give me*, because you are *bought* and you have *sold** me."
Thus John keeps the real exchange at the level of the [p. 161]
discourses, but of the discourse where the reality claims to
be [*se dit*], despite the speaking intentions.[132] These are
the verbal signifiers which signify the real exchange: the
"doing" of the word of Jesus: "What you are going to do, do
quickly" (Jn. 13:27) is interpreted, but it is interpreted only as "buying" and "giving"--which is what it is in reality.

Mark and Luke or the Incomplete Contract

By excluding the anticipation, the other Synoptic variants
are prohibited from retrospection, and at the same time the explicitly neutralizer-neutralized function of the silver sign
does not play the same role, with the exception of John where
it appears, but in an entirely different way.

---

*Again the word Marin uses has the dual meaning of "to sell"
and "to betray".

The two synoptic variants (Mark and Luke) indicate in effect the treason contract as a contract. Judas proposes to deliver Jesus, and as compensation the chief priests and the leader of the guards agree to give him the silver. But then a problem appears: the narrative nowhere reports that the silver has been given, once Jesus is delivered. The contract is concluded, but it is not totally completed. Jesus is delivered, but the silver is not given. The remarkable absence of the correlate function--its presence as absence, we will dare to say--is significant [significante]. It plays the same role at the end of the account, but in a more hidden way, as the rejection of the "silver" signifier in Matthew which escapes every grasp and leads to the place of blood and death of the stranger. Here this signifier, the expectation of which is exchanged for the other signifier, that of the Father, the Living God, or "Jesus' body" (a signifier which only existed therefore as a potential) also leaves it despite the filling of the contract by Judas, but from the text, not in the referend [le référend] that the text relates, but from the narrative of the text. Luke and Mark quite simply do not speak of it: there is an absence and silence which are--in this very text-- the zero marks of the neutralization that the silver has effectively performed, as potential reality.[133]

TEXTUAL ORGANIZATION AND VARIANTS

Let us return to Matthew. This variant can give us the general syntagmatic structure of the intermediary narrative segments between the treason contract and the death of Judas (or [p. 162] the absence of retribution of the traitor). It is outlined in the following way:

	A	B	C
I	Announcement of the treason of Judas	Eucharistic meal	Announcement of the treason of Peter
II	Realization of the treason of Judas = arrest of Jesus	(Jesus before the Sanhedrin)	Realization of the treason of Peter = the denial of Peter
III	Remorse of Judas death	....	Remorse of Peter life

The remorse of Judas appears only in the Matthean variant, as we have said. On the other hand, we have for the benefit of the structural organization, disjoined the remorse of Peter (26:75) from the narrative of his denials. In this way the correlation of Judas' remorse and Peter's remorse is revealed more clearly in the table above.

Luke's variant consists of inverting in line I, A and B (the eucharistic meal which precedes the announcement of Judas's treason) and of separating A and C by a dispute about preeminence among the Twelve. Further, it will be noted that line II, A and C and at the same time B of line III are connected. The appearance of Jesus before the Sanhedrin is transferred behind C. However, as the meal in Luke is divided into a paschal meal and a "eucharistic" meal, the latter keeps the same position in the syntagmatic structural organization. The correlation of the two treasons is reinforced by an additional trait: the allusion to Satan in connection with Judas and in connection with the disciples and Peter. The segment which separates them on the narrative line is the dispute between the Twelve for preeminence, which is resolved by the "eschatological" affirmation of the fraternal community in the Kingdom and in the transcendent meal. We are reserving for the moment the examination of Lk. 22:35-38 where we will later see the signifier correlations. The table summarizing the organization of Luke's narrative with its differences from the other two Synoptic variants can be constructed in the following way: [p. 163]

	A	B	C
I	Paschal meal	Eucharistic meal	
II	Announcement of the treason of Judas	Dispute and solution among the Twelve	Announcement of the treason of Peter
III	Arrest of Jesus = realization of the treason of Judas		Realization of the treason of Peter
IV	Remorse of Judas death		Remorse of Peter life

This table makes two difficulties apparent: I C and III
B. We propose, as a hypothesis, the following solutions: for
I C, the removal of verse 30 from segment II B: "that you may
eat and drink at my table in my kingdom, and sit on thrones
judging the twelve tribes of Israel" (Lk. 22:30). In other
words, it is necessary to introduce a third "eschatological"
meal in Luke, which we find in Mark and Matthew in what it is
convenient to call traditionally "the eucharistic institution".
Thus, in Mk. 14:25: "Truly, I say to you, I shall not drink
again of the fruit of the vine until that day when I drink it
new in the kingdom of God." And in Mt. 26:29, which is even
clearer: "I tell you I shall not drink again of this fruit of
the vine until that day when I drink it new *with you* in my
Father's kingdom." For III B, by the paradigmatic displacement of vv. 35-38 concerning hostility and which, more precisely, ought to be correlated functionally with vv. 49-53 which
are a conclusion of the realization of Judas' treason in the
narrative syntagmatic, and an introduction to the realization
of Peter's treason: III B would be the moment of the sword
and the Darkness. The table is then constructed:

	A	B	C
I	Paschal meal	Eucharistic meal	Eschatological meal
II	Announcement of the treason of Judas	Dispute among the Twelve: solution	Announcement of the treason of Peter
III	Realization of the treason of Judas	Moment of the sword and the darkness	Realization of the treason of Peter
IV	Remorse of Judas death	....	Remorse of Peter life

This structural organization of the narrative syntagmatic
gives us in a general way—it is a question of the table of the
[p. 164] direct variant (Mark and Matthew) or of the compound
variant (Luke)—some fundamental indications for our purpose:
1/ The essential correlation of Judas and Peter, that is to
say of columns A and C of the tables in which the actantial

opposition of the helper and the opponent cannot be accounted for, because the helper does not coincide with the figure of Peter. Peter--as we have been aware in the reading of earlier segments--is in effect a kind of opponent. And on the other hand, Judas functions as a kind of transcendent helper by which "the Scriptures are fulfilled". 2/ The function of the eucharistic meal is "central", since even in the case of the compound table (variant Luke) the eucharistic meal remains "central" in the function of the meal between the "ordinary" Paschal meal and the transcendent "extraordinary" eschatological meal. The problem which this centrality presents is twofold. It can be asked on the one hand what its function is in the correlation of "Judas" and "Peter".[134] On the other hand, it can be asked what type of relation it maintains in the compound table with the dispute among the Twelve and what we have called the moment of the sword and darkness. In a general way the very notion of centrality, which is to a certain extent questioned by our general hypothesis of research about the traitor, reappears in the two tables constructed for the synoptic variants. Is there not an important difficulty here in the attempt at a validation of this hypothesis?[135]

THE ANNOUNCEMENT OF THE TREASONS: DOING AND SAYING

What is therefore the signifier value of "Judas" and "Peter" in the three successive segments of the narrative from Matthew? And first at the level of the announcement? The first opposition will rest on the treason itself which is found modulated in a different way in Judas and Peter. "One of you will deliver me"; "You will deny me three times, this very night, before the cock crows" (Mt. 26:34). To deliver is opposed to deny, as the act of exchange according to material things [les choses-bien] is opposed to the act of exchange according to words; as the positive is opposed to the negative; or again as the gift is opposed to the rejection. This first opposition is [p. 165] then improved by two secondary oppositions. The indeterminate partitive ("one of you") is opposed to the specific mode of the other in the dialogue ("you"). The impersonal is opposed to the indicator of the allocuted, on the one hand; and on the other hand, the oneness of the act (of delivery) is opposed to the triplicity of the word (of denial). Finally the first of the oppositions is itself modalized by a third degree opposition, that of the indefiniteness of the moment. It is a non marked element which is opposed to the rigorous determination of the moment "that very night before the cock crowed". The correlation of "Judas" and "Peter" in "the announcement" made to one and the other displays a remarkable compensatory system. The high degree of determination of "Peter" is opposed to the weak or non-existent degree of determination of "Judas". But the overdetermination of "Peter" lays stress on a *negative word*, a verbal rejection which can be repeated three times without danger, while the overdetermination of "Judas" is articulated in a *positive act*, a *real gift* which can only take place once.

The correlation between the two "traitors", which is so apparent that it almost has a didactic value, is thus profoundly dissymmetrical in the "importance" of the two functional poles. But the essential signification of this dyssymmetry rests on the opposition of the act of Judas' *positive gift* and the *negative parole* of Peter's refusal. And the positive character of Judas' act is discovered in the discourse of Jesus which comments upon the announcement of his treason... "The *Son of Man* goes as it is written of him, but woe to that man by whom the Son of Man is delivered" (Mt. 26:24). The *gift* of the Son of Man by Judas *is* the *departure* of the Son of Man to his Father. This departure is, we know, a positive return which assures through death eternal life to humanity. Such is the scope of Judas' *gift*. By delivering the Son of Man to the political-religious community of Israel, he assures the departure *forecast by the Scriptures* of the Son to the Father, that is to say, taking everything into account, the universal religious community living from Him. To be sure, woe be to that man! But thanks to him, or better still to his additional intervention, the Son of Man goes and realizes the prophecies, the "divine plan". The curse thrown upon the traitor is a correlate of the announced scandal of Peter and the disciples, but the scandal has the value of a selective test [p. 166] to be overcome (cf. Lk. 22:31), while the curse has the value of a definite statement.

Finally, one last detail must be supplied about the announcement of the treason of Judas and Peter. Jesus says to Peter: "You will deny me...." But he says to the disciples, "He who has dipped his hand in the dish with me will be the one who will deliver me." And when Judas asks the question of Jesus: "Will it be me, Rabbi?", Jesus answers him, "You have said so." We will not repeat the analysis here which we have made elsewhere of this form of response which refers a question back to the questioner, in the form of an affirmation that the one who is questioned refuses to accept. But it is remarkable that at no place of the text is Judas denounced as a traitor by Jesus, we mean Judas in his proper name which specifies him in his referential figure. The traitor--the one who "gives" Jesus--is, unlike Peter in his verbal rejection, only defined by the "subject" as someone who eats with Jesus. Now the Twelve actually eat with Jesus. And it is Judas who denounces himself by receiving as an affirmation the question

which he poses about himself to Jesus. It is Judas who is
named as a traitor by Jesus indirectly, while Peter is named
as a "turncoat" by Jesus directly. In this new dissymmetry
the additional function of the traitor appears fully as such
which must correspond with the sole condition of eating (with)
Jesus. Less important is the proper name of the instrument
by which the Scripture is fulfilled. In this perspective
everything is interchangeable: "One of you who eats with me
will deliver me, and that is necessary in order that I can go
to the Father. Will it be me? Judas says--You are denouncing
yourself--It is you that you name as such, Jesus responds."

Consumption* and Verbal Rejection

In order to perform the necessary gift of Jesus, it is
necessary for someone, whatever his name may be, to whom Jesus
gives himself in his triple signifier of *parole*, force, and
body, i.e. a consumable and consumed body, already be exchanged
for the silver. Or even more profoundly Jesus must be exchanged as food--*parole*, assimilated and annihilated-neutral-
ized in this consumption which is the meal. A meal with Jesus
comes to be [p. 167] in the following segment the meal (of)
Jesus. While the other traitor, Peter, appears only in the
syntagmatic line of the narrative after the meal. "After the
singing of the hymn", the Son of Man has already been delivered
--consumed--annihilated as a signifier. The exchange is accomplished in its immediacy at first for the empty signifier, the
silver. Then it is accomplished for "nothing" in the pure act
of consumption, or destruction which is the very act of eating.[136]

If this is true, then Peter can be named by his proper
name and his treason attributed to him. It will only be a
verbal rejection, a negative word, and not the destructive,
neutralizing act that is the act of consuming (with) Jesus.
The gift of Jesus to the political-religious community of
Israel by Judas, in exchange for the silver, is the projective
relation of the original act of neutralizing exchange of the
signifiers which is the consumption of Jesus by "he who has
dipped his hand in the dish with me".[137]

In this way, therefore, we find in the "central eucharistic" meal a place of the articulation of two correlates of the
announcement, Judas and Peter. In this way therefore the ir-
reducibility of the before and the after in the narrative ap-

---

Consommation may mean consumption *or* consummation!

pears as the achronic narrative structure. It is truly diachronic, resolved, and hidden at the same time. The structural organization of the oppositions between the announce-
ments of Judas' and Peter's treasons finds its "ratio" after
all in the fact that Peter's treason follows Judas's beyond
the meal. The reason for the effects is on the surface and
the effects are in depth. "A text," Roland Barthes said, "has
its roots in the air."[138] That is no doubt true of this "central" moment of turning upside down of the narrative functions
in our narrative. And the figure of this irreductibility is,
in the very contingency of his name, the traitor Judas.

Let us not forget that the eucharistic meal is the point
of conjunction and identification of three signifier series of
paroles, forces, and body, in that it is the moment when the
body-bread becomes Jesus's *parole* and Jesus's *parole* in the
bread becomes his own body by the force that it contains in
itself: a moment which is already a sacrifice on the cross in
exchange for the death of a multitude. Therefore it is an initial point of foundation of the New Covenant and of the new
universal Community which will recite the narrative, and by
reciting it will be made a living being from the body, the
blood, and the very life of Jesus. It is a zero point of the
[p. 168] signifier series, a zero point of the signifiers--
signifieds to come. It was necessary *moreover* that this moment be another zero by which the first could be the second,
namely that this body-*parole effectively* be consumed, annihi-
lated and neutralized by the one who had already, some moments
before, exchanged the signifier for an empty, universal, and
equivalent signifier, another neutral of the filled, universal
community to come.[139] If everyone comes to consume, only one
is going to be consumed in a neutralizer exchange of the signifier: the one who is necessary in order that the consumption
of the others be filled with meaning to come, that is the traitor.

THE REALIZATION OF THE TREASONS

The second moment of the correlation of "Judas" and
"Peter" is that of the realization of their treasons, one by
permitting the arrest of Jesus, the other by denying Jesus
three times in the courtyard of the palace of the Chief Priest.
It will be noted that the episode which separates the two correlates on the line of the narrative is the trial of Jesus by
the Sanhedrin, which "functions" therefore like the eucharistic
meal in the preceding moment. We will note in effect that this
trial is the place of the first "affirmation" of the subject
concerning his divinity. Although this affirmation may again

be oblique, it is what will bring about his condemnation to death. In other words, the second moment of the correlation of "Judas" and "Peter" in its "central" segment is one where we are present at the beginning of the "inversion of the meaning" of the narrative, or repeating at the same time our terminology and hypothesis, the one where the series of connected signifiers in the unit(y) of the eucharistic meal comes again to diverge, but endowed henceforth with their signifieds.

The Trial Before the Sanhedrin

Let us quickly analyze this "central" point before going to the correlation itself. The trial unfolds itself schematically in three marked stages: the first by the assertion of two false witnesses who, entirely by speaking falsely, speak the truth and whose testimony concerns the destruction of the Temple and its reconstruction in three days by Jesus (let us recall Jn. 2:19 here and our previous analyses). The *signifier of the body* [p. 169] of Jesus which appears here is then referred by the Chief Priest to the *signifier of the parole*, but it is considered as a bearer of this signified of identity in the being and in the name of which we have seen the whole importance in the constitution of the signifier network of the gospel narratives.[140] "I adjure you by the living God, tell us if you are the Christ, the Son of God..." (Mt. 26:63). Then Jesus responds with the oblique response which we already know refers the question back to the questioner in the form of an affirmation. But it is remarkable that this indirect affirmation is then repeated by Jesus as a signifier of the force and the power, endowed here again—by the discourse of the subject and in this discourse—with its signified at the same time of a resurrected and eschatological return: "But I tell you, hereafter you will see *the Son of Man seated at the right hand of Power, and coming on the clouds of heaven*" (Mt. 26:64). The death sentence which follows the blasphemy consists, for the subject, of claiming divinity. It flows therefore, in a linear way, from the position of the false witnesses about the signifier of the body of Jesus as a Temple of God to be destroyed and reconstructed. These false witnesses who speak falsely and tell the truth both at the same time—speaking of the Jerusalem Temple, but talking about the body of Jesus[141]—are the "narrative actors" directly articulated in this other narrative actor which is the traitor. It is he who lets them into the syntagmatic organization, since by him the body of Jesus has been consumed, and neutralized in the eucharistic meal, a segment of the narrative which is in equilibrium with the trial before the Sanhedrin. By these brief remarks we do not pretend to exhaust the semantic content of this trial in its relation to the one which will unfold before Pilate or in its internal articulations. We are content to remove from the episode the signifier stratum which is important for our purposes, namely the dialogue by which the three signifiers of the body, the *parole*, and the force are repeated in order to receive for the first time their own signified, but in discourse.

The Kiss and the Parole

Next we can construct around this central segment the second correlation of "Judas" and "Peter", that of the realization of the treason. It appears to us to be built on the essential opposition between two kinds of signs, the kiss on the one hand, [p. 170] and language on the other. "Now the betrayer had given them (the armed men sent by the Chief Priests and Elders of the people) a sign, saying, 'The one I shall kiss is the man; seize him.' And he came up to Jesus at once and said, 'Hail Master!' And he kissed him. Jesus said to him, 'Friend, why are you here?' Then they came up and laid hands on Jesus and seized him" (Mt. 26:48-50). In another correlate, it is a servant who approaches Peter and says to him: "You also were with Jesus the Galilean" (Mt. 26:69), and Peter denied it. Then to another who again exposed him—"This man was with Jesus of Nazareth" (Mt. 26:71)—Peter denies with an oath. "After a little while the bystanders came up and said to Peter, 'Certainly you are also one of them for your *accent* (i.e. language) betrays you.'" To which Peter retorted with a denial accompanied by oaths and curses. By a kiss, a sign by bodily contact, Judas *indicates* Jesus as an object to be *delivered*, as an object-gift. His treason is in this sign-gesture. Its signification is coded by Judas, but in the same gesture, because the latter is perfectly "in place" in the situational context. The gesture is a sign of reception and reciprocal recognition, but it is also a coded sign of delivery, transmission, and betrayal of the object. The signifier *contact* between two bodies signifies the disjunction of the exchange which is carried out, the separation that the "gift" of the traitor performs. In order to separate from Jesus and to separate Jesus from his disciples in order to deliver him, it is necessary that Judas touch Jesus. It is necessary that it be with his contact. In other words, after the neutralizing exchange as *consumption of the body-food*; the surface exchange is indicated here where the *contact with the body-object* is exchanged with the *separation-transmission of this body*.

On the other hand, it is while speaking, or more precisely it is while denying by *parole* his appurtenance to Jesus, that Peter shows who he belongs to: *the rejection or the separation in language*, in the discourse, of Jesus by Peter is the lin-

guistic signifier that *Peter is with Jesus*, as one who was
"one of them"*, as one of the anonymous actors of the scene
says (Mt. 26:73). It can also be said that Peter the traitor
is betrayed by the very instrument of his treason, language.
Consequently, he uses a sign in order to separate himself from
the object, but this sign of negation and refusal is, if this
can be said, a sign of symbolic denial,[142] which passes in the
very negation to its contrary, the affirmation. In one word,
because Peter uses discourse to betray--to deny Jesus--he is
betrayed, [p. 171] and his treason not only cannot be accomplished, but it is reversed in appurtenance. The same corre-
lation-signification of doing and speaking is continued therefore from the first to the second moment, and it is modulated
here in the opposition of the sign as a gesture of contact and
of the sign as a word of refusal. And as in the preceding moment, if it is true, it is perhaps because *in the narrative*
manifested the realization of Judas's treason is separated and
connected to the realization of Peter's treason by the trial
before the Sanhedrin, i.e. by the episode in which the signifier of God, the Son (of Man) is affirmed in the discourse--
dialogue with the leaders of the political-religious community
of Israel, as Christ, Son of God. That is to say introduced--
in discourse--but for the first time as the signified in the
text. Henceforth, the signifier is found connected to its
meaning, and acts and discourse can only speak it. Even when
they deny it, their negation is a denegation by which the signified turns upside down in order to be manifested.

This analysis, which is too hasty in its tedious minute
detail, must however take into account in the realization of
the treason of Judas the episode of the resistance of Jesus's
companions who strike the High Priest's servant and cut off
his ear. This act provokes a discourse from Jesus successively addressed to the disciples and his adversaries. It is addressed to the disciples in order to turn away all violent resistance on the part of the men, and all "political" opposition
to the measures decided by the leaders of the political-religious community, for "But how then should the scriptures be
fulfilled, that it must be so?" (Mt. 26:54). The opposition
to the transmission-treason of the object-subject is here signified by a sign-gesture, the sword stroke which cuts off the
servant's ear. It is a sign-gesture of separation which is an
opposite in some way of the sign-gesture of contact which is
traitor's kiss, and whose consequences will be opposites in
the same way. The kiss has assured the transmission of the

---

*The French text is more direct, saying, "one who is *in* him"
("*en est*").

object by bodily contact. The sword stroke can only prohibit
this transmission by the separation of a part from the body.
The "separating" sign impeded the transfer of the object or
its exchange, and the exchange which it must accomplish between the political-religious community of Israel and the
other universal community that already exists in his disciples.[143]

It can be thought that this brief episode within the segment of [p. 172] Jesus's arrest is the correlate in Peter's
"treason" of another sign itself correlated inside of the segment. This is the matter of the cock-crow. May we be permitted to say that the disciple's sword stroke is to the traitor's
kiss what the cock-crow--(announced by Jesus)--is to the "traitor's" word of denial? The sign is again on the order of a
(no doubt animal) language, but it is announced by Jesus. It
is a signifier carried by a sub-human voice, but it is attributed to the prediction of God. It is what will interrupt
Peter's denials by a reminder of Jesus's word and begin the
remorse.

THE REMORSE

We will not emphasize the third moment of the correlation
of "Judas" and "Peter", the remorse. We have already analyzed
the return of the thirty pieces of silver to the Temple, and
then the throwing of them outside of the Jewish religious community in the form of a Field of Death for strangers. This is
a metaphoric-metonymic figure reversed from the signifier line
which will lead to the universal community.[144] The remorse
and the death of Judas appears to us to be strictly connected
to this turning upside down of the initial signifier of exchange and to its extinction, once its office is performed.
Judas discovers, because everything has now been *done* and *said*
--the eucharistic meal, the trial before the Sanhedrin--that
the operation of substitution and neutralization of the signifiers of which he has been the operator recovered, at the
same time as its condition and as its occultation, the arrival
of the signified in the signs: "I have sinned in betraying
innocent blood" (Mt. 27:4). Judas discovers that he was the
figure of an operation whose truth could only be perceived
once it was accomplished, because it was the dynamic necessity
of a measurable force, after the fact, simply in its trace.[145]

Just as the signifier which has served to begin the neutralizing exchange, i.e. the silver, can no longer have a narrative existence henceforth, once the substitution and the neutralization of the signifier is realized, so the textual figure

which is that of passage and transformation--once the consumption of the body-subject occurs in the ingestion of the eucharistic bread and wine, and then its transmission-delivery by the [p. 173] signifier contact of two bodies in the kiss--must finally be erased from the narrative text. Its withdrawal from the narrative and its disappearance by hanging are then correlatives of Peter's departure and his "bitter tears". But at this point again the opposition of doing and saying is pursued. The rupture of the denial by the acoustic sign in remembrance of Jesus's *parole* brings about Peter's obliteration in the signifier of the narrative, as the return of the silver to the Temple and its rejection in the Field of Death brings about Judas's obliteration in that which is the being of the text, i.e. the referend [*referend*] that the text designates.

The Two Series

At the end of this analysis of a large segment of the villainy in Matthew, it seems that we can mark out by a chain of privileged signifiers the movement of substitution-neutralization which permits the "turning upside down" of the narrative on itself and its definitive and irreversible overture to its signified: the silver in language signs, and then in material species; the bread and wine in consumable substances; the kiss as a contact of a surface and a sign-gesture; the silver as a signifier rejected in the sacred place; and finally the Field of Blood as the inverted figure of the potter's field to bury strangers in [*la mort étrangère*]. This chain of privileged signifiers is in some way doubled by another chain of signifiers carried by "Peter", which is unbalanced in relationship to the first and functions within language and the voice of the affirmation of fidelity in the reminder of Jesus's *parole*. These two chains intersect one another in the eucharistic meal where Peter and Judas consume the body of Jesus. But with this difference, this gap or this signifier staggering between the two signifier series, that one consumes his body AFTER having already betrayed him and the other BEFORE entering a situation of treason. This gap between the two series, the place where the difference is produced, and by being produced engenders the meaning of the narrative, is indeed the center of the narrative in its structure, but it is empty. It is only filled by an "other" of the text that the latter is content to designate in its absence by the text itself. It is a place of the neutral of the exchange in which the signifiers turn upside down one moment in the insignificance with reference to the narrative in order to carry then the signifieds of which they were deprived.

Chapter VI

REMARKS CONCERNING THE VARIANTS
AND GENERAL CONCLUSIONS

THE VARIANT FROM LUKE

The compound* table, when compared with the simple table
(Mark and Matthew), reveals the presence of an additional correlation braided with the large correlation of "Judas" and
"Peter". It is the articulation of these two correlations on
the syntagmatic line of the narrative which ought--it seems to
us--permit us to resolve the problem posed by the variant from
Luke. In effect, the order of narrative sub-segments is the
following: IA -- IB -- IIA -- IIB IC -- IIC -- IIIB -- IIIA
-- IIIC --. The braiding of the correlates comes into play
with lines I and II. Everything takes place as if the narrative reserved, for its temporary conclusion, the grouping of
correlates C from lines I and II. We recall that elements B
from the table are the central elements of correlations whose
connected correlates are elements A and C.

THE TWO TREASONS AND THE TWO MEALS

In other words, if in the syntagmatically designed table
the announcement of Judas's treason *follows* the eucharistic
meal instead of *preceding* it, as in all the other variants,
it is necessary to perceive that the announcement *belongs* in
reality *to the meal*. It is what marks on the one hand, the
continuity of Jesus' discourse, "this is my blood of the new
covenant which is poured out for many" (Mt. 26:28; Mk. 14:24).
However, "behold the hand of him who betrays me is with me on
the table...etc." (Lk. 22:21); and on the other hand, the
present, "him who betrays me", [p. 175] ἡ χεὶρ τοῦ παραδιδόν-
τος (Lk. 22:21) in contrast to the future παραδῶσέι of Mark's
and Matthew's text. The displacement on the syntagmatic line
of the announcement of the treason within the *"central sub-
segment"* confirms our analysis of the traitor in the eucharistic meal by reinforcing it. The traitor is a consumer of
the body and blood of Jesus; he is for that very reason his
donor.

---

complexe means both "complex" and "compound".

167

On the other hand, it will be noted that the announcement of Judas's treason precedes the "eucharistic meal" and is found correlated with the announcement of Peter's treason, beyond a dispute among the Twelve which Jesus resolves. In this way the problem of the new universal community connected to the new covenant, but also to the eucharistic meal, is presented. But in addition, just as the announcement of Judas's treason belongs to the eucharistic meal, *the announcement of Peter's denial also belongs to the eucharistic meal.* Now this meal is a meal in discourse--in language. It is the solution, projected into the eschaton, of the dispute, "Who is the greatest?" (Lk. 22:24-27). That is to say, the universal fraternal community of the New Covenant in the blood and body of Jesus. From then Simon-Peter is simultaneously the one who will *turn back* to strengthen his brothers,[147] and the one who will betray Jesus, but in *paroles.*

The direction of research that we are suggesting is therefore the syntagmatic projection of the element of the compound* table which reveals the telescoping of IB and IIA and IC and IIC. In other words, the first two lines of the table could be written:

IA (IB IIA) IIB (IC IIC)

This new transcription, which is a transformation of the compound table constructed on a ternary base with a double correlation, reveals a double binary articulation on a single line of the table, which is very significant, since the Paschal meal is found correlated with the "Who is the greatest?" dispute, and then the eucharistic meal with the eschatological meal. Just as the present treason of Judas is correlated with the future denial of Peter.

In effect, it can be thought that the dispute poses the problem of political messianism in the entourage of Jesus, and the response of Jesus repeats *on the mode of discourse*, what the Johannine variant with the washing of feet had presented in the reading *about the mode of the narrative.* "For which is [p. 176] the greater, the one who sits at table, or the one who serves? Is it not the one who sits at table? But I am among you as the one who serves" (Lk. 22:27). Will the ancient rite of the Jewish Passover not be correlated with the

---

*See the earlier note about the dual meaning of this word on p. 167.

ancient "Judaic" form of the community? From then on the eucharistic meal, which institutes the new rite of consumption
of God, which Judas betrays by sharing in it, but which he institutes in turn by the fundamental exchange which constitutes
this consumption, is articulated in the eschatological meal,
in the banquet--a fraternal judgment in the Kingdom of the
Son. This meal is a meal to come--at the end of time--that
of the realized universal community.

But that must be constituted in time and in the test--and
here is the point where the announcement of Peter's future
"treason" is articulated, in the evocation of the eschatological meal, in which Peter is simultaneously the foundation rock*
of the community and the traitor, the denegator. Peter is the
founder because he was a denegator, as Judas was the donor of
Jesus because he was a consumer. "Simon, Simon, behold Satan
has demanded to have you, that he might sift you like wheat"
(Lk. 22:31). "But I have prayed for you that your faith may
not fail; and when you have turned again (i.e. returned from
the denying flight which is the satanic sieve) strengthen your
brethren" (i.e. be the foundation of the fraternal community)
(Lk. 22:32).

The Sword Stroke and the Kiss

Line III in the compound* table introduces as the "center"
of the correlation the "realization of the treasons", which we
have called "the moment of the sword and darkness", by repeating the final sentence of Lk. 22:53 and by putting it into relation with the segment Lk. 22:35-38.[148] If this relation appears to us to be necessary to be introduced here in order to
take account of a remarkable articulation of reading, it does
not pose difficult problems to the analysis in the least. "And
let him who has no sword sell his mantle and buy one" (Lk. 22:
36). This is the advice given by Jesus to his disciples in Lk.
22:35-38. The moment is no longer in the free gift and in the
mission which is accomplished with ease and fullness, but in
the struggle and precisely in the beginnings for the purpose
of preparing for resistance and the struggle. Nevertheless,
this struggle which must effectively take place, seems indeed
to assume a [p. 177] symbolic character: "Lord shall we strike
with the sword?", the disciples ask (Lk. 22:49). And the
stroke of the sword blade [le coup de glaive] cuts off the ear
of the servant. "No more of this," Jesus then says, making
amends for the injury by healing the servant of the Chief

*See the note at the bottom of p. 167.

Priest. And Jesus adds to the intention of those "who had come out against him, 'Have you come out as against a robber, with swords and clubs?'" (Lk. 22:52). But have not the disciples also come out with swords? This is the difficulty of reading into its very articulation.

The first remark that we can present on this subject concerns the interesting correlation of the kiss and the sword stroke: "Judas, would you betray the Son of Man with a kiss?", Luke writes (Lk. 22:48 paraphrased). The kiss of Judas is not coded as a sign. It is the gesture by which *the subject* is *delivered* and *given*. On the other hand, we have the feeling that the sword stroke is coded, but without a deciphering of the code of the sign being given. The conjunction or the contact of Judas and Jesus (the kiss) is the gesture of disjunction and separation of the subject from the sphere of the helper, the delivery itself of the object. The sword stroke which cuts off the ear is a gesture of disjunction and separation to the opponent which the gesture of contact with Jesus annuls: "And he touched his ear and healed him" (Lk. 22:51) is a correlation which can be summarized in this way:

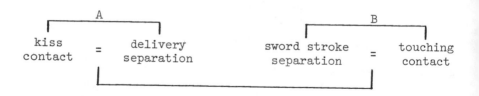

Thus narrative correlation B seems to have the function of annulling correlation A. In other words, more than Matthew or Mark, the narrative from Luke with its difference strives to insure the exchange of the object without impediment and this is why the sword stroke is effaced in its result by a "kiss" of Jesus on the instrument of transmission, the servant. It is a contact which marks the conjunction of the subject and his enemies, and the entrance of the subject into the sphere of the opponent. And it is indeed necessary that this entrance be made in one way or another, since on the syntagmatic line of Luke's narrative, the trial before the Sanhedrin will take place *after* the realization sequences of the treasons.

In this way therefore the traitor's kiss to Jesus which is the transfer of the subject-object to the opponent is found mediatized in Luke--[p. 178] because the subject-object has again not acceded to the fullness of the signified--by a "kiss" of Jesus to the opponent, a consequence of the confrontation of the helper and the opponent. It was necessary that the traitor be "doubled" in order that the transmission be carried out, that Jesus or his companions be comprised of robbers--of resisters and no doubt of political resisters--in order that the subject-object pass to the enemy in order to arrive at its essential mutation from pure signifier into signifier-signified. "Purchase some swords and provisions" in order that *"this parole of Scripture will be fulfilled in me: 'he was put in the ranks of the scoundrels'"*, Jesus declares (Lk. 22:36-37 paraphrased). It is then that Peter's "treason" in discourse which is a general correlate of the ensemble of relations that we have just studied can be introduced into the analysis.

THE JOHANNINE VARIANT

In the examination of the Johannine variant, we will limit ourselves once again to some indications of research, especially since we have already analyzed certain fragments. The essential difference which the variant introduces consists in the fact that the meal, which begins the washing of the disciples' feet and where the "treasons" of Judas and Peter are found denounced, is not a eucharistic meal in which Jesus will be consumed by the traitor in order to neutralize the total signifier of the body-*parole*.

Negative Eucharist

A certain number of consequences result from this difference the examination of which would return us to a general study of the contexture of the entire Johannine variant. The first is that the subject comes in some way to exchange itself into its significance, by using, even by provoking, the services of the traitor. By revealing the identity of the traitor by a gift of a morsel of bread to Judas, Jesus gives himself, delivers himself, or radically reverses himself into his significance. "Who is the traitor?," Peter and John ask. "Jesus answered, 'It is he to whom I shall give this morsel when I have dipped it.' So when he had dipped the morsel, he gave it to Judas, the son of Simon Iscariot. *Then after the morsel, Satan entered into him*" (Jn. 13:26-27). By a kind [p. 179] of negative Eucharist, where the bread and wine are mixed in the dipped morsel, Jesus indicates Judas to be the traitor. He indicates Judas as the one who, eating with him, gives Jesus to be eaten. The traitor is indeed one who eats with Jesus, to whom Jesus gives the bread and wine to eat and drink in the same morsel. But this gift of food is a satanic gift, a gift from the non-God.

In other words, the exchange which the traitor produces not only consists, as in the other variants, of annulling the signifier by the consumption of the *body-parole*, a prelude and condition of his transmission-treason to this other annulment of which the first figure is the death on the cross, in order to permit him to cohere with [*cohère avec*] his signified, God living in the universal community. But again the exchange performed by the traitor consists of inverting this signifier into its contradictory, of making it a non-divine signifier. And it is then, and only then, that the signifier can create a turning upside down to its signified--at this point of the text--and become the signifier-signified, the glorified Son in the glory of the Father. "When he (Judas) had gone out, Jesus said, 'Now is the Son of Man glorified, and in him God is glorified; if God is glorified in him, God will also glorify him in himself, and glorify him at once'" (Jn. 13:31-32). This is indeed the "sign" of the departure to the unique sig- nified where the signifier finds its consistency. The an- nouncement of Peter's "treason" must be understood in this perspective.

The traitor in the Johannine variant by his presence at the meal where Jesus gives himself to be eaten, permits in one single movement the transformation of the signifier into a sign, and he gives the solution to the problem of the text, the death of God and the arrival of the moral in the eternal community according to the following schema:

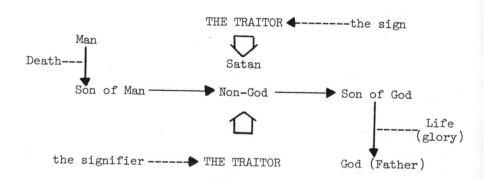

The traitor is the figure manifested in the narrative of this passage by the contradictory which John names Satan, the operator of the semantic transformation, the place which is

empty in the structure, but [p. 180] named in the narrative,
thanks to which the metonymy of the signifiers can be completed and fulfilled in the filled metaphor of the signified.

How is the Object Transmitted?

The second indication of the research refers to the
realization of the treachery. It will have been noted that
it is impossible for the subject hero to be stopped, i.e. that
the object-subject is transmitted, in short that the treachery
is realized. Twice *Jesus gives himself up as an object to be
transmitted* and twice it seems that the cohort and the guards
are separated from him. Judas leads them, and guides them in
order to perform the delivery of the object (Jn. 18:5), but
the delivery cannot be accomplished. It will only be accomplished at the moment when *Peter*, who removes the spell in
some way, strikes with his sword, the servant of the Chief
Priest, named Malchus. It is a blow given by Peter on the
body of the opponent which cuts off a part from him, his ear,
which permits the realization of the treason. The traitor or
the transmitter is Peter here, and the sword stroke is the
negative of the kiss which Judas does not give to Jesus in
this variant. While the contact of Judas with the body-object
of the subject permitted the separation and the transmission,
it is here the separation of the body of the opponent which
permits the transmission of the object to the opponent himself. It is then the helper who is the operator of this
transmission (the helper is therefore a traitor).

Therefore the Johannine variant presents a remarkable
example of an inversion of terms and functions in its difference with the three variants according to the canonical formula:

$$F \; x \; (a) : F \; y \; (b) \simeq Fx \; (b) : Fa \; -- \; 1 \; (y)$$

The function of transmission by the bodily contact (the conjunction) is to the function of opposition of the subject, as
the function of transmission of the subject is to the function
of bodily non-contact (or disjunction-separation) of the opponent. The traitor on the first side of the equation is Judas.
The traitor on the second side is Peter.

This working hypothesis appears to us to be confirmed by a
study of the correlation of "Judas" and "Peter" in this variant.
It will be noted that the narrative segment of Peter's denials
is literally braided with the judgment of Jesus by [p. 181]

Annas and Caiaphas. And is it not a servant of the Chief Priest, "a kinsman of the man whose ear Peter had cut off",[149] who provokes Peter's third and last denial, a separation in *parole* of the "traitor" from his appurtenance to Jesus? Just as he had separated in act the ear from the body of the opponent in order to permit the transmission of Jesus to the opponent. And we will note that nowhere is mention made of Peter's remorse. Because of its specific contexture of narrative and discourse, of which we have already spoken, the Johannine variant allots the function of treason, i.e. the operation of inversion of the content, to two manifest figures who, entirely by being correlates, take turns from one another: first Judas, then Peter. This is only one of the lesser paradoxes of this analysis.

CONCLUSION

The System of the Text

At the end of this very long study we would like to draw attention to some points which could constitute some useful research hypotheses for the future. First there is the construction starting from the multiple analyses which we have made of what we have called the system of the text: a system whose four variants constitute the dimensions articulated by some rules of transformations which we have given some examples of with some particular segments of the text. Clearly indeed, in this study dealing with the traitor we have extracted from the text the moments which appeared to us to be the most directly important for our purpose. And at the same time it seems difficult for us to be able to sketch out the system in its totality.

But perhaps we can indicate its heuristic function. It is twofold. On the one hand, it articulates the corpus in our arbitrarily determined boundaries and thereby accomplishes its temporary closure. "To articulate" means here to connect the elements of the corpus by some relations which are coherent between them. On the other hand, it furnishes a binding kernel for other textual elements which could ulteriorly be integrated in it. The corpus is an open corpus according to the dimensions and rules of coherence of the dimensions between them, constituted by the variants initially retained and the [p. 182] circular transformations[150] which permit us to obtain them. In this double sense, the system of the text has a heuristic function for a specific ensemble of texts and is like a crystallizer of other texts.

The Surface Figure

A second direction of the research of equal importance is suggested more particularly by this study: that which marks the return to the superficiality of the text. But as we understand it, it is by no means a question of abandoning the solid abstractions of structural analysis, the formalizable relations which permit it to construct, between the reduced elements which find their position and for that very reason their intelligibility, the ruled variances of the structures between them, i.e. the relational invariances of a specific system of structures. All these constructions can only be carried out at the price of a reduction of the lexical--semantic and syntactic--elements that the text offers to the immediate reading, and to the semic elements being defined by the different relations of position and of negation which they maintain, at the price of the establishment of schemas, models, or the most general formulas. And the system of the text is one of them-- permitting us to understand the functioning of an ensemble of texts, even to foresee certain traits of its functioning, and to require here or there necessarily the presence or absence of a segment, a group of functions, and a function.

But the question which we ran into with the traitor, in these four variant-texts, was the presence of an element from the surface which could, to be sure, be projected on the meta-linguistic levels of the analysis, but which preserved its compound* nature by being at the same time "neither one, nor the other", and also "the one and the other". It was the mediator in the structure who permitted its construction. It was the mediation itself, we know, which has the characteristic of not being any of the contraries (*ne---uter*, neither the one, nor the other) *and* of being the two contraries at the same time (the one and the other). Whether the narrative structure is expressed in its diachronic form or in its syn- or a-chronic form, this empty/filled point always exists, *in* the structure around which the diachrony pivots and reverses the [p. 183] invested contents of the narrative, by which the syn-/a-/ chronic relation of double correlation is indicated as relation. In every case, an element appears, indeed a sign which was present only one time in a formula, but starting from which and around which all the other elements developed their recurrences, their iterations, and their correlations.

We have named this empty/filled unnameable point of the structure "the traitor". He is a figure of it--it is only a

---

*See the note at the bottom of p. 167.

figure in the structure since that of which it is the figure can only be introduced in a non-structural form, that of a non-relational element, a source of all the relations. Or again, and it is in this way that we understand this return to the superficiality of the text, the traitor was, in the deep structure of the narrative, an element from the surface which manifested in depth that of which the surface is the bearer, and only that. He is the force of the narrative whose factual superficial contingency is necessary in order that the relations be knotted and articulated, in order that the structure be outlined starting from their transformations, and in order that the system of the text be constructed starting from the mutual structural representations.

The Unmotivated Substitutions

The third direction of research will then be--and we have made an attempt to do this in this study--to conceive this surface role, this figure of the traitor (as a mediator) as the exchanger of the signifiers of the text, at one manifest point of the narrative where the inversions are necessary, that is to say where the structure is going to "take", where its symmetries in negative and positive, contraries and contradictories are going to crystallize, and where the correlations are going to find their correlates by spanning it. Then the contingent intervenes, that which in an unmotivated act will substitute for the chains of signifiers a new series at one point which is at the same time the point where it annuls--neutralizes the signifiers and divides this blank space, opened in this way for the reception of the new series. Reflection about this process of substitution--annulment in the exchange --has occupied us for a long time in the preceding pages.

We can designate three forms in it (starting from the texts studied); but no doubt they are generalizable, at least in certain areas of culture. The first is the [p. 184] monetary substitution. The perfume is exchanged in discourse for three hundred denarii, the Son of Man for thirty. It is indeed a matter of a substitution of a specific signifier for a signifier which can be all the signifieds, which is none of them: the totally neutralizing signifier.

The second is the alimentary substitution, that of the food and the consumption of the body. To eat and to drink are double-sided processes. In effect, the transformation of the other into the same (into itself), the assimilation (*Eritis sicut Dei*), is preceded--perhaps it is only its other side-- by the moment of the pure destruction, the immediate annulment, and the neutral moment of every transformation. The nature of the traitor in our text will have been to continue and to be presented as the figure of this other of the assimilation, and the constitution of the signifier in a sign.

The third is the corporeal substitution: the anointing, the kiss, and the sword stroke, which are contacts of conjunction or separation, but which are inverted into the contact itself and into their contraries. The touching or touching lightly are wrenching [arrachement], schism, and rupture. Here again we note in the immediacy, in the violence, or in the blindness of the gesture, the point where the exchange is performed, in an instant, the point at which the gesture is another signifier and at first a flashing and empty instant. Quite evidentally, these three forms on which some works by scholars have already been carried out, starting from theoretical or practical (cultures, civilizations, economies) texts, are tightly connected.[151] They form a system, flowing from one another, designating one another, and being transformed one into another.

One of the most remarkable modes of this interplay of the process of substitution, of which the figurative operator is the traitor, is constituted by two "regimes" of the text: the narrative and the discourse. The narrative can be, for example, that of a meal; but this meal can only have the reality of a discourse in the text. However it is compared from this point of view, Judas selling the perfume "in discourse" at Bethany or selling Jesus "in narrative" at Jerusalem, or the eucharistic-narrative meal and the eschatological-discourse meal, etc., it will not be insignificant that the substitution is made from one regime to another, from the diegetic* to the mimetic*, or vice versa. And we will note that the privileged regime of the traitor is the diegetic.* It is the place where the decisive exchanges of the signifier are carried out, [p. 185] because it is perhaps the place where the most primitive transformation-substitution of all is performed, that by which a fragment of the real, the world, and history* becomes a text from an event [coup]. In this sense, the first traitor of the story is the one who has narrated it for the first time, *after* having lived it, *instead of* living it.

---

*diegetic--according to Plato, "diegesis" is "the poet speaking in his own name without trying to make us believe that it is another who speaks".

*mimetic--according to Plato, "mimesis" is "the poet speaking in the voice of the character himself".

178

The last direction of research is indicated in these interplays of substitution; among a great many others we would
like to allude to: the relation which maintains the space,
the body, and the text. In the preceding study of the places
of the narrative and earlier of parabolic discourse,[152] we
have explored the organizations of the space in the text, of
the text as space, and of the space as text. And we have perceived the importance at certain moments of the text of the
passage from narrative to discourse, that this discourse may
be moreover a narrative or a narrative of a narrative, or that
it possesses another value than narrative or constative, performative, imprecatory, proclamatory, exhortative, or orant
[*orante*]. In these simultaneous recoveries, in the systema-
tics of the text, and succession, in its syntagmatic, the meaning of the text is developed, not mechanically or deductively
by necessary constructions, but in the form of planes of substitutive interplays which are reciprocally or even hierarchi-
cally restrained, entirely by stirring up or reactivating one
another.

But these dynamic activations, these substitutions by
which the signifiers pass from one regime to another, and from
one modalization to another, cannot--it seems to me--be comprised by the structural models, although they cannot be comprised without them. It is necessary that some exchanges constantly occur between the construction of the model and the
surface of the text which, metalinguistically, provoke the
meanings. Our study of the traitor has attempted to be a particular work about one of these exchanges. But what it has
taught us--and indeed our study about the places of the narrative already pointed to this idea--is that the relation of the
space and the text is only intelligible beyond a simple topography, topics, or topology. That the signifier substitutions which constitute the text in its dynamic are not only in
the narrative-text [p. 186] or discourse--some journeys and
displacements, some orientations or miscarriages--but that
they call into play not only geographic but "biological" processes. There is a body of the text, as well as a space of
the text. And the space of the text is that of its body, that
is to say of the body which it dismembers, which it articulates, but also which it produces in its surface and its functions, in short in its unseizable force as such, but only in
the marks that it leaves on its surface and which the reading
and the writing of the text tirelessly retrace. The text is
thus, in its space of writing and reading, the most powerful
phantasm of the body.

But was this not the fundamental interest, the "original" interest of the texts which we studied: to put in their center this relation between the *parole*, or indicatory *parole*, the force, a transforming power of the discourse, and the body as that of the *parole* and of the recitable and consumable food, recitable as consumable--consumable as recitable? A relation which is a fulfillment of the Scripture, but by which a universal community becomes knotted. Was it not the "original" interest of the text studied in its four dimensions to connect then to this relation between the *parole*, the force, and the body, between the archaic writing and history to come, the traitor in the double figure: that of the exchanger by neutralization and annulment of the signifiers, the "donor" Judas and that of the founder of the signs by a denegative position in the language, the "founding" rock of the community, Peter.

Appendix I

ON THE NOTION OF AN INDEX:
SOME EXTRACTS FROM C. S. PEIRCE

ICON--INDEX--SYMBOL

Signs can be divided according to three classifications. First, according to whether or not the sign itself is a simple quality, an existing reality or a general law. Second, according to whether the relation of the sign to its object consists in the fact that the sign possesses a characteristic by itself or in an existential relation to this object or in its relation to an interpreter. Third, according to whether its interpreter represents it as the sign of a possibility, a fact, or a reason...

(Extracted from *"Logic as Semiotic: the Theory of Signs"*, op. *cit.*, p. 101.)*

According to the second trichotomic classification, a sign can be an icon, an index, or a symbol. An icon is a sign which refers to the object which it denotes only by virtue of characteristics which are peculiar to it and which it possesses, whether the object referred to really exists or not....

An index is a sign which refers to the Object that it denotes by the fact of being really affected by this Object. This is why it cannot be a quali-sign[1] because qualities are what they are, independently of every other thing. To the extent to which the index is affected by the Object, it necessarily has some qualities in common with the Object; and it is as a function of them that it [p. 188] refers itself to the Object. This is why it includes a kind of Icon, though of a particular kind. The index is not a simple resemblance with its Object, even with regard to what constitutes it as a sign, but it is its real modification by the Object.

(Extracted from *"Logic as Semiotic: the Theory of Signs"*, op. *cit.*, p. 102.)

---

*   This Appendix was translated from Marin's text.

1. A quali-sign is a quality which is a sign.

A sign is either an icon, an index, or a symbol. The icon is a sign which possesses a character which makes it a signifier, even if its object does not exist. Thus a pencil draws in so far as it represents a geometric line. The index is a sign which will instantaneously lose the character which makes it a sign, if its object is withdrawn. But it will not lose its signifier character, if it has no interpreter. Thus, for example, a piece of molding containing a bullet hole is the sign of a gun-shot, because without the gun-shot, it would not have a hole. But the hole exists there in the piece of iron, even if no one had the idea of attributing it to a gun-shot. A symbol is a sign which loses its signifier character if it has no interpreter. Thus an occurrence of *parole* only signifies what it signifies because it is understood that it has this signification.

The Index

An index is a sign or a representation which refers to its object, not so much because it has some similarity or analogy with it, nor because it is associated with the general characteristics that this object would be capable of possessing, but because it is in a dynamic (including spatial) relation at the same time with the individual object and with the meaning or the memory of the person who serves as a sign himself....The demonstrative and personal pronouns are in their ordinary usage "true indices", while the relative pronouns are "degenerated indices". Although they can, in effect, accidentally and indirectly refer to some existing things, they refer directly and they have no other function than to refer themselves to the images that the antecedent words have created in spirit.

Three characteristic marks distinguish the indices from other signs in representations: first, they do not have any signifier resemblance with their objects. Second, they [p. 189] refer to some individual, singular unit(s), singular collections of units or singular continuums. Third, they direct attention to their objects by a blind constraint. However, it would be difficult, if not impossible, to give an example of an absolutely pure index, or on the contrary to find a sign devoid of every indicational quality. Psychologically, the action of the index depends on the association by contiguity and not on the association by resemblance, or on intellectual operations.

An index or seme (σῆμα) is a representamen whose representative character consists in the act of being a "second"

individual.[2] If this "secondariness" is an existential relation, the index is said to be "true". If the "secondariness"
is referential, the index is said to be "degenerate". A true
Index and its Object must be of existing individuals (whether
it be a matter of things or acts). Its immediate interpretant
must possess the same characteristic. But since every individual must have its own characteristics, it follows that a true
Index can contain a "primariness" and therefore an icon as a
constituent part. Every individual is an Index stripped of
its own characteristics.

The sub-index or hypotheses are signs which are made so
principally because of a real relation with their objects.
Thus a proper noun, a demonstrative, personal, or relative
pronoun, or even the letter inscribed on a diagram denotes
their function, thanks to a real relationship with their objects, but not one of them is an index since it is not an individual.

(Extracts from *"Logic as Semiotic: the Theory of Signs"*, *op.
cit.*, pp. 104 and 107.)

---

2.   Peirce defines the sign or representamen as a *"first"*
which is connected by a triangular relation to a *"second"*
called its Object, a relationship so primary that it is capable
of determining a *"third"*, called its Interpretant and having
the same triangular relation to its Object that it maintains
to the same object. This triangular relationship is called
primary in that these three moments are connected by it in
such a way that it cannot consist of a compound of dual relations. [p. 190]

Appendix II

ON THE NOTION OF A CODE

I. We will limit ourselves to recalling here a certain number of texts: first of all, those of Roman Jakobson.[1] After having indicated two very important problems posed in structural linguistics by the rejection of the "monolithism" of language and by the recognition of "the interdependence of different structures within a single *langue*", he adds: "Without a doubt, there exists a unit(y) of the *langue* for every linguistic community and for every speaking subject, but this global code represents a system of sub-codes in reciprocal communication. Each *langue* includes several simultaneous systems; each of which is characterized by a different function."

In other words, the code is assimilated here to the *langue*; even if one must, with Jakobson, analyze this global code into sub-codes. We are referring therefore to the Saussurian concept of *langue*, "a social part of language, external to the individual which he alone can neither create, nor modify...of a homogeneous nature. It is a system of signs in which the only essential thing is the union of meaning and the acoustic image." It is therefore "a purely social object, a systematic ensemble of the conventions necessary to communication, and unconcerned with the substance of the signs which compose it".

II. As Roland Barthes emphasizes, the assimilation of the code to the *langue*, and the *parole* to the message, is not possible in Hjelmslev's perspective, since he distinguishes three planes in the *langue*: 1) the schema or *langue* as a pure form (this is the [p. 191] "system" or the "pattern" of the *langue*); 2) "the norm which is the *langue* as a material form already defined by a certain social realization, but still independent of the detail of this manifestation; 3) the usage which is the *langue* as a collection of habits of a given society".[2]

---

1. *Essais de Linguistique générale*, "Linguistique et Poétique", pp. 213-214.

2. R. Barthes, *Eléments de sémiologie*, Paris: Gonthier, 1964, p. 85ff.

III. If, however, the identification[3] is accepted, it will be necessary, as R. Jakobson suggests, to analyze closely the complex functioning of the code in the elaboration of the message. From this point of view, one can define, with Granger,[4] in contradistinction to a pure system of coding in the strict sense of the word, the superimpositions of codes that every message makes use of. A coding system, in the strict sense of the word, is a system of transcription from a *langue* corresponding to the condition of rigorous uniformity. Granger takes the example of morse code in which "the imperative and exhaustive grammar" prohibits by its nature every possibility of superimposition of multiple codes. This would be the fundamental characteristic of a code in the strict sense of the word. And the author can give, by following the works of Chomsky, Turing, and Post, and Kleene and McNaughton on automatons,[5] a purely formal definition of a code: "If X is the collection of symbols constituting the alphabet; the collection L of the words of the code will be a sub-monoid $L(X)$ constructed on X, so that: 1) There exists a part A of L which produces L by the operation of iteration $L = A$ (i.e. an iteration or a "star operation"*) 2) Every word of L is decomposable in a single way into a concatenation of words from A."

But as soon as a coding is "envisaged in its concrete realization"--even in the case of the transcription of a sequence of a *langue* into morse code--one or several codes superimposes itself on the principal code, "those which cause the independent diversity of the [p. 192] possible material representations of the symbols, by the variations of intensity

---

3. Cf. for example, A. Martinet, *Eléments de linguistique générale*, Paris: Colin, 1960.

4. G. G. Granger, *Essai d'une philosophie du style*, Paris: A. Colin, 1968, p. 188ff.

5. Cited by G. G. Granger, *op. cit.*, p. 150: McNaughton, *The Theory of Automata*; a survey in Fr. Alt, *Advances in Computers*, II, 1961. Kleene, *Representation of Events in Nerve Nets and Finite Automata* in *Automata Studies*, Shannon and McCarthy, 1956 ed. Chomsky, *Formal Properties of Grammars* in Luce, Bush, Galanter, eds., *Handbook of Mathematical Psychology*, II, 12--1963. See also M. Gross and A. Lentin, *Notions sur les grammaires formelles*, Paris, 1967.

*On "star operations", see R. Barthes, *S/Z*, trans. R. Miller, New York: Hill and Wang, 1974, pp. 13ff.

and rhythm of manual operations which their transmission implies.

IV. The distinction which Granger introduces then between *a priori* and *a posteriori* codes is of very great value, and at the same time it is heuristic and explicative. The *langue*, from this point of view, possesses some *a priori* codes which are its syntax and its semantics, whose rules, entirely by remaining unformulated, constitute the basic pattern. The *a posteriori* codes would then be those which necessarily generate the usage of the *langue*. It would then be a matter of "free systems extemporaneously constituted and readable *a posteriori* in the message". The analysis must then be aimed at the specific organization of those free systems according to different approaches that Granger characterized under three headings: 1) a "variation" of "entropy" of the messages compared with a middle entropy of a corpus; 2) the presence of "supra-codes" superimposed, properly speaking, on the lower codes; 3) the possibility of a "transformational" origin of neutral messages".[6] We are referring to them. As far as we are concerned, our analysis would belong to headings 2 and 3 (it is in this sense that we speak of a "code articulated in an open way") in the position of carrying out the transfer of all the remarks that we have just made at what Benveniste calls "a meta-semantic" level, the level whose objects are the texts, the works and the artistic objects. Thus we ought to presuppose with R. Barthes, and before him with Propp and Greimas, a *langue* of the narrative whose unit(y) would constitute the global code.... [p. 193]

---

6. G. G. Granger, *op. cit.*, p. 193.

Appendix III

ON A TOPONYM

With the toponym "Mount of Olives" and moreover with the
"Temple" (see the following page) a fundamental problem is
posed, which concerns not only the theory of the proper name,
but likewise the very hypothesis which we are attempting to
validate. Can the Mount of Olives (τό ὄρος τῶν Ἐλαιῶν) be
considered to be a true proper name? Because in the expression, "Mount" and "Olives" are common nouns, and at the same
time they can enter into some signifier paradigms. The same
remark can be made concerning the term "Temple" (τὸ ἱερόν).
The objection is found at the level of a consideration of what
could be called the lexicon, by taking "Mount of Olives" or
"Temple" as some simple, isolated, or independent nouns outside of their contexts of use. These names can then be interpreted by an enunciation of their definition, i.e. by
transposing them into one or several series of interpretants.
For example, the paradigm will be used according to the meaning: "Mount of Olives" will become a "mountain or elevation
of earth where olives, or trees of the species X producing
some fruits of that kind are planted in a Mediterranean climate". Likewise "Temple" will be transformed into "a holy
edifice where religious ceremonies are organized".

On the other hand, when the analysis is carried out on a
text, at the beginning on a narrative and its singular curve,
as is the case here, the common nouns can then have access to
the "dignity of the proper", to the extent to which, in the
context of use, at the level of the narrative syntagms and in
the constitution of the [p. 194] narrative paradigms, "Mount
of Olives" and "Temple" designate and indicate this elevation
on the other side of the Kidron, facing Jerusalem. It is a
named place [lieu-dit], or indeed the only holy edifice (or
that which the Jews want to be unique) where they practiced
their worship. We must therefore consider where they appear
in the narrative to be a quasi-index whose value is uniquely
referential: this hill in the world in Palestine; this temple
at Jerusalem. It could, moreover, be noted that the other two
geographic determinants of the Mount of Olives, Bethany and
Bethphage, are analyzable and reducible into common nouns--
as well as proper nouns. And henceforth the proper nouns,
Bethany and Bethphage, can enter into some signifier systems
by etymological analysis, for example that of a *house* (Beth-),
as *Mount* of Olives could be that of a mountain, and *the Temple*

that of a Temple. And it is understood that the analysis of
Cl. Lévi-Strauss in *la Pensée sauvage* [*The Savage Mind*] can
develop, according to this half-etymological, half-functional
line of research, the "etma" referring to the function and
vice-versa.

In this same perspective, it can moreover be shown that
Mount of Olives, by the specific appurtenance of the olive in
a specific botanical species referring to some faunistic, cli-
matic, economic associations, refers or rather enters into a
connoted system that could be signified by the term "Mediterranean". But that is not our problem here, nor any longer our
level of analysis. What interests us is not the proper noun
considered as such, but its integration in some specific discursive ensembles, the passion narratives, and its correct
function in these ensembles. But in these ensembles, the
proper names appear indeed--at first glance--as a quasi-index
with a purely referential value--therefore as an in-signifier.
They have to receive their significance from the narrative
which, at least essentially, will not be fundamentally that of
the olive as a tree of some species, which is found in a Mediterranean climate. What we are trying to show is the way in
which the story (or one story) has taken on these names which
--at first sight once again--indicate, and only indicate, a
place of space, to the point that today for one whose culture
understands this narrative as an archetypical story, the Mount
of Olives first designates this story, before indicating a
geographic place. [p. 195]

In the narratives which we are studying, a compound transformation is performed on these names that an "ancient" story
has already strongly bestowed with meaning and that a more ex-
tensive analysis will have to take into consideration. For
example, as far as the Mount of Olives is concerned--by a
reference to Isaiah...and also for the Temple, it does not
follow at all that in the narratives that we have restricted
to something narrated, the names Mount of Olives or Temple
indicate, on the surface of the text, some specific places of
geographic space that the narratives come to bestow with meaning by some compound operations dealing at the same time with
the signifier and the signified, with the form and the substance of the content. One of these no doubt essential operations will consist, we shall see, in substituting for "Jerusalem" or "the Temple" some generic names for these toponyms.
The city will be used for Jerusalem, or else they will tend to
be obliterated completely--the Temple is no longer mentioned
in the Passion narratives until the resurrection of Jesus.
These common nouns are then indeed different from the "common" origin of Mount of Olives or Temple. [p. 196]

Appendix IV

ON THE DOUBLE

I would like to present in all its generality the problem of duplications within the narrative. One of the approaches to the problem would be, with C. Lévi-Strauss, to consider duplication as a transforming mediation of the initial contradiction. In the present case it would be John who would be the double of Jesus, and not Jesus who would be the double of John, because John dialectically "prepares" for, if that can be said, the story of Jesus which is the story of the opposition of God and man, and Life and death. The story of John, in other words, is *in the narrative*, the representation of the story of Jesus in a narrative within the narrative, which establishes it as the second scene [*scène*] in which the "adventures" of the hero are reflected and produced. We have therefore a case [*affaire*] in the narrative discourse, of a process of duplication of the representation very similar to that which F. Boas and C. Lévi-Strauss have analyzed, one in his *Primitive Art*, the other in his article (published in *Renaissance, Ecole libre des Hautes Etudes de New York* 2-3 [1944-45], pp. 168ff., reprinted in chapter XIII of *Anthropologie structurale*). Finding in the notion of a mask the key to the duality between the setting [*decor*] and the face, the role and the actor, Lévi-Strauss writes: "Their role (the masks in windows) is to offer a series of intermediary forms which insure the passage from the symbol to the signification, from the magical to the normal, from the supernatural to the social. Therefore they have the function of masking and unmasking." The story of John masks and unmasks the story of Jesus, but these two functions are distributed on the syntagmatic line according to two segments articulated by the remark [p. 197] of Herod about Jesus. This remark would correspond precisely to the moment described by Lévi-Strauss when the mask, "by a kind of bifurcation inside out", opens itself into two moieties. The mask of "John" by opening itself makes the moieties of Death and Life appear, which is precisely the "problem" of the story of Jesus. Just as the baptism of Jesus by John would correspond to the "split-representation" in which the actor himself is duplicated in order "literally and figuratively to display the mask at the cost of the wearer". [p. 198]

Appendix V

A READING OF THE 30/300 DENARII
IN LES ROMANS DE LA TABLE RONDE

The intra-textual relation between the numbers 300 de-
narii/30 denarii which we constructed by correlating some
Johannine and Matthean variants has been perceived by the author of *Les Romans de la Table Ronde* which makes from this
correspondence the essential argument for the treason of Judas. It will be noted that the numeric interplay on the point
of meaning in the text which we are reading is found invested
by the medieval author with an economic and institutional signification that he finds in the society which is contemporary
to him. As a seneschal of the house of Jesus-Christ, Judas
has the right on certain days to the tithe of the income of
Our Lord. The correspondence between the two numbers "opens"
a meaning which is indeed *the economy of exchange of the signifier*, but this "open" economy is found invested-specified
by an *economic institution* taken from the historical context
which masks the "aperity" in it, or which closes the productivity in it. This would be the constraint effect of a reading in the system of the text, a reading by which the narrative is recited according to a modality whose signification is
only of textual reflection. We owe to Gilbert Lascault the
knowledge of this text:

"At the time that our Lord was of this world, those of
Rome had put in the country of Judea a bailiff of the name of
Pilate. This Pilate had in his service a knight named Joseph
of Arimathea, who was a high constable of his house, and who,
having met Jesus-Christ in several places, loved him with all
his heart, but did not dare to confess it because of the other
Jews. Because Our Lord had a great many enemies and few disciples, besides, among them, [p. 199] was found one, Judas,
who was not as good as he had wanted. And the others hardly
loved Judas at all, because he was not really gracious; moreover nor did he love them.

Judas was a seneschal of the house of Jesus-Christ, and
for this reason he had a right on certain days to the tithe of
Our Lord's income. Now precisely one of these days, Madame
Saint Mary began to anoint the hair of her son with perfume.
Judas was very angry, because he calculated that this ointment
was worth exactly three hundred denarii and consequently Madame Saint Mary had defrauded him of thirty denarii. In order

193

to recover them, he decided to meet with the enemies of God.

Seven days before the Passover, these men met with a man named Caiaphas in order to examine how they could seize Jesus. Judas went to this meeting. Upon seeing him, those who were there kept silent or changed the subject, because they believed him to be a very good disciple. But he told them that if they wished he would sell them Our Lord for thirty denarii. They answered that they would willingly bribe him, and as one of them had the thirty denarii, he paid him. Then Judas explained to them how they could take his Master, and he advised them not to confuse him with James, who resembled him a great deal for he was his first cousin.

--But, Sire, how do we recognize Jesus-Christ?, they asked.

He responded:
--The one whom I will kiss, seize him."

> (*Les Romans de la Table Ronde*,
> edited by Jacques Boulenger,
> cols. 10-18, 1971, vol. I,
> pp. 156-157) [our translation]

NOTES FOR THE INTRODUCTION

1. Homeostasis is the processes of a stable state implied in a referential communication. Cf. our note 34, p.

2. E. Benvéniste, *Problèmes de Linguistique générale*, Paris: Gallimard, 1966, p. 130. [Our translation.]

3. C. Lévi-Strauss, *Anthropologie structurale*, Paris: Plon, 1958, pp. 70-71. [Our translation.]

4. E. Benvéniste, "Sémiologie de la Langue (2)," *Semiotica* (Mouton) 1 (2, 1969), p. 135. [Our translation.]

5. C. Lévi-Strauss, "Introduction à l'oeuvre de Marcel Mauss" in Marcel Mauss, *Sociologie et Anthropologie*, Paris: P.U.F., 1955.

6. Cf. Michel de Certeau, "L'articulation du 'dire' et du 'faire'", *Etudes théologiques et religieuses* 45 (1, 1970), pp. 25-44. Cf. also n. 3, p. 91; n. 46, p. 106; n. 78, p. 121 above.

7. C. Lévi-Strauss, *La Pensée sauvage*, Paris: Plon, 1962, pp. 285, 286.

8. One will be referred here, moreover, to Goldstein's distinction between *"zeigen"* and *"greiffen"* in his *Etudes sur l'Alphasie*, as well as to Husserl's analysis in his *1re Recherche logique* and to the commentary of Jacques Derrida in *La Voix et le Phénomène*, Paris: P.U.F., 1967. See also the fine work of Tran Duc Tao in *La Pensée* on the gesture of indication.

9. R. Jakobson, *Essais de Linguistique générale*, Paris: Ed. de Minuit, 1965, pp. 177, 178.

10. P. Ricoeur, *Le Conflit des Interpretations-Essais d'Herméneutique*, Paris: Ed. du Seuil, 1969, p. 93.

First Part

NOTES: THE PLACES OF THE NARRATIVE

Chapter One

1.   On the problem of the proper name, the following studies can be cited: A. H. Gardiner, *The Theory of Proper Names. A Controversial Essay*. 2nd ed. London, [p. 201] 1954, discussed by C. Lévi-Strauss, *La Pensée sauvage*, Paris: Plon, 1962, pp. 266-270 in particular. Read also R. Jakobson, *Essais de Linguistique générale*, Paris: Ed. de Minuit, 1963, pp. 177-178. The problem is taken up again and investigated thoroughly by Jacques Derrida, *De la grammatologie*, Paris: Ed. du Seuil, 1968, who discusses the thesis of C. Lévi-Strauss. In another area, see our own studies on the proper name and the pictorial figure in *Etudes sémiologiques*, Paris: Klincksieck, 1971.

2.   We have tackled the problem of the proper name in a study of the pseudonymous and the anonymous concerning the relationship of the Pascalian text and its "author", as this relationship appears in the text itself; and on the other hand, in a study to appear on proper names in the *Utopia* of Sir Thomas More, which presents through their "etymology" the very question which we are raising in this text: the relation between reference and significance. See on this subject our study in collaboration with Gilbert Dagron, "Discours utopique et récit des origines", *Les Annales* (E.S.C.), March, 1979, pp. 290-327.

3.   According to the remarkable suggestion of R. Barthes in "L'analyse structurale du récit. A propos d'Actes X-XI", *Recherches de Sciences religieuses* 58 (1, 1970), p. 21, it would be necessary to generalize and investigate it thoroughly.

4.   On the concept of level, read E. Benvéniste, *Problèmes de linguistique générale*, Paris: Gallimard, 1966, the study on "the levels of linguistic analysis", pp. 119-131.

5.   See our study, "Essai d'analyse structurale d'un récit-parabole: Matthieu 13,1-23", *Etudes théologiques et religieuses* 46 (March, 1971), pp. 35-74. Cf. also the theological section of *Le Récit évangélique*, eds. C. Chabrol and Louis Marin, Paris: Bibliothèque de Sciences religieuses, 1974.

6. We are distinguishing problematic and problem in our terminology. The problematic is a collection of problems forming a network or system, which implies that it is articulatable according to multiple combinations or different developments, of which the preceding page gives an example. It is the metalanguage of problems and questions. Pascal gives in the conclusion of his *Traité des ordres numériques* an excellent description of the problematic as a possibility of multiple developments of a network of problems: "If one does not know how to turn the propositions around in every sense and that one only makes use of the first slant that has been considered, one will never go very far. It is these different paths which open the new consequences and which, by some assorted enunciations on the subject, draw some propositions which would not seem to have any relation to the terms from which they were first conceived."

7. We are repeating here the definition that Peirce gives of the index by itself and in its opposition to the symbol. It will be found in appendix I: *Philosophical Writings of C. S. Peirce*, ed. Justus Buchler, New York: Dover, 1955, p. 104 and p. 107.

8. C. Lévi-Strauss, by posing the question of the integration of proper names in code systems, asks himself if this operation, which consists of "determining the significations by transforming them into the terms of other significations" would be possible "if it were necessary to follow the teaching of the logicians and certain linguists and admit that the proper names are according to Mill's formula 'meaningless', devoid of signification". *Op. cit.*, p. 228. [p. 202]

9. Our study "Textes en representation" in *Critique*, Nov. 1970, can be read on this subject.

10. R. Jakobson, *op. cit.*, pp. 177-178.

11. See also on this point the analysis of the proper name "Schulze" in E. Husserl, *Recherches logiques*, "4° recherche".

12. We are using the term "discourse" here in its most general meaning: an expression of the *langue* as an instrument of communication, a totality whose unit(y) is the sentence. Cf. E. Benvéniste, *op. cit.*, pp. 129-130 and also *idem*, "Sémiologie de la langue", *Semiotica* 1 (1-2, 1969).

13. Read on this subject, G. Genette, *Figures*, Paris: Éd. du Seuil, 1969, p. 101ff.

14. See on this topic the analyses of A. J. Greimas about the anthropomorphic character in the logical categories of the deep grammar, in his *Du sens*, Paris: Ed. du Seuil, 1970, pp. 166-167.

15. Read on this point, A. J. Greimas, *Sémantique structurale*, Paris: Larousse, 1966.

16. This is the passage in the terminology of Greimas from the anthropomorphic categories to the logical categories of the deep grammar.

17. In other words, the term meaning passes here from signification to the direction or to orientation, a passage which is that of the text to space, i.e. a moment when the space of the text is established.

18. The notion of a productive scene is an essential notion that it would be necessary to develop by distinguishing, as we did below, but no doubt very quickly, product and production. The product is the closed textual object which delivers, in its superficiality of reading, the referential reality of its discourse about the mode of reflection. That is why we are speaking of a specular [i.e. mirror] product, hence the power of "the reality effect" about which Barthes has spoken so well. The deconstructive reading of the text in the form of a semiotic analysis will consist of making apparent in the product the marks of its own production, marks which it bears as traces of the constitution of the meaning. One of these traces, which is perhaps privileged, is the network of the places of the text-space in the organization of the toponyms (cf., on the notion of production, M. de Certeau, "Faire de l'histoire-problèmes de méthodes et problèmes de sens", in *Recherches de Sciences Religieuses*, 58 [October-December, 1970], 481-520).

19. A new ambiguity appears at this point in the organization of the narrative, the analysis of which would arise from the phenomenology of the reality effect. A narrative--because it is narrative--gives what is there to be seen in the space of the text, i.e. that which has the simple consistency of a discourse. Under what conditions therefore is the narrative this form of discourse which evokes the "reality" under the species of potential, inchoative figures which its reading makes apparent? The syntagmatic organization of the narrative discourse in its specificity which rigorously makes the most of an apparent *contingence* of the narrative events constitutes no doubt one of these conditions. The semiotic analysis must dissolve this appearance by producing this strictness, by articulating it, as A. J. Greimas does with power in his

narrative grammar, in an achronic, logical organization which gives its texture to the surface discourse. But by dissolving this appearance, it is the specular evocation of the reality which is equally dissolved and the worldly referent reintegrates then the organization of the signifiers in the different [p. 203] developments of meaning. On the other hand, what appears at the end of the analysis at the same time reducing and integrative is another form of reference, that of a space of communication of the discourse whose features, circuits, and limits are themselves marks in the discourse. On this latter problem, in the present study our analysis of the parable of the two sons, p. 65, may be read, and in a more general way here again E. Benvéniste, *op. cit.*, p. 56 and ff. and p. 130. "Those who are in communication have precisely this in common, a certain reference of situation, for want of which communication as such does not take place, the 'sense' being intelligible, but the 'reference' remaining unknown." On the integrative analysis and its relationship with the figure, see our study, "Sur la description de l'image" from *Communications* 15.

20. The notion of a geographic, or better still cartographic space should be introduced here into the analysis and at the same time into the text which is being carefully read: What is the function of the geography map in its illustration of the narrative? And how does the map itself perform a certain reading of the space of the world subject to the same general laws as the reading of the narrative? But also what are its properties? Different maps of the same region at the end of our copy of the Bible, that from l'Ecole biblique de Jerusalem, would obviously show that there is a map of the Palestine of the Old Testament, and a map of the Palestine of the New Testament. Between them, some names are erased, others appear. The same is true for the two Jerusalems. What is there to say, except that we are dealing here with two reading developments [*parcours*] by these "objective figures" which are the maps, two discourse-developments differently accentuated, or differently articulated, and in which in a space which is no longer that of the world, but not yet that of the narratives properly speaking, certain types of transformations are organized which are not yet those of the text, but are close to them, and which prepare for them, by which the worldly referent, or "reality", begins its integration into discourse. See on this problem of the geography map, our *Etudes sémiologiques*, Paris: Klincksieck, 1971, pp. 151-180.

21. A new problem to be pointed out here in the passage, but which we are setting aside by a methodological decision as we indicated below, is the matter of the closure of the text, or of the narrative in all its dimensions. It is one of the

most fundamental methodological questions of structural analysis. See on this subject, our analyses, *op. cit.*, pp. 203-276 and also p. 287ff. As far as the biblical text is concerned, the question becomes: What is the Book? This is a major theological problem, but it is also one of the semiotic problems of the reading. Where does it begin? What is its origin? What is its end?

22. On the notion of a methodological decision and its theoretical implications, cf. Michel de Certeau, *op. cit.*, *Recherches de Sciences religieuses* 58 (October-December, 1970), pp. 481-520.

23. In the spatial and *topic* sense of the term: "to walk in the opposite direction".

24. See Appendix II on the notion of a code.

25. This insignificance is presented in a hypothetical way here.

26. We are borrowing this expression from an unpublished work of Alain Cohen. [p. 204]

Chapter II

27. We are using this term hero in the sense of a particular investment of the "subject" actant according to the model elaborated by A. J. Greimas.

28. But we will see that, except for some references about some points, which it is true are essential, our analyses will be concerned with the three Synoptics.

29. Which signifies that "Jesus" is the name of this actor (or of this character) of the narrative who carries or conveys the directions of the space in the text.

30. We are considering the four gospels, and especially the three Synoptics, as four or three variants of the same narrative. But again it is necessary to define precisely their relationships to the "sameness" of the narrative, and to the analysis which we are making of it. The four or three variants do not constitute, in our mind and in our methodological view, three or four examples of one essence, a "Narrative of the Passion", which would be the truth and which they would

reproduce with more or less exactitude. If that were the case, we would choose after examination—but according to what criteria of meaning, reading, or materials?—the best variant for a particular passage. One of the methodological postulates of structural analysis would rejoin here what is classically called textual criticism and end, in the best of cases, in the establishment of a detailed critical apparatus of the text. The variants in the species are not variants at all of a "same", but they are in a reciprocal position of variation or difference. Each being a variant of the other three and the narrative being only the system—which is postulated at least before being demonstrated—of the differences between the variants, differences that the analysis has the purpose of displaying in the different levels where it is developed. That signifies that the narrative is not this linear series of "actions" and "events", even in the case of the most transparent narrative, but a complex, stratified ensemble in which the variants offer at some point or moment of the text the hierarchies of their transformations. But there is another problem presented by the variants, which is connected with what we have evoked concerning the corpus. Are there not other constitutive variants of the text of this narrative? Apocryphal gospels, didactic commentaries, or figurative representations, or in an even more general way, all the documentary traces of one tradition of this narrative in its text, in the triple sense of the term of tradition: the practical effect of its content or its proclamation; its historical transmission connected to this effect or to its development in the economic, political, social, and cultural "contexts"; and the textuality of the discourses of which this narrative is or has been the object. All these reference elements are in an *inter-voire*, a trans-textuality which belongs rightfully to our topic. But, however, we are limited—as far as we are concerned—to the three Synoptics and the gospel of John. The texts do not have a greater value for us because of their antiquity. Behind these texts there are no other texts, written or oral, which are even more ancient, and therefore "more authentic". It is in this way that in our *Etudes sémiologiques*, we have integrated [p. 205] into our "biblical readings" a work on this fragment (discursive, it is true, and non-narrative) of the Passion narrative: "This is my body", commented upon by the Port-Royal logicians. Nevertheless, it is necessary to pose in an internal way the problem of the limit of the corpus, which is introduced here in an external way. Can a text engender the limit of the corpus of texts where it will be studied in its differences? Can it close the circle of its differences by which a meaning is pronounced?

31. See the questions posed by the preceding note.

32. See the words from the research group already published, and in particular in our *Etudes sémiologiques*, p. 227ff.

33. See Appendix III.

34. By an application of the hypothesis of the "text as a productive scene".

35. See on this subject our study about "The neutral term and philosophical discourse" (forthcoming) and also in *Etudes sémiologiques*, "Lectures bibliques", the analysis of Pilate's question to Jesus and the response which is given to him. Every question is, in general, neutralizing, and particularly the question dealing with being, "Who are you?". It is equally an essential point of our second part: "The Semiotics of the Traitor".

36. We are drawing attention here to this qualifying mark of the hero before the test, which is one of the characteristics of the narrative according to Propp and A. J. Greimas.

37. See the following study, "The Semiotics of the Traitor".

38. It is in this way that we are setting aside from our analysis the indications concerning the meetings and the conversations of the Pharisees which are hetero-topics in relation to the narrative analyzed--to the places of our text.

39. We are speaking here of sequence from the point of view of the places of the narrative, because they manifest the opening and closure of a process which is then "completed". Jesus goes from the Mount of Olives to the Temple and returns from the Temple to the Mount of Olives. This process thus constitutes a totality integrating the ensemble of the topic elements of the narrative.

40. A final stage of a transformation, to the extent to which we shall consider that the binary opposition is in this area the strongest and the simplest opposition and that it can be *methodologically* considered to be the τέλος of the analysis. But in another sense, the opposition peculiar to Luke could be taken as the starting point of an inverse transformation, aiming by the introduction of intermediary elements to overcome an opposition thought and experienced [*vécue*] as irreducible. This is reminiscent of the remarks of Lévi-Strauss about the mythic narrative. Henceforth a transformational circularity of the toponymic variants is defined by which the *rules* of

that which the narrative displays are found laid down in the
enchained and successive syntagms of the narration: in short
a syntax.

41.   Here the difference between a place and a space appears in the narrative, which would correspond to the opposition that could be made between the productive scene and the
setting.   The space *between* two places is essentially nameless,
but it can--as is the case--be semantically invested by the
passage of the actor.   The interest of the analysis in the
narrative of the space which is displayed between two sequen-
tial poles is to introduce a third "compound".

42.   The first time during which the vendors have been
chased from the Temple; the second which is opened by the
healing at the public bath of [p. 206] Bethesda; the third at
the time of the Feast of Tabernacles when Jesus withdraws in
the evening to the Mount of Olives (Jn. 7:2); the fourth at
the time of the Feast of Dedication when the question of his
messianic identity is clearly presented (Jn. 10:22-23).

43.   See the following study, "The Semiotics of the Traitor".

44.   We will come back again to this point.   Let us point
out that from now on when "Jerusalem" appears it is in the
discourse and not in the narrative.

45.   See the remarks about the anointing at Bethany in our
study, "Les femmes au tombeau", *Etudes sémiologiques*, "lectures bibliques", pp. 216-217.

46.   The expression in the text itself of the translation
of the name "Golgotha" as "the place of the skull", or the
introduction into the "insignificance" of the name--*into the
narrative*--of its etumon [*sic*] has an important signifying
value.   The lexicon, to repeat the term which we have used
following A. J. Greimas, instead of remaining in the order of
the paradigms, makes its appearance in the syntagm.   It is the
mark of a transgression of the paradigm-syntagm opposition,
however essential to the organization of the narrative.   It is
at the same time the index of the intervention of the narrator
in the account and equally a mark of reading, a sign of the
reader.   We are taking into consideration in our work only the
first level of significance of this "translation".

47.   An operation of superimposition or covering, like
this, is accomplished in what could be called a meta-textual
space, a neutral epistemological space in which the system of
variants is established according to a certain point of view--

the distribution here of the toponyms and their substitutes--a
system which is properly the textual space. But the operation
which should make the object not only of a terminological indication but moreover of a methodological justification is that
by which we superimpose the variants, and articulate them on
the condemnation to death of the hero (cf. below). The justification for the superimposition of the variants should, in my
opinion, be sought in the narrative redundance which character-
izes them. It is because all four of them tell the same story
that we feel ourselves intuitively authorized to juxtapose them
in metatextual space, leaving the strictness of this juxtaposition to be displayed by some more specific reasons (here the
toponyms, their substitutes or articulation of the space in the
text). Thus the narrative redundance, at the level of the
global narrative in the book among the four Gospels and particularly the three Synoptics, permits us to annul or limit the
"chronic"* effects of the narrative itself. On the other hand,
the rabatment* of the system thus constituted around one moment
of the narrative and which permits--as we wrote below--the
structural equivalence of certain places in their "before" and
"after" names to be displayed; this moment is justified by the
implicit presence of a narrative model articulated in two superficial "alienation" and "reintegration" phases in which V.
Propp and A. J. Greimas will be recognized.

48. See on this point our work "les femmes au tombeau" already cited.

49. We are giving this remark here as a simple working hypothesis suggested by our analysis of the toponyms in the four
(or three) variants. Its demonstration (or at least its confirmation) could only occur [p. 207] in a general and "complete" analysis of the passion narrative. It is a matter here
of a simple orientation of reading.

50. That we will consider, once again, as some variants,
not of an original text, but as inter-representatives [entre-
représentatives] (in a position of circular, reciprocal representation).

51. We say historical because, as far as the names of
places are concerned, we consider the texts of the Old Testament to constitute a "chronological" opening of the system of
toponyms that we are analyzing in the Passion narrative as a
closed system.

---

*chronic--i.e. temporal.
*rabatment--i.e. folding back of a triangle, etc.

52. Here indeed appears, as we pointed out in note 47, the logically "anterior" position of Propp's and Greimas's narrative model. We are using it for operative effectiveness because our purpose is not to analyze the Passion narrative globally, but the system of the places of this narrative.

53. We are introducing here a reference to the schemas of communication in order to recall--and it is one of our fundamental hypotheses here--that this narrative, or more precisely the narration of this narrative, is equally a proclamatory and constitutive discourse of a community which comes into existence by relating it. It is not a question here of an apologetic or dogmatic presumption, but of a hypothesis which validates from numerous marks in the text itself, marks of recitative narrative or a reception of the message.

Chapter III

54. That is to say the toponymic variants in their references to the functions and the actants of the Passion narrative. In other words, in their references to the general forms of structural intelligibility of this narrative: which includes here again the logical priority of Propp's and Greimas's narrative model.

55. We mean by that the sense of the text in relation to the problem of the toponyms.

56. By this qualificative we simply aim to characterize this meal "nominally". Therefore it prejudges nothing about its real or symbolic signification.

57. Cf. our note 47 on the methodological justification of this process of covering or superimposition inside of the model.

58. The paradigmatic organization "puts into perspective" --if that can be said--episode 1 and episode 2 from the point of view of the structuration of the space of the narrative. But this perspective is no longer the temporal or chronic perspective of the narrative: episode 1 earlier, episode 2 later, in the time of the narrative with the irreversibility of the referential (be it illusory) time, and irreversibility of the time of reading. It is an achronic perspective of the model in heuristic work: a form of equivalence. However this equivalence is not identification. The arrival at the city does not repeat or reproduce the entry to Jerusalem, while being a structural equivalent of it. (The places in one and the other

"representation" enter into some relations of the same form.)
It is the structural equivalence which is inductive of the
paradigmatic relation of an order which it does not contain,
since it [p. 208] restricts itself to displaying the parallelism of the two ensembles of local relations, but from which it
authorizes the question since, noting the parallelism, we ask
ourselves in that case what kind of relations these two ensembles maintain. We are characterizing this vertical or se-
cant between the two planes as a relation of implication-ex-
planation. The arrival at the city is the implication or the
concentration of the entry into Jerusalem. The latter is the
explanation or the development of the arrival at the city. It
could be said, to give a picture, that episode 2 is the scaled-
down model of episode 1 in the double sense (which marks the
reversibility of the relationship) of the expression, because
episode 2 constitutes the archetypical model of episode 1, its
"final cause", but it is at the same time cut on the pattern
of episode 1. Does it reintroduce time in a model which as-
serts itself to be achronic? It could be thought so, but it
is a matter of a reversible time, in retroactive positive and
negative moments, a theoretical or epistemological time which
has nothing more to do with the linear, successive time of the
surface reading or with the trite image of "referential" time.

59. On this apparent schema, see our methodological remarks from the preceding note on the structural equivalence
between the two journeys in relation to the places. We should
add that this inductive structural equivalence of the relation
of order is itself induced by a comparative surface analysis
dealing with some textual marks and indices.

60. On the strongly invested semantic value of the sign
"ass's foal--she-ass or wild donkey", in relation to the
"royal" messianic entrance of Jesus, the Old Testament [vé-
téro-testamentaires] references abound, but in a remarkable
ambiguity that a precise and complete analysis of the messianic entry ought to take into account. Because if the horse and
the chariot are signs of kingship, asses possessed in large
numbers are a sign of wealth in Jgs. 10:4 or 12:4. Gen. 49:
11; Jgs. 5:10; 1 Kgs. 1:38 and 1:5; Isa. 2:7; 62:11; Jeremiah
17:25; 22:4; Zech. 9:9 should be consulted. But it is not
this value which interests us here, but the simple definition
of the ass's foal as a means of transport, of a spanning of
space, as an instrument of articulation of a spatiality.

61. The written form used displays two parallel planes
of the induced structural equivalence.

62. We will come back to this point in our study of
Judas.

63. The relation of order between the parallel planes of the structure begins here to "cut out" [*"travailler"*] and produce some retroactive relations.

64. We are only formulating here some hypothetical anticipations suggested by the local signifier system.

65. This point is capital. We are referring to our analysis of the parable of the sower in Matthew 13:1-25.

66. This is a new example of an application of the relation of order between the planes of the structure.

67. Hence the difficulty, even the impossibility, of using a simple analogical "code" in order to decode a "double meaning", a characteristic process of hermeneutics.

68. In another sense, the implicative and explanatory system of the places that we are seeking to put into place could be defined as the result of a structural organization multiplied by a syntagmatic succession. [p. 209]

69. In this sense, the text is indeed a productive scene.

70. Here again we are referring to our n. 58, p. 41.

71. See on this subject our n. 41, p. 30.

72. Carrying a jug is in effect an act with a socially feminine connotation in this context. Cf. for example, the episode of the Samaritan woman, Jn. 4:7.

73. See on this subject our study already cited on the parable of the sower.

74. A citation from Mark, "Is it not written, 'My house shall be called a house of prayer for all the nations?' But you have made it a den of robbers" (Mk. 11:17). Cf. Isa. 56:7: "Their burnt-offerings and their sacrifices will be accepted on my altar, because my house will be called a house of prayer for all peoples"; and Jer. 7:11: "Has this house, which is called by my name, become a den of robbers in your eyes?"

75. A Temple whose name is the very Name of God, according to the citation from Jeremiah.

76. It is in this way that the inter-representation of the variants form a productive system of meaning, in the articulation of their structures.

77. It will be noted that, the more we progress into the
analysis of the secondary variants, the more we are forced to
invest semantically the topic signifier system, and thereby we
articulate little by little the "significations" of the narrative considered as such, in the system which is our only object of study.

78. It would equally be suitable to make an analysis of
Lk. 13:31-35 in this perspective. Let us emphasize only some
points in this study: first of all the affirmation of power
presented on the part of Jesus, "I cast our demons and perform
cures today and tomorrow" (Lk. 13:32); then the indication of
the third day, a day of consummation for Jesus (τελειοῦμαι);
accomplishment and final conclusion; and finally the reprimand
to Jerusalem which is the announcement and preparation in the
discursive mode for the obliteration of the toponym of the
city as well as that of the Temple which has lost its name because it will be left to the Pharisees: "Behold, your house
is forsaken. And I tell you, Ye will not see *me*..." (Lk. 13:
35).

79. See on this subject, our work on "the eaten *parole*"
in our *Etudes sémiologiques* and the conclusion of Part II of
this work.

Chapter IV

80. We enter here into the analysis of a new dimension of
the generative system of meaning, which functions in some way
in relation to the system previously analyzed as an elevation
to a second power, to a second order or work of the system.
Power is here employed in the double arithmetic (multiplication of the number by itself) and energetic (productive of
meaning by a constitution of significance) sense.

81. And it is known that the rhetorical place, before being a logical reservoir of reasoning premises, was an imaginary mnemonic space where the orator situated his arguments,
the spatial enchainment of the places representing the order
of development of the arguments. See on this subject the
fine book of Frances Yates, *The Art of Memory*, London, 1967.
See also note 13, p. 93.

82. In other words, by a direct or indirect, even cryptic,
citational interplay. [p. 210]

83.   That does not mean that we set aside as illusory, the problem of the historical reference. But the inter-representative systems which we are studying as textual systems induce in the immediately readable [*le lisible immédiat*] a referential effect which is, *itself*, an illusion of reading. Just as the mimetic representation in a painting induces a figurative effect of specular reference about which all the theories are constructed, i.e. all the ideologies of the painting.

On the distinction between a code and a cipher, see P. Ricoeur, *Le Conflit des Interprétations, Essais d'Herméneutique*, Paris: Ed. du Seuil, 1969, p. 59, note 1: "The code," P. Ricoeur writes, "assumes a correspondence, an affinity of contents, i.e. a cipher." Repeating this idea in a note, he adds, "this cipher value is first apprehended in the emotion", as Lévi-Strauss remarked in *La Pensée sauvage*, pp. 50-59. P. Ricoeur concludes: "The comparisons, correspondences, associations, intersections, symbolizations which is the subject on the following pages (53-59) and which the author [Lévi-Strauss] does not hesitate to compare to hermeticism and emblematicism, places correspondences--the cipher--at the origin of the homologies between differential variations belonging to different levels, thus to the origin of the code." We repeat this problem in our introduction. Let us point out only one question here. Is the ordinary cipher, as P. Ricoeur suggests, only an understanding of the double meaning? In the parable, the meanings proliferate and the code which permits its decipherment is not a closed system of an operation of "interpretation", but an open interplay of articulations between the multiple levels of the narrative, and between the different isotopies, which seem to us to be the infinite cipher of the narrated story [*l'histoire racontée*]. On the notion of an infinite cipher being equal to zero, see our *Etudes sémiologiques*, pp. 166-172.

84.   On the relationship of the subjects of discourse to the parabolic narrative, see our study on the "Parabolic Narrative", *art. cit.*

85.   Certain parables are repeated in the text, but outside of the Passion narrative, at another point of the narrative syntagmatics. Cf. our instructions from the following page.

86.   We can try to give the formula of the hypothesis to be validated:

$$[(P_1 \simeq P_2 \simeq P_3 \simeq \ldots Pn) \, t_1 \simeq (P_1 \simeq P_2 \simeq P_3 \simeq \ldots P_n) \, t_2 \simeq$$
$$(\ldots) \, t_n] \simeq [N_1 \simeq N_2 \simeq N_3 \simeq \ldots N_n]$$

Or by developing N:

$$N_1 \ [(P_1 \simeq P_2 \simeq \ldots) \ t_1 \ \ldots \ t_n]$$

a formula in which P = parable, t = variant text, N = narrative segment, and the sign ( ) = the textual "framing" at the levels indicated by the exponent: t for the fragment of the variant text considered, N for the narrative segment.

87. We have tried to show this elsewhere concerning the parable of the sower in Matthew.

88. Our note 78: it must, however, be noted that the induction of meaning of the expression: "I am consumed" is only accomplished directly in the French translation; in Greek it equally functions, but in a metaphoric form. In the sacrament the τελειοῦμαι of the fulfillment and the end has, for a metaphoric and sacramental point, the eucharistic meal. [p. 211]

89. The putting in relationship of the three variants of the parable displays in this way three practical possibilities in the decipherment of the parabolic narrative: an implicit decipherment by juxtaposition of the narrative and of a citation itself coded, a juxtaposition which is a "zero" mark of reading (Mark); a symbolic decipherment by a "picturesque" transposition of the code of the citation (Luke); an explicit, but partial, decipherment and in another lexicon of the parabolic narrative and of the citation (Matthew).

90. Or at the very least of a vast architecture.

91. It is convenient, at this point of the analysis, to point out some extra-textual correlations, but which are inside of the Book: thus Hag. 1:9-10 and 2:15-19 in which the construction of the Temple is connected to the production of the fruits of the earth or Isa. 8:14 in which Yahweh is a sanctuary and a stone of offense, a rock of stumbling, a trap and a stone to the inhabitants of Jerusalem. See also Zech. 1:12-16 in which the reconstruction of the Temple is connected to the destruction of the arrogant nations or Jer. 51:26 which concerning Babylon indicates that of the "destroying mountain", "I will stretch out my hand against you, and roll down from the craigs, and make you a burnt mountain. No stone shall be taken from you for a corner and no stone for a foundation, but you shall be a perpetual waste..." (Jer. 51:25-26).

92. It is necessary to evoke here the ambivalence of the iconography that Christendom has devoted to the "mystic" press-house: a press-house not of wine, but of blood, therefore of

death, but which is at the same time the regeneration of those who bathe in it or drink of it. Cf. also the intoxication from new wine during Pentecost (Acts 2:13-15).

93. The same duality of "high-low" contraries is found in the citation from Jeremiah given in note 91, p.

94. This is an important hypothesis of reading which we are introducing here which, if it were validated, could constitute the general rule of articulation and the creation of the three "scenes" of the narrative.

95. It is equally necessary to evoke the proper name of the domain where Jesus goes with his disciples to await his arrest, "Gethsemane", the translation of which we know is "a press-house for oil". Nevertheless, we cannot, except by an extra-textual correlation which is not absolutely necessary, take this toponym into consideration in its translated form. More serious would be the reproach of not having represented the toponym in our analysis, or of having done it in an incidental way. "Gethsemane" is found, according to Mark and Matthew, only once as an index of the place where Jesus suffers his death agony and is arrested. Like other toponyms, Emmaus or Bethphage for example, we do not think we ought to study it, except when considered as an index or topical quasi-index. In effect, the question of its integration into several (at least two) signifier systems is not presented in its subject. Our working hypothesis is not relevant to its purpose. It is the recurrences of the toponyms in the narrative "chain" which constitute the very subject of the problem that we are studying. It does not follow at all that the translation of Gethsemane, which does not appear in the text (unlike that of Golgotha which does), is an extra-textual interpretant of great value, since the isolated toponym and what as such has only one "referential" function is perfectly integrated at the level of its translation in the signifier system that the text of the narrative puts into place in all its complexity. [p. 212]

96. A characteristic question of the process is to be in a "double bind", in a double shackle or constraint which "wedges" the receiver-sender into two equally unacceptable alternative responses. See on this subject the study of Alain Cohen on the parable (to appear). The expression and its analysis are borrowed in the later works of Gregory Bateson. (Cf. also Anthony Wilden, in a work to appear soon.)

97. This is no doubt one of the most fruitful questions which could be posed to the biblical text, especially because the narrative which is narrated is also a proclamation, a reci-

tative of the community which narrates itself by narrating the narrative. The narrative must therefore contain in its textuality the marks of transmission and reception in this narrative to have this function.

98. Cf. the notes from the preceding page.

99. See again on this point our study of the parabolic narrative, *op. cit.*

100. We will develop this point in our study of Judas.

Chapter V

101. However, it will be noted that Jesus will respond to the double question of the people concerning the moment and the sign of the destruction of the Temple by a prophetic description of the destruction of Jerusalem and thereby, cosmological and eschatological, of the coming of the Son of Man. It can no longer be a question of the Temple as an object of the referend [*référend*] of discourse. It has become a pure place of *teaching parole*: this very *parole in* the subject who delivers it. Cf. Lk. 21:37-38. It will equally be noted that this transformation from the place of *parole* into the subject of *parole*, this same subject who pronounces the transformation, but who does so negatively, will find his positive completion in an ultimate transformation, that of the subject of *parole* into a body spoken-to-be-eaten [*parlé-à-manger*].

102. It is discourse in an extratextual position in relation to our narrative, but it constitutes a useful correlation to it. On the other hand, we must inscribe it in the space of the toponyms in order to be able to take it into consideration at the level where this study is situated.

103. It could almost be said to be in another "genre" in the literary sense of the term.

104. See our n. 97.

105. "He went on ahead, going up to Jerusalem" (Lk. 19:28).

106. Thus in Lk. 19:47: "he was teaching daily in the temple..."; and in Lk. 21:37-38, especially, "every day he was teaching in the temple, but at night he went out and lodged on the mount called Olivet"....

107. In this perspective, the paradoxical idea of a text passing to textual being--ontological proof--can be ventured.

108. "The installation of the desolating sacrilege in the holy place" (cf. Mt. 24:15), and the return as a Man into the World with power and great glory (cf. Mt. 24:27-30).

109. The royal judgment of the Son of Man (Mt. 25:31-46).

110. The problem of the creation by separation has been masterfully presented and studied [p. 213] for Genesis 1 by P. Beauchamp in *Création et séparation*, Paris: Bibliothèque de Sciences religieuses, 1970. [The original text erroneously numbers this footnote note 115.]

111. In his work *Die Gleichnisse Jesus* (English trans. *The Parables of Jesus*, New York: Scribner's Sons, 1963), Joachim Jeremias examines the validity of the parabolic comparison. "The application of the parable to the return of the Son of Man is strange; for if the subject of discourse is a nocturnal burglary, it refers to a disastrous and alarming event, whereas the Parousia, at least for the disciples of Jesus, is a great day of joy." P. 49 the same remark, cited by J. Jeremias, from E. Fuchs, *Hermeneutik*, Bad Carlstatt, 1954, p. 223: "The application is, in my opinion, inconsistent (with the parable itself)." J. Jeremias finds a "psychologist" solution, by removing the reference to the Son of Man and by constructing what could be called "the situation of reception" of the parable by the hearers of Jesus, a construction based on the references to the Flood and to the destruction of Sodom. "Here, too, although of extreme antiquity, events which overwhelmed men un-prepared are used by Jesus as a warning of terrors to come. He sees the approaching Fate, the disaster at the door....Jesus wishes to arouse them to open their eyes to the peril of their position....Thus would Jesus' hearers have understood the parable of the Housebreaker: as a rousing cry to the crowd in view of the oncoming eschatalogical catastrophe." By this comparison, it seems to me, the interest of structural analysis is perceived in a short narrative which resolves the contradiction opened by a surface allegory, thanks to an articulation of the narrative into opposed and correlated functions: closure vs. opening = entry vs. rejection + conservation vs. rupture. However, it is necessary to add that the psychologist reconstruction of the situation of reception leads Jeremias to that of a second stratum in his commentary, the situation of interpretation of the Church. The ambiguity of coding of the parable is then found resolved by the interference of these two situations. "Jesus addressing the crowd, emphasized the sudden irruption of the tribution...while the attention of the early church was directed

at the end of the tribulation", p. 51.

112. One should read the analysis of the Parable of the
Ten Virgins in Joachim Jeremias, *op. cit.*, pp. 51-53. There,
as in the parable of the thief, the interpretative solution of
J. Jeremias rests on two chronologically and historically dis-
tinct situations in which the parable is received: that of
the hearer of Jesus--"How then must his audience have understood the parable especially if we regard the audience as con-
sisting of the crowd?"--and that of the Church which relates
the parabolic narrative anew, which recites it: "an essential
change of emphasis took place: the warning cry intended to
awaken the crowd from sleep became an exhortation to the band
of disciples, and the parable became an allegory of Christ,
the heavenly bridegroom and the expectant Church", p. 53. As
far as the first of these situations is concerned, one should
read, *op. cit.*, pp. 171-172, the discussion about the "reality"
of the marriage ceremony in which Jesus would have assisted and
in the course of which he would have pronounced the parable.
The goal of this analysis is perceived. It aims to construct
for the parabolic narrative a double articulation by which
some rich inflections of meaning appear. But it is limited by
historicist and psychologist presuppositions. It conceives,
in effect, this double articulation as that of two historical
moments [p. 214] (which exists, to be sure, but the meaning
which is shown in it does not exhaust the meaning of the text)
and as that of the reception of the narrative (which constitutes only one of the aspects of the communication of a message). For this reason, see the discussion of G. Bornkamm,
"Die Verzogerung der Parusie" in *Memoriam E. Lohmeyer*, Stutt-
gart, 1951, pp. 119-126 and R. Bultmann, *op. cit.*, p. 119:
"This is a Church formulation completely overgrown by allegory
and having a strongly emphasized referent to the Person of Jesus."

113. See the analysis of the parable in J. Jeremias, *op.
cit.* p. 58 and ff. See in particular the interesting note 51
on p. 61: "Burying according to rabbinical law was regarded
as the best security against theft."

114. See our study of parabolic narrative in *Etudes théologiques et religieuses* 46 (1, 1971), p. 67.

Second Part

NOTES: SEMIOTICS OF THE TRAITOR

Chapter One

1. We repeat at this point the model worked out by A. J. Greimas, in *Sémantique structurale*, Paris: Larousse, 1966, starting from the works of Propp and Souriau. Its canonical form is the following:

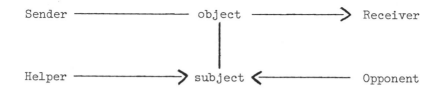

2. By introducing the term "subject" here we do not intend to present, in a surreptitious way, a somewhat metaphorical thesis, but only to indicate one of the aspects of the referential illusion provoked by the presence of the proper name of the character in the text. Even if while included in a metalinguistic discourse constructed about the text, the character is found dissociated or integrated in some (or one) of the functional classes. It does not follow at all that the act of reading the story necessarily performs this interplay of attributions due to the name-index.

3. To speak of an *exterior* of the text is not contradictory with *the referential illusion* of the proper name and the character. The latter consists of presenting, in a gesture which, in many respects, is a homologue of the natural thesis in Husserl, a reality of which the narrative would be the duplication. It is a question indeed of a lure [*leurre*] in the double sense of bait and deception. Some profound indications about the original movement of duplication of reality in Occidental discourse [p. 215] will be found in *Les Maîtres de Vérité dans la Grèce archaïque* of M. Détienne. And we have said that at the level of the reading, this emergence of the double was a necessity, a constraint which is due no doubt to the reading of the written text, which has a material "reality"; but of a very strange nature since by speaking silently of some thing, it is only a space traversed to its outside: a

material reality whose meaning is the movement of its own transcendence. Some conditions of possibility of the bait and deception of the referend [*référend*] of which the text would be its double will be found there. The exterior or the other of the text is thus contained for us in the very constitution of the text as a text which is only accomplished as meaning by a constant displacement outside of itself, than by a gesture of transcendence. Every effort of structural analysis consists, in our point of view, in being manifested in this gesture or in this displacement, as the swimmer is carried by a wave. Henceforth, the referential illusion that the displacement makes possible in it is the stop and like the seizure by things. It consists in giving to the text a substantial reality, but in a mirror; to represent the things themselves and the world and to exhaust itself in this function of reflection.

4. We are taking this term in its current meaning, that does not attempt to say that this meaning does not maintain some relationships with its recent use by M. Foucault in the *a priori* historical sense, a condition of reality of the narrative statements [*énoncés*] of a discourse, including some laws of coexistence and transformation of these narrative statements [*énoncés*], a collection of rules which characterize a discursive practice. The gospel text equally constitutes an archive, in the sense that this text includes in itself its rules of reading, that it can always be reread and redefined in a new discursive practice: a text which is perhaps only a metatext or again whose narrative is that of the way in which one can, in which one must, read the narrative. This reading--we will show a little further on--is not only recitation, but also gestualization and ritualization. And it is equally in this sense that this text, as a possibility of institutional ritualization, functions like the archive of M. Foucault: "a system which establishes the narrative statements [*énoncés*] as some events having their conditions and their domain of apparition and like some things (including their possibility and their field of utilization)"; or again "a system of functioning of the narrative statement-thing [*l'énoncé-chose*]". *L'archéologie du savoir*, Paris: Gallimard, 1969, p. 166ff.

5. We are using this term in Saussure's sense, defining "semiology" as the general science of signs, such as, for example, customs, etiquette, rites, institutions, and objects, which are indeed those which we are referring to in this sentence.

6. Perhaps it would be necessary to examine the notion of narrative origin that we are introducing here. Let us state

precisely, however, that what we do not mean here to make of
this narrative, an original text [un text d'origine], but only
to note that for the groups, the community, or the institution
considered, the gospel narrative is indeed a narrative-origin
[un récit-origine] in the sense in which this narrative relates the origins of the Christian community by relating the
life Jesus-Christ and by writing down his teaching [ensigne-
ment = enseignement?] and equally when this community was established by the recitation of this narrative. Its very essence is to repeat, tell again, and interpret this narrative.
On the other hand, the problem--and it is considerable--pre-
sents itself of knowing if, even on this plane, one can consider the gospel narrative to be the narrative origin [récit-
origine] without ascribing it to [p. 216] the Old Testament,
or to the texts of the Judaic religious tradition. See our
methodological remarks in our study of the parabolic narrative, art. cit.

7. We have used as a reference the books of O. Cullmann,
Die Christologie des Neuen Testaments, Tübingen, 1957, in its
English translation, The Christology of the New Testament,
trans. Shirley C. Guthrie and Charles A. M. Hall, Philadelphia: The Westminster Press, 1959; and from F. Hahn, The
Titles of Jesus in Christology. Their History in Early
Christianity, The World Publishing Co., p. 112: "Jesus Christ
means Jesus Messiah. Already the letters of Paul, the oldest
Christian writings we possess, have a tendency to fix the word
Christ as a proper name, although the passages in which Paul
writes 'Christ' before Jesus (i.e. Christ Jesus) serve as a
reminder that he is still aware of its real meaning." Χρισ-
τός as a translation of the Hebrew mashiach: "the anointed
one". Analyse du langage théologique: le Nom de Dieu (Actes
du Congrès international Rome, janv. 1969), Archivio di Filos-
ofia, direction E. Castelli 39-1969 and Paris: Aubier, 1969
should also be consulted.

8. We are referring at this point to our analyses of the
problem of the proper name, ibid, Part I, "The Places of the
Narrative" and in our Etudes sémiologiques.

9. See on this subject, C. Lévi-Strauss, La Pensée sauvage, p. 227 and f.; p. 240 and f., pp. 248-249 and p. 283 and
f.

10. FIRST PART: "The Places of the Narrative", p. 28f.
and pp. 46-47.

11. See on this subject, our study of Acts 10:1-11:18 in
Exégèse et Herméneutique, Paris: Ed. du Seuil, 1971, pp. 213-
238. However, it will be noted that this analysis presents the

methodological problem of the ethnological reference outside
of the text itself. To what degree is it right to use this
reference in the structural analysis of a specific text? The
problem is not one of excluding it, because every text--and
the latter perhaps more than any other--is read by an interplay of external references to the text, but to be explicit
in its mode of integration to the reading or to the meta-reading.

12. The notion of a sphere of action is a notion introduced by Propp in chap. 6 of his *Morphologie du conte*: "De
nombreuses fonctions se groupent logiquement selon certaines
sphères. Ces sphères correspondent aux personnages qui ac-
complissent des fonctions. Ce sont des spheres d'actions."
[= "Many functions logically join together into certain
spheres. These spheres correspond to their respective per-
formers. They are spheres of action." Propp, *Morphology of
the Folktale*, 2nd ed., p. 79.] After having isolated 7
spheres of action, Propp indicates that "le problème de la
distribution des fonctions peut être résolu au niveau du problème de la distribution des sphères d'actions entre les personnages." French trans., Paris: Ed. du Seuil, 1970, pp. 96-
97. [= "The problem of the distribution of functions may be
resolved on the plane of the problem concerning the distribution of the *spheres of actions* among the characters." Propp,
Morphology, 2nd ed., p. 80.]

13. It is convenient to note here the importance of the
notion of place of τόπος which has the historical and functional characteristic of articulating the space *in which* the
discourse is pronounced in the space, *starting from which* the
discourse is composed. It is known in effect that the τόποι
was not only the repertory or the reserve of arguments or
questions which allowed the orator, by dismembering the body
of the "subject" into elements or discursive instruments, to
display his discourse on the individual case in the general
models of his method. The τόπος also constituted the space--
the scene in other words--of representation of the discourse,
whether this scene was real or imaginary. They were the
places of the space in which the orator put the constituent
parts of his discourse and which permitted it an easy and un-
broken utterance. Thus the space of *logical articulation* of
the discourse, thanks to which [p. 217] the orator *"invenit
quid dicat"* is represented or projected by and in the space of
corporeal action, of the verbal gesticulation of which it is
very often forgotten the discourse was equally made: an un-
broken space animated only by some differences of parts of the
edifice, of the place where the orator spoke or even by those
of the compound interior image that was given to him before
speaking. It is a matter therefore of a dramatizing, or

rather again, of a staging of the discourse, by which, as in the theatrical representation, the discourse is figured, is given to be seen. The fragility or uncertainties of the rigorous opposition which has been attempted to be made between an image, figure, and word-discourse is seized with an example perfectly justified historically. On the historical aspect of the question, and for much of the bibliography, see Frances Yates, *The Art of Memory*, London: Routledge and Kegan Paul, 1967.

14. An ontological subject considered as a product of the referential illusion.

15. See on this subject Propp, *op. cit.*, and the interpretations of A. J. Greimas, *op. cit.*

16. This identity is only perceptible on the plane of metadiscourse criticism. A fiction-writer can relate, for example, the psychological evolution of his hero who will retrace the changes in himself, or his life from the cradle to the grave. In this sense, the subject "will change", and will not remain the same. But he will traverse the story "as himself..." by the substantial identity of an "ego", a support, a substratum of all his changes, or an identity which his name marks in the narrative itself.

17. We are following closely here the analysis of A. J. Greimas, *op. cit.*

18. Diverse relations of opposition of the significative units in the "narrative, according to a typology of relations between the similar element and the different element of the opposition".

19. It is understood from our preceding remarks that the character in his proper name is the figure, in the sense at the same time rhetorical and representative of one or several roles, of a system of relationships. The proper name acts in the space of the meaning like the theatrical or rhetorical figure in the space of the scene.

20. For this hypothesis the importance of Jacques Derrida's text dedicated to the notion of structure, *L'écriture et la différence*, Paris: Ed. du Seuil, 1967, pp. 409ff. will be noted. We have not thoroughly investigated in our text the ambiguity of the notion itself of the subject which refers, on the one hand, to the character as a proper name in its transit into the story, and on the other hand, to the "content" of the story as summarized in the name of the book in reading. It will have been noted that the name of the book—

or its title--is the proper name of the story, as is the name of the character, and that these two proper names function according to a process of reference: because the proper name of the character refers to this "ontological" stability which possesses what in its narrative displacement inside of the book illusorily produces the story, just as the title which gives the "subject" of the book refers to the productive subject of the book which has given him his name. Technically moreover, the title reunites the name of the subject of the book and the name of the one who has produced it, the author. Does the gospel have a title? And as such does it possess a subject? The indecisiveness among the terms for the Bible, the Book, the Scriptures--the only book *par excellence*--or for the Gospel--Message and Good News--should show, if necessary, the metalinguistic operation of which this book is the bearer. If it has a subject, [p. 218] it is the very fact of being a subject of discourse. Therefore this aspect is in some way a self-producer [*autoproducteur*] of the biblical gospel text which is produced by producing the very conditions for its reading and its transmission. It is after all one of these operations of production that we have attempted to describe.

21. There is a remarkable study by Paul Beauchamp about "the notion of covenant as a central structure in the Old Testament" which repeats a very interesting text from Ernst Bloch about the notion of a structure and a center. *Recherche de Sciences religieuses* 58 (1970), 161-193. It remains to be asked if the notions of structure and center are compatible by themselves. It does not seem the least possible to us to make the center the productive place of the structure without the structurality. In that case, one would find Derrida relevant.

22. See on this subject, E. Haulotte, "Fondation d'une Communauté de Type universel: Actes 10,1-11,18", *Recherches de Sciences religieuses* 58 (1, 1970), 63-100.

23. The notion of narrative dynamics which originates from a metaphorical energetics deserves an explanation. Considered as an illusory representation of events distributed along a temporal line, the narrative manifests the irreversibility characteristic of every temporal unfolding. The structural analysis of a narrative aims to construct the a-chronic form of the relations existing between the elements of the narrative. But can it integrate, i.e. submit to the structure *the moments of the narrative*, when the very possibility of a structural construction is produced? Now this moment, in this narrative and no doubt in every narrative, is at the same time that of the greatest determination--but prospective for the future of the story--and that of the greatest contingency, but in the present of the story. It is this double dimension which

we have called "a punctual mark of irreversibility" and which
refers back to the notion of a narrative dynamic, or a force
which would manifest itself in the forms of the narrative. It
is because this moment possesses this double dimension that
its specificity can pass unnoticed, because it functions in
the narrative like a kind of release of the relations which
will constitute--once extracted--the surface narrative structure, in which, at the same time, it disappears. But the very
fact of its introduction into the narrative and the release
itself does not belong to the order itself of the structure
which they permit. Far from being the elements of an "inferi-
or" order which would be reduced at the time of the structural
analysis of the narrative, they belong to the superior order
of the conditions of emergence of the structure. They indicate, in the narrative, the point of intrusion of its exteri-
or, and that is why we speak of a force, designating by this
term the non relational aspect of this moment--a condition of
possibility of relations.

24. We are repeating the term "shifter" introduced by
Jakobson in his famous article on "The Shifters and the Verbal
Categories of the Russian Verb", by keeping its fundamental
sense of a double structure "shifting" the conventional rule
defining the sign with the existential indication of the utterance by the utterer. It is the exceptional moment, or more
precisely the exceptionally apparent moment, when the *langue*
as a system, the "code", is projected, not only in the message,
but in the act, in the event of utterance of the message. In
other words, it is the moment when a relational element of the
system of the *langue* (and which possesses its signification
inside [p. 219] of the system) can only make it signify in an
act, by indicating the exterior of the system. It is the exchanger in the message of the values of the code and which can
only transgress its rules, since it can only refer to the "exterior" of the code, to its other in its very utilization. We
are suggesting that a character (and therefore an element
originating from the narrative message) represents this exist
from the code into the narrative: a place of exchange around
which and by which the elements of the code are in transit in
order to be structurally constituted in the message.

25. The contradiction is here defined as a figure in the
form of the text. Also the negative term does not refer to
some negativity of a Hegelian type of which the character of
the traitor would be the bearer. It signifies only that it
is, because it does not belong to the structure of the narrative that the "treacherous" event makes it possible.

26. And in this is manifested the impossibility of considering the origin in the occurrence, the place of the open-

222

ing of the structural relations. This place is considered
only in its metaphor which has taken the figure of the personage of the traitor.

27. It is remarkable, in effect--and we will return to
this later on--that the traitor combines, in his figure, the
two ensembles of elements connected by relations of opposition.
He is a personage or a figure with a double structure (hence
his function of exchange). Thus the slang expression shows
this: "He has double crossed me" in order to say "He has betrayed me", which signifies: "He has been the double 'negative' of the 'positive'." Thus Judas, one of the Twelve,
"double crosses" Jesus to the chief Priests and Pharisees.
More precisely still, his is the figure, the representation
of the separation between these two ensembles. The one who
signifies that the center of the structure which he represents
is an empty center, like spacing. The traitor is thus a compound figure. He is the one *and* the other, but who represents
a structural neutral, and the one who is *neither* the one *nor*
the other in the structure, its center beyond opposition.

28. We are speaking of a vertical separation to the extent to which the traitor as a personage belongs to the narrative manifestation, and that he is--at this level--the figure
of an empty center in the immanent structure. The following
schema reveals that:

level of the narrative manifestation

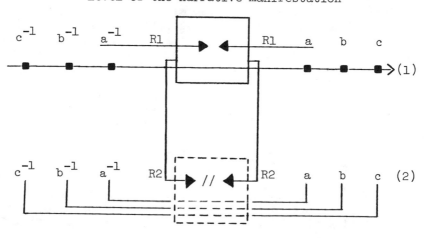

level of the immanent structure: connections of correlatives

■   = the personage of the traitor

R1,R1 = metonymic catachresis

The event of treachery [or villainy] is inserted by metonymic contiguity into the succession of the narrative. [p. 220]

R2 R2 = the vertical separation of the symbol representing the empty center in the immanent structure

29. Resorting to the Greek text has here a purely illustrative value. Our earlier analyses have shown us that the traitor was the figure of an exchange in the narrative, a shifter between a code and message. We exemplify these analyses by the Greek word signifying "traitor" in the gospel text. We could also have resorted to the etymology of the French word.

30. These categories constitute the opposition subjacent to the two narrative modes distinguished by Greimas: the deceptive and the truthful. Must one not wonder about the introduction of Being and Appearing which seem to be a metaphysical pair destined to establish the scientific analysis or give it some frameworks [*cadres*]?

31. Thus there is no narrative "suspense" in the text present in the reading, since this intervention of the narrator is "de-realizing". It contributes to dissipate the referential illusion in order to establish the text at another level.

32. The terms which we are using could be debated--"to discover" [*découvrir*] and "to denounce" [*dénoncer*]--but our analysis remains pertinent whatever terms may be used.

33. We are limiting ourselves to the four gospels. No doubt an enlarged work would have to include an examination of the apocryphal gospels.

34. This secondary hypothesis ought to confirm our earlier analyses, once it is verified. The traitor in the narrative structure is a mark of freedom or an opening of the structure. There is a necessity of the story, which is related, a necessity which will reveal the rigorous correlations of the structure. But it cannot appear and function as such: it requires a "release". That does not belong to the same order as the structure. It is opposite it like the contin-

gent, the exception which makes the structural necessity possible. On some articulations of this kind, see the recent works on the general theory of systems, and in particular: Paul Wetzlawick, Janet Beavin, and Don Jackson, *The Pragmatics of Human Communication* (New York: W. W. Norton, 1967), W. Buckley, *Sociology and Modern System Theory* (Englewood Cliffs, N.J.: Prentice-Hall, 1967), and Gregory Bateson and Jurgen Ruesch, *Communication: The Social Matrix of Psychiatry* (New York: W. W. Norton, 1967). See also Anthony Wilden, "Analog and Digital Communication: on the relationship between negation, signification and the emergence of the discrete element", *Semiotica* 6 (1972), pp. 50-82.

35. The constitution of two series, transcendent and historical, presents an important methodological problem. By what collection of reductions or alignments can one put into perspective the events of the text or the transcendent intentions? The examination and the solution of this question arises from our subject. A hypothetical approach would consist of classifying the gospel text into two large ensembles: one or more narratives and the discourse. It could be possible that the first transcendent series arose instead from the discourse, [p. 221] and the second story from the narratives. But a study of the interferences would be even more interesting. As far as our own analyses are concerned, let us say only that we are giving this distinction between the two series as an "exploratory" model.

36. We present here inductively, starting from the text and its commentaries all through history, the problem of the death of God as a fundamental antinomy in the gospel text considered as narrative. Can this antinomy be reduced to what C. Lévi-Strauss discovered as "the origin" of the mythical narratives which he examined in *Anthropologie structurale*? Methodologically, we have carried out this reduction on the following pages without our considering however what is here *the* truth of the text. It is only a very general operative disposition which permits us to verify the productivity of certain formulas established by Lévi-Strauss for the North American myths.

37. It will have been understood that the factual and historical series finds one of its codes in the transcendent series which constitutes it as a story written in cipher, as a signifier of the transcendent signified which is specified and realized. Henceforth the story as such possesses the necessity of every story, but at the same time, at one point of this narrative, this necessity is combined with the very necessity of the signified God who cannot without contradiction be confessed to be mortal.

38. C. Lévi-Strauss, *Anthropologie structurale*, Paris: Plon, 1958, p. 227f. and in particular, p. 243.

39. C. Lévi-Strauss, *op. cit.*, p. 248. Cf. the commentary of E. Meletinsky, "L'étude structurale et typologie du conte", in V. Propp, *Morphologie du conte*, Paris: Ed. du Seuil, 1970.

40. We are referring here to note 36, p. 106 and to our introduction. The question of knowing if the antinomy "Eternal vs. Mortal" is a mythical antinomy appears to us to be able to be set aside in the name of the operative necessities of the procedure of analysis.

41. We note at this point a transformation of the duality of the personage which we have already analyzed: a narrative figure of the empty center of the structure. It is also in the articulation of the structure and of the event in the emergence of a new organization. See on this subject the works of Anthony Wilden.

42. C. Lévi-Strauss, *op. cit.*, pp. 252-253.

43. E. Meletinsky, *op. cit.*, p. 215. See also on this subject Köngas and Miranda, "Structural Models in Folklore", *Midwest Folklore* (Indiana University) 12 (4, 1962), pp. 137-138, and in particular: "When analogy is not specifically 'linear' or 'non-linear', Lévi-Strauss's formula is 'non-linear', i.e. it implies a permutation of roles, functions, and terms. This permutation is necessary according to our interpretation, to account for structural patterns in which the result is not merely a cyclical return to the point of departure after the first force has been nullified, but a spiral-like step, a new situation different from the initial one, not only in that it nullifies it, but also it consists of a state which is more than a nullification of the initial...." From our point of view, the traitor functions like the additional neutralizing element coupled with the mediator and which permits the mediator to accomplish his mediatory function with a gain--that is to say [p. 222] the establishment of a *new* structuration and not a simple return to the earlier structure, a compromise moment.

44. The notion of effectuation of the myth as narrative is explained by the distinction of the narrative manifestation and the narrative structure and the effective taking into consideration of the first level. The structure of the myth can--in the case which interests us--do without the traitor. However the structure of the myth is not a myth. It is not even its truth or essence. The myth is first of all a narrative, a

recitation in which an additional element appears which permits the effectuation of it, but which is the other of the
structure, of another order, a condition of extra-ordinary
possibility. Thanks to it--which is an addition of the center, the myth is told and by being told, by being effectuated,
the structure is reorganized at another level since an innovation appears in it which marks this dissymmetry of Lévi-
Strauss's formula.

Chapter II

45. We are referring here to note 20, p. 102. See also
on this subject the remarks of R. Barthes in *Recherches de
Science religieuse* 58 (Jan.-Mar., 1970), 17-38 and our remarks
in *Etudes sémiologiques*. It is essential to emphasize the decisive importance of the fact that a metalinguistic position
is introduced into the message since the content of the message is to give the rules of its reading (= function of the
code in the analysis of R. Jakobson).

46. On *parole* power, we draw attention to the work of M.
Détienne, *Les Maîtres de vérité dans la Grèce archaïque*, Paris:
Maspero, 1966, and in another perspective, that of the analytical philosophy of speech-acts, the work of J. L. Austin, *Quand
dire, c'est faire*, Paris: Ed. du Seuil, French trans., 1970.
See also E. Benvéniste, in *Le Vocabulaire des institutions
européennes*, Paris: Ed. de Minuit, 1969, his studies on *Rex*
or *Dico*....

47. This point is essential in our view, namely the connection of the verbality or function of the *parole* and of the
orality or function of assimilation in itself and of transformation in itself of the exterior element: the food.
Therefore it is no longer a matter here of eating the body
of God in order to assimilate his force, but of assimilating
his *parole* as food, a consumable body: which is entirely different. The theophagy is mediated here by the theology. No
doubt it may be possible to reduce this theology to the archaic theo-phagy; but the mediation, i.e. the relation, is
more fundamental than the reduction to one of its poles.

48. We have ascribed the Judaic institution to the position of opponent, in the sense of the actantial model of A. J.
Greimas, with its difference on the one hand from the disciples (helper), and on the other hand from the universal community (receiver). This term is not absolutely satisfying,

because we should also inscribe the men or the crowds or the demons. Nevertheless, as far as the problem of Judas or the traitor is concerned, it is indeed the Judaic institution which will be the most important investment of the "opponent" actant. [p. 223]

49. On the notion of the epistemic space of the model and on the construction of the notion of the subject in this space, see our study of the parabolic narrative. It is naturally a matter of a conventional notion resulting from the construction itself of the model. However, it would be necessary to pose the question of the nature of the model's space and accordingly that of the operations of which the model is the place. The "subject" is thus an artifact resulting from an experimentation inside of the model.

50. Thus we would have--if our hypothesis of reading is proven valid--a remarkable case of "shifting" in the sense of Jakobson, since the reading code of the message is constituted by the message itself or at the least by one of its moments.

51. Dt. 8:3; but cf. also Amos 8:11; Neh. 9:29, etc.

52. Dt. 6:16.

53. See, on this subject, the first part, "The Places of the Narrative", pp. 54-58.

54. Dt. 6:13.

55. The *parole* of praise or adoration, as well as that of cursing, is indissolubly verbal and behaviorial. See on this subject, M. Détienne, *op. cit.*, p. 51f.

56. To what extent have we the right to assimilate the signifier of the body to the modalization of the will? It will be recalled that, according to A. J. Greimas, this modality corresponds to the opposition of the subject and the object, as the tension of a desire in quest of an object intended to fill this lack which is the desire. In other words, the subject is defined by this lack to the extent to which this lack is shown to be absent and whose return and possession are marked by the signs of this possession. It is not our purpose to apply the theme of the will as the desire, so defined, to the signifiance of the "body" in the texts which we are studying. Let us only point out that by a transformation of the communicable *parole* into a consumable body, the subject gives himself as an object in which the desire finds its fulfillment by and in the signs: on the one hand, the *parole*, on the other hand the bread; the signs of linguistic

exchange becoming the signs of a substantial identification. The body as a signifier will therefore be focused in our text on the point of identification--the eucharistic institution-- the index of the desire of the "subject" actant in quest of its fulfillment, namely the transformation of its *parole* into its body as a consumable object *given to be* eaten.

57. The passage from the "negative" to the "positive" has no other meaning than that of the negative and positive valorizations which immediately appear in the reading of our texts.

58. We are referring here to our earlier analyses, pp. 96-97, and to our reflections on the notion of narrative dynamics.

59. This point is essential to our analysis. It implies a definition of the neutral and neutralization which is the fundamental moment of every dialectic transformation. See on this subject, our study "The Neutral and the Philosophical Discourse" in *Neutrality in Academics*, London:/Montreal, 1971, or from a more particular point of view, the study of Köngas and Miranda already cited.

60. The unmotivation of an act--that is to say the fact that this act is never found inserted inside of the narrative as a text read in a simple or complex chain [p. 224] of psychological or physical causes is an important element of the process of neutralization: because the act then appears isolated, independent in relation to the narrative enchainments, i.e. in the ensemble of relations which link the narrative segments--and sequences--to one another. It interrupts the metonymic contiguity of the functions in the narrative, and opens a spacing in the narrative into which the narrative will be able to be structured on another level. The unmotivation as a factor of neutralization thus appears to be a kind of narrative violence. It causes violence in the narrative. On this point, one will read with interest M. Bakhtine, *Problèmes de la Poétique de Dostoiewski*, Lausanne: Slavica, 1971, and in particular, pp. 158-159.

61. However, John only makes more explicit what the gospel narrative is in general: being a message about the transmission of messages or a narrative of the conditions and circumstances of communication of the narrative.

62. The intervention of the narrator, to which we shall return, decodes the enigmatic purpose of Jesus. But this decoding is contemporary with the moment of reading. It is found in the relationship between the transmitter and the receiver. Elsewhere, the continuation of the story, the narra-

tive of the Passion relating the death, the shrouding, and the
resurrection of Jesus, but in a future of reading, in a text
which is again absent. The narrator is in some way the delegate of this absence or this future already happened in order
to make it contemporary with the present moment of reading.
Thus the character at the same time linear, successive, and
irreversible of the reading is found weakened or annulled to
the benefit of the notion of a text whose parts react on one
another because they coexist with one another. However, it
will be noted that this annulment is only carried out by the
projection to a metalinguistic level of what will happen much
later as a moment of the narrative. "But he spoke of the
temple of his body" is a meta-communication. Therefore the
metacommunicative value of the metaphor can be concluded from
that. The "condensation" here affects the chronological organization of the narrative.

63. Metonymic in the sense in which the subject of the
action is taken for the place where the action unfolds the
embodied for the embodier. But in another sense the formula
is metaphoric, because the "subject" is in relation to the
whole story what the capstone is to the edifice of the Temple,
that by which the story is held together, coheres, or is structured. It will not be forgotten that "structure" is first of
all an architectural term. The fall of the subject is indeed
the fall of the Temple, of the edifice, and also the fall of
what the edifice represents or that of which the edifice is
the place for the institution and the Judaic community: a
dissolution of a structure therefore by a metonymic process,
but also a moment of change of a structure by a metaphoric
process which indicates the level (substance or form) where
the new structure must be reestablished: the body of Jesus
as a universal, spiritual food.

64. Cf. Part I, p.

65. Cf. note 6: It is convenient to examine here the notion of fulfillment of the narrative to which we have made a
brief allusion in our first chapter, p. 92, in its relation to
the narrative. It has no doubt some relation with the relation of the rite and of the myth than the former or the first,
the practical illustration of the second. And in one sense,
in effect, the ceremonial recitation [p. 225] of the narrative
finds its origin in the narrative which reproduces it. It is
indeed the very body of Jesus Christ which is at each moment
of the story the constitutive food of the universal community
starting from the original narrative where it became so "for
the first time". But at the same time, the rite produces
elsewhere the narrative of its origin, since it metaphorically
signifies it. The narrative of origin has metaphorically de-

stroyed the Temple and has really constructed it as a consumable body-sanctuary. The rite which reproduces it metaphorically constructs the consummable body, and really destroys the *parole* of the original narrative. It would be necessary to develop this point by emphasizing the transformations intervening between institutional ritual and original narrative in the ceremonial (ritual) recitation of the original narrative [*récit d'origine*]. These transformations would serve to enlarge the indications supplied by C. Lévi-Strauss in his essay "Structure et dialectique" in *For Roman Jakobson*, The Hague, 1956, pp. 289-294 and would open the way to the analysis, which is at the same time dialectical and structural, of the notion of tradition.

66. Namely Judas as a political partisan (see our remarks from chap. IV) and Judas as a treasurer or financier of the community of the Twelve (cf. the Johannine variant).

67. We are emphasizing the reflexive because the return of the signifier to itself and in itself is marked in it, a return marked by the *"meum"* of the eucharistic formula employed at the time of the Last Supper. The possessive of the first person is a "shifter" by which the message, in order to be reduced to its lowest terms, refers back to an other-of-the-message, but which, in the present case, is nothing else than the subject itself of utterance, the one who says *"meum"*. But it is also true that this return is at the same time a gift of food.

68. "Knowing their thoughts, he said to them, 'Every kingdom divided against itself is laid waste, and no city or house divided against itself will stand; and if Satan casts out Satan, he is divided against himself; how then will his kingdom stand?...But if it is by the Spirit of God that I cast out demons, then the Kingdom of God has come upon you. Or how can one enter a strong man's house and plunder his goods, unless he first binds the strong man? Then indeed he may plunder his house'" (Mt. 12:25-29).

69. "*And whoever says a word against* the Son of Man will be forgiven; but whoever speaks against the Holy Spirit will not be forgiven, either in this age or in the age to come... brood of vipers! how can you speak good (*language*) when you are evil? For out of the abundance of the heart the mouth speaks. The good man out of his good treasure brings forth good, and the evil man out of his evil treasure brings forth evil. I tell you, on the day of judgment men will render account for every careless word they utter; for by your words you will be justified, and by your words you will be condemned" (Mt. 12:32-37).

70. "For as Jonah was three days and three nights *in the belly of the whale*, so will the Son of Man be three days and three nights *in the heart of the earth*" (Mt. 12:40).

71. Verses 48-50: "'Who is my mother, and who are my brothers?' And stretching out his hand [i.e. making a gesture] toward his disciples, he said, 'Here are my mother and my brothers! For whoever does the will of my Father in heaven is my brother, and sister, and mother'" (Mt. 12:48b-50).

72. Here are some fragments from this dialogue. First the disciples: "Send her away because she is crying after us" (Mt. 15:23)...then the woman: "But she came [p. 226] and *knelt before* him, *saying*, 'Lord help me'." And the response of Jesus, "It is not fair to *take the children's bread* and throw it to the dogs." And the retort of the woman: "Yes, Lord, yet *even the dogs eat the crumbs that fall from their master's table*" (Mt. 15:23-27). It is a retort which is truly "inspired" by the strict articulation of the *parole*, the food (the dogs), and the force (the masters).

73. "I have compassion on the crowd, because they have been with me now *three days*, and have *nothing to eat*; and I am unwilling to send them away hungry, lest they faint on the way" (Mt. 15:32).

74. See our commentary in Part I: we are citing vs. 4: "'An evil and adulterous generation seeks for a sign, but no sign will be given to it except the sign of Jonah', so he left them and departed" (Mt. 16:4).

75. This point is very important and ought to be closely connected--in our minds--to the institution of the ceremonial meal and consumption of the body-*parole* of Jesus. This passage at the same time prepares and opposes it. In effect, the proper meaning of the question is to carry out the neutralization of the object on which it bears. The question puts the object, suspected of being inside of the language, in the very time of the question up to the one who answers it, reinstalls it, or reinsures it in the being. "Who is the Son of Man, according to the people?" signifies therefore the neutralization in expectation of the response of the signifier being of Jesus --and this response, as we will see in our analysis to follow, will only be supplied with the eucharistic meal and the treason. But it is opposed to this true response because it only seems to require a verbal communication in return out of neutralization, while the subject itself will have to be communicated as an object, at first sold [or betrayed], then consumed.

76. "Blessed are you, Simon Bar-Jona! For flesh and blood has not revealed this to you, but my father who is in heaven. And I tell you, you are Peter, and on this rock I will build my church and the powers of death shall not prevail against it" (Mt. 16:17-18). The text is remarkable because it presents the problem in all its breadth of the proper name which it has been seen subtends all our work. Let us summarize this movement of the name--its displacement through this text: 1) first the index, or the quasi-index, the word of interpellation of the individual in his singularity, "You, Simon...". 2) Then the integration of the name in the kinship relationship which determines then the individual in his name by his relation of filiation, i.e. according to the flesh and blood. 3) Hence as a consequence, the impossibility of keeping the proper name "Simon", to the extent to which it is articulated in a classifying table of kinship according to the filiation, since the same Simon speaks, better named the Other according to the Father, gives him the name which is the one which the Father gives, and by giving it to him integrates him into a true relationship of filiation: the Son of Man, a metonymic relation, redundant of filiation is the Son of the Living God, right relation, correct appellation. (But the Father is in the Heavens, therefore this filiation is not according to flesh and blood.) 4) Also Simon, Bar Jona (i.e. Son of Jonah) must be de-nominated. By losing his proper name, he acquires metaphorically a common name "rock", but a common name which conquers its property functionally: Simon by becoming the rock [i.e. Peter], becomes the founding rock of the Church. His new naming is no longer according to the relation of filial kinship (the flesh and blood), but according to the function of the [p. 227] name in the community of which he is the chief. We have therefore passed by displacement of the proper name from the singular index to the "social" function by the mediation of a double appellation of kinship of the interlocutors which determines the displacement.

77. It is a question of a naturally narrated act in the text. The text will only become an act in its turn in the institution and the rite of recitation.

78. We are referring here to the theory of J. L. Austin of the performative enunciations. Cf. J. L. Austin, *Quand dire, c'est faire*, trans. Gilles Lane, Paris: Ed. du Seuil, 1970 and especially the first and eighth conferences which are enough in the actual state of our analyses to give the philosophical background for our purpose. We are thinking in effect of considering two coupled functions named "Peter" and "Judas" which, between them, constitute a complete performative in Austin's sense: the production of an enunciation and

the execution of an action. It happens therefore that to say
something is to do it. But the definition must equally include the taking into consideration of the circumstances: "It
is always necessary to consider that the *circumstances* in which
the words are pronounced may be adapted in a certain way."
Otherwise the enunciation is empty, null, and non operative.
The question of the completeness of the circumstances adapted
is therefore essential in order to respond to that of the validity of the performative. Let us say that as far as our
text is concerned, the validation of the proclamation of
Peter, "You are the Christ, the Son of the living God" (Mt.
16:16) could only be established by the construction of a
circumstantial context by the action of Judas that the narrative told us.

79. See our chapter V.

80. Here is the text of Mt. 17:4-5: "And Peter said to
Jesus, 'Lord, it is well that we are *here*; if you wish, *I will
make three booths here,* one for you and one for Moses and one
for Elijah.' *He was still speaking,* when lo, a bright cloud
overshadowed them, and a voice from the cloud said, 'This is
my beloved Son, with whom I am well pleased; listen to him.'"
It is interesting to compare this interruption of the profane
discourse by the transcendent word, with the interruption of
the discourse of Peter to Cornelius and his family by the fall
of the Spirit (Acts 10:44-45).

81. These are verses 9-13 of chapter 17 in Matthew.

82. The expression "productive force of the signified" is
not very clear. Perhaps it would be more acceptable in reference to note 23, p. 103 concerning the notion of narrative dynamics. It appears to us in effect that, from the beginning,
the interplay of serial signifiers, while manifesting Jesus,
manifests him as the signifier of the Father, to which the
signified is never connected, but constantly hidden. We have
seen, with the proclamation of Simon Peter, a fine example of
the "failure" of this coalescence of the signifier with its
signified. It is necessary therefore that this process of
annulment or neutralization of the signifiers expose therefore the signified, but by arranging the place which is at the
same time empty and central where it can then be shown. It is
this movement of indication of the signified in this central
and neutral zone that we qualify by a realizer force to the
extent to which by it the overthrow of the structure and its
restructuration will be provoked at another level (the passage
to the universal type of community).

83. Hence the intervention in this perspective of Being and Appearing in order to classify the dialectic of the traitor as mediation. [p. 228]

84. We think that this notion of "textual practice" is important. It must be understood in the perspective which was ours from the beginning, of a return of the analysis to the surface of the text in its central place. If, in effect, the narrative structure constitutes, from an epistemological point of view, the theory of the text, we mean by textual practice this surplus that the text in its manifestation adds to the structure, while making it possible. It is a textual practice which is nothing else than its reading, but again unconscious of itself.

85. Here are some citations of these texts: "Jesus came into Galilee preaching the gospel of God, and saying, 'The time is fulfilled, and the kingdom of God is at hand; repent, and believe in the gospel'"(Mt. 1:14-15). Or in Mk. 1:21-22: "And they went into Capernaum; and immediately on the sabbath he entered the synagogue and taught. And they were astonished at his teaching, for he taught them as one who had authority, and not as the scribes."

86. It is a question of the violent confrontation with the demon or the healing of the ill or the possessed.

87. We are repeating here the terms of the functional model of A. J. Greimas, "mandate" and "mark". The baptism of Jesus by John in this perspective, can be considered as the qualifying test in the course of which the hero receives the mark which qualifies him for his mission, which may be a matter of the Spirit of God descending on him like a dove (Mt. 3:16; Mk. 1:10; Lk. 3:21-22) or a voice coming from the skies (Mt. 3:17; Mk. 1:11; Lk. 3:22b). Moreover, a kind of confrontation [affrontement] can be noted between John and Jesus which is a true test (Mt. 3:14-15 or Lk. 3:15-17).

88. See Appendix IV.

89. A characteristic inversion of the metacommunicative processes.

90. See on this distinction our remarks in Part I: "The Places of the Narrative", and in our article on the parabolic narrative.

91. The opposition of the active and the passive introduced here is a modalization at the same time syntactical and semantic of the subject/object axis.

92. We are referring to note 60, p. 112 concerning the notion of motivation. See also on this subject the work of Kenneth Burke, *A Grammar of Motives and A Rhetoric of Motives*, Cleveland:/New York: The World Publishing Company, 1962 (1st ed. 1945-1950).

93. Cf. our note below on the problem of the double. It is a matter here of a new example of integration of the code in the message, but by noting that this integration itself is coded by a grid of second level ciphering, which is the order of the narrative itself.

94. We are using here the term introduced by Ch. Perelman and Olbrechte-Tyteca in their *Traité de l'argumentation*, Paris: PUF, 1958. We are referring to that term.

95. On the signification of δόξα, we have consulted G. von Rad, *Old Testament Theology*, trans. D. M. G. Stalker, New York: Harper and Row, 1965, and in particular vol. 2, p. 358; Hans Conzelmann, *An Outline of The New Testament*, trans. John Bowden, New York: Harper and Row, 1969, and in particular, pp. 175-176, 343, and 345-346.

96. In other words, in the Synoptics it is the narrative itself which must function as its own commentary, essentially by some modifications of the chronological order of the functional distribution.

97. Hence the semiological interest in considering the text as a system [p. 229] formed by the projections of four (or more) narrative structures, in the species of four variants which we have taken into consideration.

98. There is an important problem here which appears in the Johannine utilization of metanarration or the metalinguistic discourse: that of the articulation of the (ritual, ceremonial, etc...) institution and of the narrative which is given as its origin. It would seem that the discourse (in the sense of the metanarration) is in some way powerless to be constituted as an "original founder" [*"origine fondatrice"*] of an institution, while the narrative has this capacity. A discourse is repeated, but it does not "reproduce", if that can be said, unlike the narrative and its recitation which is literally production anew of what the narrative gives as representation. The narrative illusion fully acts here like a reference to the "reality" that the recitation of the narrative re-produced. But no doubt there is more. The very fact of being narration confers a *power*, an essential productive force, but it is one which will be converted into a dogmatic-institutional system in order to be congealed. Some reflec-

tions similar to ours will be found in the text of Harald Wein-
rich, "Structures narratives du mythe", *Poétique* 1 (1, 1970),
25-34, in particular, pp. 28-29.

99. Here is the text: "Truly truly, I say to you, you
seek me, not because you saw signs, but because you ate your
fill of the loaves. Do not labor for the food which perishes,
but for the food which endures to eternal life, which the Son
of Man will give to you; for on him has God the Father set his
seal" (Jn. 6:26-27).

100. Thus in Jn. 6:60-61, and above all in 6:66: "After
this many of his disciples drew back and no longer went about
with him."

101. This important affirmation should be noted: "the
flesh is of no avail" (Jn. 6:63), and its opposition to the
spoken *paroles* which are "life". We are referring here to our
earlier remarks about theophagy and theo-logy. It is the *parole* which becomes flesh and blood in the eucharistic banquet.

102. Let us cite, for example, Jn. 5:38: "...you do not
have his word [*parole*] abiding in you, for you do not believe
him whom he has sent." Or the following verses 42: "But I
know that you have not the love of God within you" and 43:
"I have come in my Father's name, and you do not receive me;
if another comes in his own name, him you will receive."

103. Here is Jn. 6:64: "'But there are some of you that
do not believe.' For Jesus knew from the first who those were
that did not believe, and who it was that should betray him"
and verses 69-70: "we have believed, and have come to know,
that you are the Holy One of God" (the Twelve said). Jesus
replied: "Did I not choose you, the twelve, and one of you is
a devil?" Naturally this is a question of Judas. It will be
noted in Jn. 6:64 that the traitor appears in the discourse as
one of those who do not believe, but who extends his un-belief
almost to delivering him: which appears to us to authorize the
putting into perspective of the traitor as early as chapter 2.

104. This is a matter of the passage in which Jesus gives to
Judas a mouthful of bread dipped in the wine as a sign of recognition of his treachery for Peter and John. "At this moment,
after the morsel, Satan entered into him. Jesus then said to
him: 'That which you have to do, do it quickly'" [Jn. 13:27].

105. We are drawing attention in general to the interest
that a list of names can present, and in particular the lists
of proper names. In effect, in a list like the one which we
are studying, the proper names which figure in it receive [p.

230] a property by the very fact of being cited in it: that
of belonging in the ensemble that the list closes, namely the
Twelve. The list is therefore a paradigm in the narrative
which has an important semantic value. The Twelve "are opposed" in this way to the anonymous disciples or the crowds
who follow Jesus. On the other hand, the proper name acquires
by its appurtenance to the list a signifier value and no longer only an indicative function. For this very reason, Peter,
John...Judas are apostles: the apostle Peter, the apostle
John....Moreover, the closed paradigm of the enumeration can
also be considered as having a signifier value considered as
a syntagm. In other words, the order in which the names are
cited in the list assumes a value, a sense (which is socio-
logical, for example, if the list obeys some rules of prece-
dence; phonetic, if it observes the alphabetic order; historical or chronological, if the names of individuals are arranged according to the dates of appurtenance to the group,
etc...). The list is thus a new, particularly significative
example of an integration of the code in the message.

106. We are not trying to say that the homonymy reveals an
"intention" of the narrator concerning those who bear the same
name, but only that the presence of proper homonyms induce a
peculiar reading effect in which the bearers of the same name
are found necessarily arranged in the class of those who bear
the same name, therefore of those who have something in common. From here the induction of a similarity of meaning connected to that is found, in the poem, starting from the phonic
couplings. See on this subject, Nicolas Ruwet, "Analyse structurale de la poésie; à propos d'un ouvrage récent", in *Linguistics*, 2 (December 1963), 35-59. The work in question is that
of Samuel R. Levin, *Linguistic Structures in Poetry*, The Hague:
Mouton and Co., 1962.

107. By that we mean that in order to understand the meaning and the value of the term "Zealot", we are forced to de-
viate from the proposed text and to resort to other texts. It
will be objected that this departure could be carried out with
most of the terms of the narrative. That may be true, but we
do not need a majority of the terms of the narrative in order
to produce meaning in our reading: that is the difference.
On the other hand, Zealot appears here as a determinant of the
proper name whose "referential" value we know immediately,
therefore from going out of the system of the *langue* and the
system of the narrative to its immanence. See on this subject
in O. Cullmann, *The State in the New Testament*, New York:
Scribners' Sons, 1956, chapter I, "Jesus and the Resistance
Movement of the Zealots".

108. O. Cullmann, *op. cit.*, p. 15: "The name of Judas Iscariot has still not been satisfactorily explained. The Codex Sinaiticus at John 6:71 disects Iscariot into *Ish Kariot*; that is, man from Kerioth. But we know of no place by this name. We may therefore quite properly consider whether Iscariot may not be a Semitic transcription of the Latin word 'Sicarius'. (Cf. the reading *Skarioth* found in the Codex Bezae and the Itala.)"

109. See also on this point the works of C. Chabrol, in C. Chabrol and Louis Marin, *op. cit.*

110. Let us cite, for example, some excerpts from Matthew's text: "A man...said [to Jesus], 'Lord have mercy on my son, for he is an epileptic and he suffers terribly....I brought him to your disciples, and they could not heal him.'...'O faithless and perverse generation,' Jesus responded, 'How long am I to be with you? Bring him here to me.'" And Jesus healed the child. The narrator [p. 231] repeats: "Then the disciples came to Jesus privately and said, 'Why could we not cast it out?' He said to them,...'Because of your little faith.'"

111. For an analysis of this difference, one should consult R. Bultmann (*History of the Synoptic Tradition*, trans. John Marsh, Oxford: Blackwell, 1963, p. 68). He presents it as an example of a "tendency" [*travail*] of rewriting the tradition. "The apophthegm in Mk. 14:3-9 is a clear example of the tendency of the tradition. In Mk., the the [*sic*] murmurers are just τινές, in Matt. 26:8 they have become the μαθηταί and in Jn. 12:4, they finally turn into Judas. Besides this, in John, the woman who anoints Jesus is named Mary and Martha is said te [*sic*] have waited at the meal at which Lazarus was host. Finally in the apocryphal fragment Pap. OX,V,840 one of the questioning opponents is named—the Pharisee and High Priest Levi. This incursion of novel-like tendencies can be observed again later in other types of literary forms." What R. Bultmann analyzes diachronically as an unfolding of the tradition, we note synchronically as a differential interplay of the system of the text. It is also a question of a tendency [*travail*] of rewriting of the text, but in which the chronological anteriority must not privilege a specific text, in the present case Mk. 14:3-9, according to Bultmann.

112. These manipulative operations of the text are only justifiable by their productivity, i.e. the richness and the breadth of the correlations that they allow to be produced.

113. Cf. our study, "Les femmes au tombeau", *Langages* 22 (June, 1971), "Sémiotique narrative: le récit biblique", pp. 39-50.

114. These last correlations deserve an explanation: the *present* corpse of Lazarus with its mark: the odor, is opposed to the *absent* corpse of Jesus with its mark: the wrappings and the shroud (Jn. 20:5-7). And the call of Jesus to Lazarus which provokes a movement from the inside of the tomb to the outside, where the resurrection is signified, is opposed to the movement from the outside to the inside of the tomb where the women encounter the Angel, a proclaimer of the presence of Jesus elsewhere: an absence of Jesus and presence elsewhere signified by the message indicating the resurrection here.

115. Cf. the works of C. Chabrol, *Langages* 22 (June 1971).

116. Here it is: "Then turning toward the woman he said to Simon, 'Do you see this woman? I have entered your house, you gave me no water for my feet, but she has wet my feet with her tears....You gave me no kiss,...but she has anointed my feet with ointment'" (Lk. 7:44-46).

117. R. Bultmann points out as a tendency of the "romance", the introduction of Lazarus as a guest of the meal at Bethany in John (cf. our note 111). However, it is necessary to put the presence of the resurrected Lazarus at the meal into relationship with a particularly interesting remark by the same author (*op. cit.*, p. 215) about the resurrection of Jairus' daughter in Mk. 5:43. "There is a final typical feature (of style) in the request that the restored girl should be given something to eat, v. 43, which here serves the motif of demonstration. This is particularly clear in this instance, for if the request is interpreted as a medical prescription, it results in a grotesque combination of the rational and miraculous. Rather the reality of the [p. 232] resuscitation is demonstrated in that ghosts (*revenants*) do not themselves eat human-food." The author supports this remark with a note: "Thus the risen Lord in Lk. 24:41-43 shows that he is no 'πνεῦμα' by his eating food." The interest in this remark is completely perceived, not only as far as the participation of Lazarus in the meal at Bethany is concerned, but also for our general thesis about the relations of the *parole*, the force, and the body, this last element being directly connected to the food.

118. Cf. from this point of view, our study of the parabolic narrative cited earlier.

119. It is necessary to introduce here the problem of the signifiance of numbers inside of the text. (For another example, see the indications concerning the yield of the crop in the parable of the sower.) It is no longer a question of allegorizing and making a "numerology", but simply of drawing

attention to a call of a signifier echo especially to emphasize that it is devoid in itself of a signified. We do not
draw any conclusions about the mystic value of the cipher
3(00); but we note the phenomenon of a signifier echo 300/30,
and the induced effect of meaning which it creates, a phoneme
very similar to the value of the phonic couplings in a poem.
Cf. Appendix V also.

120. We are saying that it is a matter of the signifier
"Resurrection of Lazarus", because we are reading the narrative of a festival meal with the resurrected one whose episode
immediately precedes that of the anointing.

121. It would be necessary, in effect, to establish inside
of texts of this kind a lexicon and a topic of the sensitive
qualities, which would note the way in which they are articulated inside of a text or an ensemble of texts. This articulation, it seems to us, must be a signifier not only on the
extra-textual plane of anthropology, but in an immanent way
in order to illuminate the vectors in the narrative.

122. Cf. our chap. V.

123. An anthropological interest, because this text represents the entire hospitality ritual as a prelude to the meal
taken in common.

124. In one sense, and from this point of view, the narrative text presents itself as the "textualization" of the body
of Jesus or as the text-become-body of Jesus. It is a phantasm of the text which refers no doubt to a phantasm of the
body divided (articulated) into topic-regions, or places of
reception of a specific category of acts.

125. This ambivalence, or more precisely this displacement
of the position of the subject between active and passive,
could constitute a new indication of the corporeal phantasm
which appears to us to traverse this text. Cf. in particular,
J. Laplanche and J. B. Pontalis, *Vocabulaire de la Psychanal-
yse*, Paris: PUF, 1968, p. 156, s.v. "Fantasme".

126. Here is an excerpt from the dialogue between the en-
voys of the Pharisees and John (Jn. 1:25-27), "They asked him,
'Then why are you baptizing, if you are neither the Christ,
nor Elijah, nor the prophet?' John answered them, 'I baptize
with water; but among you stands one whom you do not know,
even he who comes after me, the thong of whose sandal I am not
worthy to untie.'" And in verse 31: "I myself did not know
him; but for this I came baptizing with water, that he might
be revealed to Israel." And in verse 33: "I myself did not

know him; but he who sent me to baptize with water said to me,
'He on whom you see the Spirit descend and remain, this is he
who baptizes [p. 233] with the Holy Spirit.'" Verses 35 and
40-41 reveal to us that the first disciples of Jesus were re-
cruits from the group of John's disciples, from which it can
be assumed that they had been baptized in water.

Chapter V

127. It is less a matter in our analysis of a hero "opponent", than that of an additional and complementary hero at
the same time whose function is to begin the exchange of signifiers. See on this subject, our analyses and preceding
notes, especially notes 17, 34, etc.

128. This representative conjunction in the traitor signifies his mediatory function of contradiction.

129. On the articulation of the figure and the place, we
refer to our note on the notion of τόπος. Naturally it is a
matter here of a particular textual place, but which is named
in the personage of the traitor.

130. We are using here the term "contract" introduced by
A. J. Greimas in his works on Propp's *Morphology of the Folktale*. The contract connects, in A. J. Greimas' model, the
sender and the receiver to the dimension of the communication
modalized by the "knowledge". It is perceived that the contract between Judas and the leaders of the political and religious community is a contract in the sense that this term
has in ordinary language. But, moreover, it functions like
the semiotic contract to the extent to which it introduces
the tests of the hero, and this permits the relation of sender
and receiver and the transmission of the Good News. But in
addition it intervenes by a displacement of its function outside of the model.

131. A chronological order is an integrating dimension to
the extent to which it implies some engagements to come, some
recurrent reciprocities of exchange. Descartes has well ap-
preciated what excluded contracts and promises in the old days
from temporary morals, because the contract necessarily implies
an organization, an ordinance of the time to come.

132. This is a remarkable example where the discourse is
by itself a bearer of a meaning, apart from intentions to
speak, beyond or on this side of them. We have attempted to
generalize this form with the notion of a parabolic structure

of the ordinary language in which language overflows the speaker who makes use of it, by a kind of excess of meaning. He has said more and another thing than what he wanted to say. This is another case of a transgression of the opposition of the system and the *parole*.

133. The notion of a zero correlate could be introduced here, whose function would be to make it or them possible correlations, therefore which would possess for that very reason a metalinguistic function since it only enters in the correlations in order to constitute their interplay of correspondence. It is a function of the code in the message itself. At the same time, the relation between the notion of a zero correlate and that of neutralization as an empty moment or of annulment is perceived then, permitting the exchange of the signifiers. The notion of a zero correlate would be a neutralization of the text by which the text finds its code or one of its codes of deciphering. On the notion of zero, see Lévi-Strauss, *Introduction à l'oeuvre de Marcel Mauss*, Paris: PUF, 1955; [p. 234] *Anthropologie structurale*, pp. 70-71 and pp. 175-176. See also Anthony Wilden, art. cit., *Semiotica* 6 (1972).

134. See below, note 136.

135. See our *Etudes sémiologiques*, pp. 240-242.

136. To eat a share is thus a function of destruction with the sacrifice. Moreover, we are presented in the species with a meal, a sacrifice in which one must not refuse to recognize the neutralizing function. Cf. Lévi-Strauss, *La Pensée sauvage*, pp. 295-302.

137. Mt. 26:23.

138. R. Barthes, "L'analyse structurale du récit", in *Recherches de Science religieuse* 58 (1, 1970), 17-38.

139. There is an important point here which it would be convenient to develop, especially by some precise analyses of certain texts from *Acts*. See on this subject, E. Haulotte, "Les Actes: modèles économiques", in *Christus* 16 (April, 1968), p. 140 [sic].

140. See our analyses below on the question of the identity of Jesus and his names.

141. A new example of a parabolic structure of discourse.

142. We are distinguishing here negation in the grammatical sense and denial in the psychological sense, "a refusal of

an affirmation which I have enunciated or which is imputed to me". By using the expression "symbolic denial", we are referring to the article by Freud in 1925: "Die Verneinung". Everything takes place in effect as if Peter, who denied belonging to the group of disciples, affirmed for that very reason his appurtenance. And in a psychological situation of non-recognition or absence in the discourse considered very characteristic, the crowing of the cock will have the function of a signifier of anamnesis. Yet that very language in which Peter denies *"en être"*, presents him as *"en étant"*. See on this subject, La Planche and Pontalis, *op. cit.*, pp. 112-113-114 s.v. "(Dé)négation". We are using the term "symbolic" in the sense of the Freudian text: "In the middle of the symbol of the (de)negation, the mind frees itself from the limits of repression." The denials of Peter have the symbolic function of (de)negation to the extent to which they realize in language a neutralization of the signifier with a view to the position of the signified.

143. The importance of the "body" in the entire interplay of contracts, suppressions, touches, etc., which is related to our indications on the ritual map of the body of Jesus, can only be emphasized here.

144. It is a question indeed of an inverted metonymic figure of the universal community. In effect, we recognize in it the oppositions of the field of death and the place of life, the foreigner and the universal, the individual corpse and the collective body, etc. The Potters' field is therefore an inverted metaphor of the community of the disciples, and then of the Christians. But in the line of the narrative, it is the mark of an episode, a moment in the series of the signifiers, namely the silver. These remarks corroborate the indications supplied p. 168 on the silver as the neutral of the community. (Cf. n. 139.)

145. It is convenient to understand this sentence at the same time in relation to the content. Judas, an instrument of the transcendent fulfillment of the Scriptures, discovers that he has been a simple instrument. He has become a tragic hero. And in relation to the form of the text, he is the figure of an immanent constitution of the text which, once accomplished, demands its narrative obliteration. The personage must then disappear from the representative scene of the text. The fact that the operation [p. 235] is displayed in this double level signifies an exterior of the text which collects the death of Judas, where it is transformed from a narrative requirement into a referent event.

146. The following schema could represent the syntagmatic correlation of Judas and Peter:

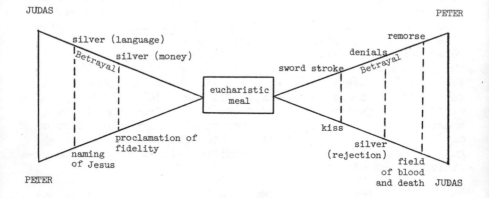

Chapter VI

147. Here is the text from Luke: "I have prayed for you that your faith may not fail; and when you have turned again, strengthen your brethren" (Lk. 22:32).

148. Verse Lk. 22:53 draws to a close with the following sentence addressed to those "who had come out against him (Jesus)": "But this is your hour, and the power of darkness." On the other hand, here are some extracts from verses 35-38: "'When I sent you out with no purse or bag or sandals, did you lack anything?' They said, 'Nothing.' He said to them, 'But now, let him who has a purse take it, and likewise a bag. And let him who has no sword sell his mantle and buy one. For... this scripture must be fulfilled in me, "And he was reckoned with transgressors [i.e. villains]"'"...(Lk. 22:35-38).

149. Jn. 18:26.

150. We are qualifying the transformations as "circular" in order to emphasize that there is not an original version of which the other versions would be variations. All the variants are on the same plane. They reciprocally signify them-

selves, or more precisely they signify by this very reciproci-
ty. This is clearly to adopt a viewpoint very different from
that of historical critical research and in particular of the
methods of form criticism. "The aim of form-criticism is to
determine the original form of a piece of narrative, a domini-
cal saying or a parable. In the process we learn to distinguish secondary additions and forms, and these in turn lead
to important results for the history of the tradition." R.
Bultmann, *op. cit.*, p. 6.

151. For example, C. Lévi-Strauss, *La Pensée sauvage*,
Paris: Plon, 1962, or Jean Joseph Goux, "Numismatiques I-II",
Tel Quel No. 35 (1968) and No. 36 (1969).

152. Cf. our study on the parabolic narrative.

SELECTED BIBLIOGRAPHY

The Bible we have used as the biblical reference text was translated into French under the direction of l'Ecole Biblique de Jérusalem, Paris: Ed. du Cerf, 1956. For the Greek text we have used *The Greek New Testament*, ed. R. V. G. Tasker, Oxford: Cambridge, 1964.

Austin, J. L. *Quand dire, c'est faire*. Paris: Ed. du Seuil, 1970.

Barthes, R. *Essais critiques*. Paris: Ed. du Seuil, 1964.

_____. *Le degré zéro de l'Ecriture. Eléments de sémiologie*. Paris: Gonthier, 1968.

_____. *S/Z*. Paris: Ed. du Seuil, 1970.

Benvéniste, E. *Le vocabulaire des institutions indo-européennes*. Paris: Ed. de Minuit, 1963.

_____. *Problèmes de linguistique générale*. Paris: Gallimard, 1966.

Gardiner, A. M. *The Theory of Proper Names, a Controversial Essay*. 2nd ed. London, 1954.

Granger, G. G. *Pensée formelle et sciences de l'homme*. Paris: Aubier, 1960.

_____. *Essai d'une philosophie du style*. Paris: A. Colin, 1968.

Greimas, A. J. *Sémantique structurale*. Paris: Larousse, 1966.

_____. *Du sens*. Paris: Ed. du Seuil, 1970.

Hjelmslev, L. *Essais linguistiques*. Cercle linguistique de Copenhague, vol. XII, 1959.

Jakobson, R. *Essais de linguistique générale*. Paris: Gallimard, 1966.

Ladrière, J. *L'articulation du sens*. Paris: B.S.R., 1970.

248

Laplanche, J. and J. B. Pontalis. *Vocabulaire de la psych-analyse*. Paris: P.U.F., 1968.

Leach, E. R. *Genesis as Myth and Other Essays*. London: Jonathan Cape, 1969.

Lévi-Strauss, Claude. *Anthropologie structurale*. Paris: Plon, 1958.

_____. *La pensée sauvage*. Paris: Plon, 1962.

Meletinski, E. "L'étude structurale et typologie de Conte", in V. Propp, *Morphologie du conte*. trans. French. Paris: Ed. du Seuil, 1970.

Peirce, C. S. *Philosophical Writings*. ed. J. Buchler. New York: Dover Editions, 1955.

Propp, Vladimir. *Morphologie du conte*. trans. French. Paris: Ed. du Seuil, 1970.

Ricoeur, Paul. *Le conflit des interprétations. Essais d'her-méneutique*. Paris: Ed. du Seuil, 1969.

Saussure, Ferdinand de. *Cours de Linguistique générale*. 5th ed. Paris: Payot, 1955.

Works consulted:

Bultmann, R. *History of the Synoptic Tradition*. trans. John Marsh. Oxford: Blackwell, 1963.

Conzelmann, H. *An Outline of the Theology of the New Testament*. trans. J. Bowden. New York: Harper and Row, 1969.

Cullmann, O. *The Christology of the New Testament*. trans. S. G. Guthrie. Philadelphia: Westminster Press, 1959.

Goguel, M. *Jésus et les origines du Christianisme. L'Eglise primitive*. Paris: Payot, 1957.

The Gospel According to Thomas. coptic text established and translated by A. Guillaumment--M. Ch. Puech, G. Guispel,

W. Till, and Yassah Abd Al Masih. Leiden: E. J. Brill/
New York: Harper and Row, 1959.

Hahn, F. *The Titles of Jesus in Christology*. New York and
Cleveland: The World Publishing Company, 1969.

Jeremias, J. *The Parables of Jesus*. trans. S. M. Hooke.
New York: Scribner Sons, 1965.

Kümmel, W. G. *Promise and Fulfilment*. Studies in Biblical
Theology. London: SCM Press, Ltd., 1957.

Rad, G. von. *Old Testament Theology*. trans. D. M. G.
Stalker. New York: Harper and Row, 1965.

Recherches de Sciences religieuses 58 (no. 1, Jan.-Mar., 1970).
(This issue contains articles by X. Léon-Dufour, R.
Barthes, E. Haulotte, and Louis Marin.)

"Sémiotique narrative: récits bibliques." eds. C. Chabrol
and L. Marin. *Langages* 22 (June, 1971). (This issue
contains articles by C. Chabrol, M. de Certeau, E.
Haulotte, E. R. Leach, L. Marin, and G. Vuillod.)

INDEX OF PROPER NAMES

NOTE: We have italicized the names of the narrators to contrast them from the names of characters who are marked with
an asterik: for example, *John* as a narrator from the fourth
[second?] century, and *John as a character in the narrative.

INDEX OF BIBLICAL REFERENCES

Old Testament

New Testament

[Trans. note: Unfortunately due to the number of typo-
graphical errors in the French text, it was impossible to simply reuse the original Scripture index with adjusted page numbers. Hence an entirely new index was compiled omitting the
questionable references (e.g. some to blank pages), and adding
some new ones which were originally omitted. It should also
be noted that other printing errors were present in the French

text (e.g. the omission of n. 146 on *French* p. 172-175, etc.).
Prof. Marin promised to supply these corrections to us, but
for some reason was unable to do so.   Thus we have simply re-
produced the 1971 ed. as closely as possible in English.]